TONIGHT AT 8.30

Ten one-act plays

WE WERE DANCING, THE ASTONISHED HEART,
'RED PEPPERS', HANDS ACROSS THE SEA, FUM OAK,
SHADOW PLAY, WAYS AND Mᵃᵗ⁻⁻   MILY
              AL^r

Coward wrote this collec   he plan
that he would star in ther.   D0878612   wrence.
Intended to showcase Co   ...uiple talents, the
plays vary in tone and prov.   ...vᵢₛ with a mix of acting, singing and
dancing. Running the plays in trios on successive nights, what resulted
was a sparkling, fast-paced and remarkably varied selection of
theatrical gems, well-received by their audiences and still enjoyed
today. Gertrude Lawrence wrote to Coward in 1947, 'Dearest Noël,
wherever I go . . . all I hear is *"Please revive Tonight at 8.30!"*.'

'*Tonight at 8.30* surprises as much as it delights as, in some of the plays,
Coward takes us to a world far removed from that of the wealth and
glamour of the debonair London socialites who dominated much of
his earlier work. But The Master's polish and sparkle are never far
away as music and song intertwine with the wit and insight of one of
our greatest ever playwrights.' *Chichester Festival Theatre*, 2006

Noël Coward was born in 1899 in Teddington, Middlesex. He made his
name as a playwright with *The Vortex* (1924), in which he also
appeared. His numerous other successful plays included *Fallen Angels*
(1925), *Hay Fever* (1925), *Private Lives* (1933), *Design for Living* (1933), and
Blithe Spirit (1941). During the war he wrote screenplays such as *Brief
Encounter* (1944) and *This Happy Breed* (1942). In the fifties he began a
new career as a cabaret entertainer. He published volumes of verse
and a novel (*Pomp and Circumstance*, 1960), two volumes of autobio-
graphy and four volumes of short stories: *To Step Aside* (1939), *Star
Quality* (1951), *Pretty Polly Barlow* (1964) and *Bon Voyage* (1967). He was
knighted in 1970 and died three years later in Jamaica.

Noël Coward

TONIGHT AT 8.30

Ten one-act plays

We Were Dancing
The Astonished Heart
'Red Peppers'
Hands Across the Sea
Fumed Oak
Shadow Play
Ways and Means
Still Life
Family Album
Star Chamber

Introduced by Barry Day

Methuen Drama

Methuen Drama

1 3 5 7 9 10 8 6 4 2

Tonight at 8.30 first published in 1936 by Heinemann and republished in 1958 in *Play Parade* Vol. 4
Subsequently published by Eyre Methuen in 1979 in *Collected Plays: Three* and *Four*, and by Methuen Publishing in 1999 in *Collected Plays: Seven*

This edition first published in 2009 by Methuen Drama

Methuen Drama
A&C Black Publishers Limited
36 Soho Square
London WID 3QY
www.methuendrama.com

A CIP catalogue record for this book is available from the British Library.

ISBN: 978 1 408 11345 5

Typeset by Deltatype Ltd, Birkenhead, Merseyside
Printed and bound in Great Britain by
CPI Cox & Wyman, Reading, Berkshire

Cover photo: Fiona Byrne and Patrick Galligan in *Brief Encounters*.
Photo by Shin Sugino

CONTENTS

INTRODUCTION

After a nine-week tour, in Manchester (two weeks), Leeds, Glasgow (two weeks), Edinburgh, Liverpool, Newcastle and Birmingham, *Tonight at 8.30* opened at London's Phoenix Theatre on 9 January 1936 and closed on 20 June after 157 performances. The US company opened at the National Theatre, New York, on 24 November that same year, after a try-out in Boston, and played for 118 performances. Both engagements could have been extended indefinitely, had it not been for Noël's personal antipathy to long runs. There were always new plays clamouring to be written, new words and music waiting to be heard . . .

In 1935 Noël took on a significant creative challenge – to revive the form of the one-act play. In the fledgling phase of his career he had tried his hand at it. In 1917 – under the rather clumsy pseudonym of 'Esnomel' – he had collaborated with his young friend and would-be playwright, Esmé Wynne, on *Ida Collaborates* and *Woman and Whiskey*. The more mature twenty-one year-old Noël wrote *The Better Half* in 1921, the unproduced *Mild Oats* in 1922 and *Weatherwise* in 1923. And that appeared to be it. The one-act format seemed to have seen its best days and, besides, in the Coward brain a host of full-length and, he hoped, more commercial plays were clamouring to be released.

His reason for deciding to write nine – in the end, ten – of them and play them in trios on successive evenings was not the simple desire to show that he could master anything he cared to turn his hand to but – as he says in his own introduction – his belief in the 'star system'. The public – in the West End and on Broadway – had enjoyed watching him and Gertrude Lawrence play together in *Private Lives* back in 1930. Presumably they would enjoy seeing them team up again in not one but many incarnations?

Gertie always had a singular fascination for him. In the mid-1930s – just before *Tonight at 8.30* – he mused on her complexity as a person and an actress . . .

> I see her now, ages away from her ringlets and black velvet cap, sometimes a simple wide-eyed child, sometimes a glamorous *femme de monde*, at some moments a rather boisterous 'good sort', at others a weary, disillusioned woman battered by life but gallant to the last. There were many other grades also between these extremes. She appropriated beauty to herself quite early, along with all the tricks and mannerisms that go with it. In adolescence she was barely pretty. Now, without apparent effort, she gives the impression of sheer loveliness. Her grace in movement is exquisite, and her voice charming. To disentangle Gertie herself from this mutability is baffling, rather like delving for your grandmother's gold locket at the bottom of an over-flowing jewel-case.

As he wrote them, he sent them to his old friends, Alfred Lunt and Lynn Fontanne, his co-stars in the 1933 *Design For Living*. On 15 September Lynn is writing to him about the first batch:

> I have read them all and am very excited. They are quite extraordinary . . .
>
> Oh, how I wish we could see some of the rehearsals. But, of course, you will do it here some time and then we shall see it.
>
> Love, love, love and good luck, my little sweet.

Then, when she'd read all nine plays, she realised the scope of what he was attempting.

> I have a hunch that changing bills like that and doing so many different things does not do the thing you had expected of it, i.e., that giving so much variety would lighten the work. I have a feeling that the job of work in the theatre of three hours hard every night is only intensified by the fact that the plays are each different and so involving further tension. And, of course, extra rehearsals, which means you are never out of the theatre. An awful lot of work to bite off in one season, Duckie! But perhaps the entertainment part will come when

you have them all and can toss them off in another season . . . such as the New York one. Or am I wrong?

Alec Woollcott wrote . . .

I am enchanted with all I hear about your one-act plays . . . Sybil Colefax wrote me a great deal about them and, whereas I could read only a few words of her comment, they seemed to indicate that she had been favourably impressed.

When the first bill opened in Manchester in October of that year 'to bigger business than has ever been known', Noël replied . . .

Darling, beastly Acky-wee,

Your horrid little note arrived just as I was about to ravish my Manchester public but now that they are safely ravished, I can write . . . You will be bleakly interested to hear that the short play idea is so far a triumphant success. We are now playing two bills of three plays each and by the time we get to London three bills of three plays each.

They are all brilliantly written, exquisitely directed, and I am bewitching in all of them.

Yours in Christ,
Noël

The first play, *We Were Dancing*, is generally considered the weakest. Set at a dinner-dance in Samolo – Noël's mythical South Sea island which was to be revisited several times in subsequent plays and his only published novel, *Pomp and Circumstance* – it tells of two married people who fall in love while dancing. Unfortunately, they are not married to one another. They decide to run away together but then the madness of the moment passes.

Noël described it as 'a light episode, little more than a curtain-raiser. It was never intended to be anything more than this and, unlike its author, it fulfilled its promise admirably.'

Not everyone agreed. Lynn put her finger on what was wrong . . .

Aside from some very funny lines, which you can always

write, I don't like it at all, and I don't suppose you do either. I can tell you where I think it seems bad, and that is at the beginning when you, as an audience, should believe that these people have fallen in love, and it only seems very silly. I don't apologise for not liking it, because I am certain that when you read it again you will hate it and very probably replace it, and I hope you do.

Ms Fontanne's hopes were not fulfilled. Nor were MGM's, when in 1942 they made a film starring Norma Shearer, which they claimed was 'based in part on the play by Noël Coward'. It suffered the fate of so many of the early screen adaptations of his work and failed to find an audience.

The Astonished Heart is the story of a happily married psychiatrist who falls madly – if that isn't an inappropriate word for a psychiatrist – in love with his wife's friend. Torn by the emotional stress he was only used to seeing in others, he commits suicide.

Lynn liked this much better . . .

> What a lovely title! I recognise our psychiatrist . . . Oh, it's awfully good. It is amazing how gradually he becomes unbalanced. It gives one a strange feeling of drowning. I love the almost Proustian psychology of jealousy.

Another old friend of Noël's – Sir Edward Marsh, the doyen of first nighters – had his reservations. While he admired '*Red Peppers*', *Hands Across the Sea* and *Fumed Oak* 'almost on the other side of idolatry', he had his doubts about this one . . .

> For some reason it left me quite cold and I now think the reason was the scene in which, after hurling Gertie [as the mistress, Leonora] to the ground, you sit down on the sofa and talk to her. This was unconvincing, partly because it didn't seem likely that she would put up with it, but much more because I couldn't believe that any man above the grade of a coal heaver or bargee, finding that he had hurled a woman to the ground, could be carried even by the most extreme stress

of emotion into a denial of the elementary instinct (and perhaps it is the result of centuries of breeding) to pick her up again.

While Marsh's explanation has a quaint ring to modern ears, his perception was instinctively accurate.

Noël himself considered the play 'more ambitious in intent [than *We Were Dancing*], but I thought then and still think that its theme, the decay of a psychiatrist's mind through personal sexual obsession, was too esoteric to appeal to a large public. It gave us, however, good opportunities for dramatic acting and provided a strong contrast to *We Were Dancing*, which preceded it, and "Red Peppers", which followed it.'

It was made into a film in 1950. Michael Redgrave was cast as the psychiatrist, Christian Faber, but it became clear to Noël, as he viewed early rushes, that Redgrave was uncomfortable in the part. He decided to play it himself and found himself proving his own thesis. What the sheer theatricality of a stage performance could just about handle looked overly melodramatic on the cinema screen. The critics agreed. In the short story 'Star Quality' Noël poked a little fun at it himself. Two of the characters go to the cinema, where they see 'an exquisitely acted but rather tedious picture about a psychiatrist who committed suicide'.

Toward the end of his life he lamented, 'Poor old *Astonished Heart*, I should love to see it again, just to find out if it really was as bad as they said it was.' He never did see it but he might be interested to see it now emerge as something of a minor 'cult film'.

The 'Red Peppers' – George and Lily Pepper – are a music-hall act who have been touring the provinces for years, still using the bewhiskered routine that George's parents used before him and slipping further and further down the bill. After a disastrous performance Lily tells George – certainly not for the first time – just what's wrong with the act.

LILY: I'm sick of you and the whole act. It's lousy, anyway.
GEORGE: The act was good enough for my mum and dad and it's good enough for you.

LILY (*with heavy sarcasm*): Times have changed a bit since your mum and dad's day, you know. There's electric light now and telephones and a little invention called Moving Pictures. Nobody wants to see the 'Red Peppers' for three bob when they can see Garbo for ninepence.

Noël described it as 'a vaudeville sketch sandwiched in between two parodies of music-hall songs. We always enjoyed playing it and the public always enjoyed watching us play it, which, of course, was highly satisfactory.' In fact, it was rather more than that. You can feel the pain under the patter. Noël himself had been brought up in a world where 'twice nightly variety' was an unquestioned staple of show business. Good, bad or indifferent, as long as an artiste gave of his or her best, Noël gave them his heart and wished them all the best. To the end of his life he had perfect recall of the songs and jokes he'd heard there in his youth and his re-creation of an act like the 'Red Peppers' goes deeper than simple satire.

Once again. Lynn summed it up . . .

'Red Peppers' is very fine and very funny. Their utter third-ratedness is so awfully pathetic. You know exactly why (aside from the pitiful business of their act) they have never been and never could be successful.

So what would happen to George and Lily? Well, the Second World War would inevitably suck them into ENSA, where they would bore the troops in many a foreign field. They'd return to find the variety palaces being turned into bingo halls. But just around the corner was that Valhalla called . . . television. They'd survive.

And besides, don't we British have a reverse reverence for something that's *so* bad it's almost good?

Noël described *Hands Across the Sea* as

a satire on the confusions of a London society woman suddenly faced with the unexpected arrival of two colonials with whom she once stayed while travelling in the Far East. It is a gay, unpretentious little play and it was acted by Gertie with incomparable brilliance. I cannot think of it without remembering the infinite variety of her inflexions, her absurd, scatter-brained conversations on the telephone, her frantic desire to be hospitable and charming, and her expression of blank dismay when she suddenly realised that her visitors are not who she thought they were at all. It was a superb performance in the finest traditions of high comedy.

It is an ensemble piece that has something of the surrealism of the Marx Brothers' cabin scene in *A Night at the Opera* – except that it pre-dates that frenetic masterpiece by several years. What Noël did not say was that it was also a thinly-veiled parody of the superficial social life of his friends, Louis and Edwina, Lord and Lady Mountbatten. The Mountbattens saw the play and completely missed that point. In fact, it never really sank in. As late as 1968 Mountbatten is writing to Noël, 'Can you confirm that it was written with malice aforethought, or did it just turn into a naval couple because you had so many naval friends?'

In *Fumed Oak* Henry Gow is seen to be living a life of silent desperation, nagged by wife, daughter and mother-in-law alike. Finally, he rebels, tells them all precisely what he thinks of them – and leaves.

Noël described it as 'a comedy based on the good old "worm will turn" theme. I loved Henry Gow from the moment I started writing him, and I loved playing him more, I think, than anything else in the repertoire.'

Lynn considered it had 'enough material for three acts. It's wonderful. But it seems dreadfully extravagant to use all those rich plots for one-acters. Won't Gertie hate playing that unsympathetic wife? I love his remaining absolutely speechless during the first scene. It's a sure-fire trick, darling, and very exciting. I love the old mother in that.'

And Noël himself had a soft spot for feisty senior ladies, who turn up as characters in several plays and films. It may have been a way of exorcising the less appealing aspects of his mother and his Aunty Vida who so dominated his early years.

*

'To get to my favourite,' wrote Lynn, '(and, of course, you already know it is the best), *Shadow Play*. Oh, darling, it is so extraordinary! I think I like it best of anything you have ever written. It is curious how that strange form of writing swings one vibrantly out into space, right out of the world somewhere in the stratosphere. It will undoubtedly be an enormous success . . .'

Victoria and Simon Gayforth are going through a difficult time in their marriage which was 'so lovely in the beginning'. Vicky fears that a divorce is imminent and takes sleeping tablets. In her drowsy state she begins to confuse past, present and her fears for the future. Simon rouses her and reassures her that all will be well. They will always come back to each other, as English people return from abroad 'to the white cliffs of Dover'.

The originality of *Shadow Play* lies not in its plot or even in the integration of the songs but in the disintegration of the timescale. We are drawn into Vicky's schizophrenic dream state and made to piece things together for ourselves. As Noël has Vicky say, 'Small talk, a lot of small talk – with other thoughts going on behind.' One is tempted at this remove to call it Pinteresque – except that Pinter is Cowardesque.

Nothing in his earlier work seems to presage what he attempts here and he might not even have appreciated it fully himself. He refers to it as 'a musical fantasy . . . a pleasant theatrical device which gave Gertie and me a chance to sing as romantically as we could, dance in the moonlight and, we hoped, convince the audience that we were very fascinating indeed. It always went extremely well, so I must presume that we succeeded.'

But there was much more to it than that.

On 2 November Noël is writing to Woollcott from Leeds, where they are playing.

> I've finished the seventh play – *Family Album* – a Victorian dainty with music and now I'm racking my brains to think up two more to make up the third bill!
>
> Our success really is fantastic – we were sold out here completely two weeks before we arrived. It takes ages after

each performance to get out of the stage door and we have to have special police to control the crowds!

The 'Victorian dainty' is set in 1860 and has the Featherways family 'celebrating' their unlamented father's passing. It is then revealed that just before his death he had written a new will disinheriting them all. It had been witnessed by his spinster daughter, Lavinia, and their aged butler, who had then proceeded to destroy it after his death. The festivities may now continue.

In his own notes he describes it as 'a sly satire on Victorian hypocrisy, adorned with an unobtrusive but agreeable musical score. It was stylised both in its décor and its performance, was a joy to play, and provided the whole talented company with good parts.'

Ways and Means was set in a familiar Coward milieu – the Côte d'Azur. Stella and Toby Cartwright are penniless 'professional guests'. Their way of life is to move elegantly around, sponging on one host after another until it is made clear that it is time to move on. On this occasion they are saved by a plot twist. But *next* time . . . ?

'A twentyish little farce', Noël called it. 'I never cared for it much, but as an "opener" it served its purpose.'

The most influential play in the set would turn out to be *Still Life*.

Laura Jesson and Alec Harvey are two perfectly ordinary people. She is a suburban housewife, who visits the nearby town religiously every week to shop, change her library book at Boot's and have a modest lunch at the local Kardomah Café. He is a doctor who puts in a day a week at the local hospital. Both are happily married. At the station, waiting for her train home, she gets a piece of grit in her eye from a passing express. Alec offers to remove it. Their paths accidentally cross again the following week . . . and the week after that. Almost without realising it, they fall in love but – being English – they do nothing about it. They part but each of them has had their life profoundly changed by their brief encounter.

Noël considered it to be 'the most mature play of the whole

series . . . It is well written, economical and well-constructed: the characters, I think, are true and I can say now, reading it with detachment after so many years, that I am proud to have written it.'

Brief Encounter, the film that was made of it in 1945, is now generally regarded as one of the great British films of all time, despite the fact that, when it was first released, local audiences seemed embarrassed to see ordinary people like themselves falling in love. Fortunately, we are now made of tougher emotional stuff and Britain can take it! French and American audiences had no such trouble.

The one that got away was *Star Chamber*. It played one matinée and was never revived. Noël makes no reference to it.

The setting is the bare stage of a West End theatre, where a committee meeting of the Garrick Haven Fund, a theatrical charity for destitute actresses, is being held. The committee – a random collection of people, all of them involved in the theatre in one way or another – are clearly more concerned with their own interests than those of their wards. The meeting breaks up with no real business having been done.

Gertie played Xenia James, a 'star' actress, who, when not talking to her incontinent Great Dane, proceeds to act the part of sympathetic president. Gertie Lawrence as – Gertie Lawrence. Noël's role is that of Jimmy Bolton ('The Man Who Made Kitchener Laugh'), a second-rate comedian who is always 'on' and always ignored since everyone has heard his stories endless times. Archie Rice anticipated by twenty years.

There's a touch of Max Miller in the relentless patter but Noël always implied that he had had Leslie Henson in mind, a performer who had always bored him. Sad that a part that would prove to have a life of its own in Osborne's hands should have made its exit after a single matinée. Not even an evening performance!

There may well have been another reason for Noël's dissatisfaction with the piece. Just before writing it he had taken over the presidency of the Actors' Orphanage from Sir Gerald du

Maurier. He realised that he was satirising people who, whatever their personal affectations, were doing valuable work. He took his own charitable work seriously and he truly appreciated others who did the same.

Star Chamber went dark.

The first major revival of *Tonight at 8.30* that was attempted was in 1947, when Gertie wrote to Noël,

> Dearest Noël,
> Wherever I go ... all I hear is '*Please* revive *Tonight at 8.30*!!!' So many people who saw those plays want to see them again and it would seem that millions who didn't see them feel furiously frustrated. Personally, I do not cherish the thought of doing them again without you ... but it stands to reason that someone will get the bright idea of reviving *8.30* and we shall only have ourselves to blame ... Please cable me 'Yes' or 'No', as I shall hold off everything else until I hear from you.
> Much love,
> Gert

Noël was not happy at the thought. He was rarely in favour of – as he put it – 'cooking his cabbage twice' but he was aware that Gertie was in one of her periodic financial meltdowns. He reluctantly agreed to a provincial US tour of six of the plays with his life companion, Graham Payn, playing Noël's original roles.

The tour itself was a moderate success. Nonetheless, Noël held firm to his conviction that it should not play on Broadway – until Gertie twisted his arm. He had been right in the first place and the show soon closed. It had not been a happy experience – with one exception. At a matinée in San Francisco Graham was too ill to appear and Noël took his place. It was the last time Noël and Gertie were to share a stage. It brought back so many memories. 'Sometimes I would look across the stage at her – and she would take my breath away.'

Barry Day
2008

PREFACE

Ladies and gentlemen, the idea of presenting three short plays in an evening instead of one long one is far from original. In fact, if one looks back over the years, one finds that the 'triple bill' formula has been used, with varying degrees of success, since the earliest days of the theatre. Latterly, however, that is during the last quarter of a century, it has fallen from favour. Occasionally still a curtain-raiser appears in the provinces but wearing a sadly hang-dog expression, because it knows only too well, poor thing, that it would not be there at all were the main attraction of the evening long enough.

Its spirit is further humiliated by the fact that the leading actors treat it with the utmost disdain, seldom leaving their star dressing-rooms to glance at it, let alone play it. Therefore it has to get along as well as it can in the hands of small-part actors and understudies who, although frequently far more talented and charming than their principals, have neither the name, authority nor experience to triumph over rustling programmes, banging seats and a general atmosphere of bored impatience.

A short play, having a great advantage over a long one in that it can sustain a mood without technical creaking or over-padding, deserves a better fate, and if, by careful writing, acting and producing I can do a little towards reinstating it in its rightful pride, I shall have achieved one of my more sentimental ambitions.

From our point of view behind the footlights the experiment will obviously be interesting. The monotony of repetition will be reduced considerably, and it is to be hoped that the stimulus Miss Lawrence, the company and I will undoubtedly derive from playing several roles during a week instead of only one, will communicate itself to the audience, thereby ensuring that a good time be had by all.

All of the plays included in the programmes have been written especially. There has been no unworthy scuffling in cupboards and bureau drawers in search of forgotten manuscripts, and no hurried refurbishing of old, discarded ideas.

The primary object of the scheme is to provide a full and varied evening's entertainment for theatregoers who, we hope, will try their best to overcome any latent prejudices they may have against short plays and, at least, do us the honour of coming to judge for themselves.

Noël Coward

WE WERE DANCING

A Comedy in Two Scenes

We Were Dancing was produced in London at the Phoenix Theatre on 9 January 1936, with the following cast:

LOUISE CHARTERIS	Miss Gertrude Lawrence
HUBERT CHARTERIS	Mr. Alan Webb
KARL SANDYS	Mr. Noël Coward
CLARA BETHEL	Miss Alison Leggatt
GEORGE DAVIES	Mr. Edward Underdown
EVA BLAKE	Miss Moya Nugent
MAJOR BLAKE	Mr. Anthony Pelissier
IPPAGA	Mr. Kenneth Carten

TWO OR THREE UNNAMED MEMBERS OF THE COUNTRY CLUB

————————

Scene I.   *Veranda of the Country Club at Samolo.*
             Evening.
Scene II. *The same. Early morning.*

TIME: The Present.

Scene I

The scene is the veranda of the Country Club at Samolo.

On the right is a room in which dances are held every Saturday night. For these occasions a dance-band flies up from Pendarla by the new Imperial Inter-State Airways. The band arrives in the afternoon, plays all night and departs early on Sunday for Abbachi where it repeats the same procedure for the inhabitants there, returning wearily on Mondays to the Grand Hotel, Pendarla where, during the week, it plays for the tourists.

When the curtain rises the veranda is deserted. A full moon is shining over the sea and, far away, above the chatter and music of the dance-room, there can occasionally be heard the wailing of native music rising up from the crowded streets by the harbour.

IPPAGA, a Samolan boy, crosses the veranda from right to left carrying a tray of drinks. He is yellowish brown in colour and, like most Samolans, comparatively tall. He wears a scarlet fez, a green, purple and mustard-coloured sarong, black patent-leather shoes, silver earrings and three wooden bracelets.

As he goes off on the left the dance music stops and there is the sound of applause.

GEORGE DAVIES and EVA BLAKE come out of the dance-room. GEORGE DAVIES is a hearty, nondescript young man dressed in the usual white mess-jacket, black evening trousers and cummerbund.

EVA, equally nondescript, is wearing a pink taffeta bunchy little dress, pink ribbon in her hair and pink shoes and stockings which do not quite match. She carries a diamanté evening bag and a blue chiffon handkerchief round her wrist. She also wears a necklace of seed pearls and a pendant.

The dance music starts again. EVA looks furtively over her shoulder.

GEORGE enters first and walks up to balcony and calls:

GEORGE: Eva! Eva!

3

EVA: It's all right, they're playing an encore.

GEORGE: Come on, then.

EVA: Where's the car?

GEORGE: I parked it at the end of the garden where the road turns off. My boy's looking after it.

EVA: He won't say anything, will he?

GEORGE: Of course not. He's been with me for years.

EVA: Oh, George!

GEORGE (*impatiently*): It's all right – come on—

EVA: Where are we going?

GEORGE: Mahica beach, nobody ever comes near it.

EVA: Oh, George!

GEORGE (*taking her hand*): Come on—

They go off right.

The band is playing a waltz and the stage is empty for a moment.

LOUISE CHARTERIS and KARL SANDYS come dancing in from the left. They are both in the thirties, soignée and well-dressed, and they dance together as though they had never been apart.

They waltz three times round the stage finishing in the centre with a prolonged kiss. The music ends, there is the sound of applause. Two women and a man come in. They stop short on observing LOUISE and KARL, they whisper together for a moment and then go back into the dance-room.

LOUISE and KARL remain clasped in each other's arms oblivious of everything.

The music starts again.

HUBERT CHARTERIS and CLARA BETHEL come out of the dance-room. CLARA is a nice-looking, grey-haired woman in the forties. HUBERT her brother, is about the same age. He has dignity and reserve and looks intelligently British.

They both stand for a moment looking at KARL and LOUISE who, still entranced with their kiss, have not even noticed them.

HUBERT (*quietly*): Louise.

LOUISE (*jumping*): Oh!

CLARA (*reproachfully*): Louise, really!

LOUISE and KARL step a little away from each other.

LOUISE (*with a social manner*): This is my husband. (*She hesitates and turns to* KARL.) I'm afraid I didn't catch your name?

4

KARL: Karl. Karl Sandys. (*To* HUBERT *and* CLARA.) How do you do?

HUBERT (*with perfect control*): The car's here, I think we'd better go if you're ready.

LOUISE: I'm not ready.

CLARA (*going towards her*): Come along, Louise.

LOUISE: I can't go, really I can't.

HUBERT: This is most embarrassing, please don't make it worse.

LOUISE: I'm sorry, Hubert. I do see that it's all very difficult.

KARL: I fear I was partly to blame.

HUBERT (*ignoring him*): Please come home now, Louise.

LOUISE (*gently*): No, Hubert.

HUBERT: I'm afraid I must insist.

LOUISE: We have fallen in love.

KARL: Deeply in love.

HUBERT: I would prefer not to discuss the matter with you, sir.

LOUISE: That's silly, Hubert.

HUBERT (*sternly*): Please come away.

LOUISE: I've told you, I can't.

KARL: Have a drink?

HUBERT (*irritably*): Good God!

LOUISE: That is a good idea, Hubert, let's all have a drink.

KARL: We might also sit down.

CLARA: Listen, Louise, you can't behave like this, it's too idiotic.

LOUISE: It's true, can't you see? It's true.

CLARA: What's true? Don't be so foolish.

KARL: We're in love, that's what's true, really it is, Mrs. – Mrs.—

LOUISE: Bethel. This is my husband's sister, Mrs. Bethel.

KARL: How do you do?

CLARA: I appeal to you, Mr. – Mr.—

KARL: Sandys.

CLARA: Mr. Sandys – please go away. Go away at once.

KARL: That's quite impossible.

HUBERT: I detest scenes and I am finding this very unpleasant. I don't know who you are or where you come from, but if you have any sense of behaviour at all you must see that this situation is intolerable. Will you kindly leave the club

5

immediately and never speak to my wife again in any circumstances whatever?

LOUISE: It's more important than that, Hubert, really it is.

KARL: It's the most important thing that has ever happened to me in my whole life, Mr. – Mr.—

LOUISE: Charteris.

KARL: Mr. Charteris.

HUBERT: Once more, Louise, for the last time, will you come home?

LOUISE: No – I can't.

HUBERT: Very well. Come, Clara.

> *He turns to go away,* LOUISE *catches his arm.*

LOUISE: You can't go, either. I know you hate scenes and that you're trying to be as dignified as possible, and that I'm apparently behaving very badly, but it's true, this thing that's happened, I mean – we have fallen in love—

HUBERT: Please let go of my arm, Louise, and don't be ridiculous.

LOUISE: Look at me – look closely – I've been your wife for thirteen years. You're wise and intelligent and you know me well – look at me!

CLARA (*anxiously*): Please go, Mr. Sandys.

KARL (*shaking his head*): No.

HUBERT (*to* LOUISE): I'm looking at you.

LOUISE (*emotionally*): Well – don't you see?

> HUBERT *looks quickly at* CLARA *then at* KARL *and then back to* LOUISE *again.*

HUBERT: Yes – I see.

CLARA: Hubert.

> MAJOR BLAKE *comes in from the dance-room. He is a red-faced, elderly man.*

MAJOR BLAKE: I say, have you seen Eva?

HUBERT: What?

MAJOR BLAKE: I can't find Eva.

CLARA: I think she went home.

MAJOR BLAKE: She can't have, the car's there.

CLARA: She told me she was driving back with the Baileys.

MAJOR BLAKE: Oh, did she, did she really?

CLARA: She told practically everybody in the club that she was driving back with the Baileys, I'm surprised she didn't mention it to you.

MAJOR BLAKE: Oh, she's all right then – thanks – thanks awfully.

CLARA (*after a pause*): You'll be able to pick her up on the way home.

MAJOR BLAKE: It's hardly on the way, it means going all round by the Woo Ching Road.

HUBERT: Why not telephone her?

MAJOR BLAKE: They won't have got there yet, it's an hour's drive.

CLARA: Why not wait until they have got there?

MAJOR BLAKE: Yes, I suppose I'd better. Anybody feel like a Stengah?

HUBERT: No, thanks.

MAJOR BLAKE (*to* KARL): Do you, sir?

KARL: No, thank you.

MAJOR BLAKE: All right – I shall go back to the bar—

KARL: Bar.

MAJOR BLAKE: Thanks very much.

He goes out to right.

KARL: Who is Eva?

CLARA: His wife.

KARL: And who are the Baileys?

CLARA (*with irritation*): Does it matter?

KARL: I don't know.

LOUISE: They live in that large reddish-looking house at the top of the hill.

KARL: I've never been to the top of the hill.

CLARA: Good-night, Mr. Sandys.

KARL: Good-night.

CLARA (*with almost overdone ordinariness*): Come along, Louise.

LOUISE: Don't be silly, Clara.

CLARA: I'm not being silly. I'm acutely uncomfortable. You're behaving abominably and putting Hubert in an insufferable position. For heaven's sake pull yourself together and be

7

reasonable. You talk a lot of nonsense about being in love. How could you possibly be in love all in a minute like that—?

KARL: We are.

CLARA: Please be quiet and let me speak.

LOUISE: Hubert, do make Clara shut up.

CLARA: You must be insane.

HUBERT: Shut up, Clara.

CLARA: And you must be insane, too, I'm ashamed of you, Hubert.

LOUISE: It's no use railing and roaring, Clara. Hubert's much wiser than you. He's keeping calm and trying to understand and I'm deeply grateful to him—

CLARA: Grateful indeed!

LOUISE: Yes, if he behaved as you seem to think he ought to behave, it would only make everything far worse. I suppose you want him to knock Mr.— (*To* KARL.) What is your first name?

KARL: Karl.

LOUISE: Karl – in the jaw?

CLARA: I don't want anything of the sort. I want him to treat the situation as it should be treated, as nothing but a joke, a stupid joke, in extremely bad taste.

LOUISE: It's more than that, Clara, and you know it is, that's why you're scared.

CLARA: I'm not in the least scared.

HUBERT: You'd better allow me to deal with this, Clara, in my own way.

CLARA: There is such a thing as being too wise, too understanding.

LOUISE: You're usually pretty intelligent yourself, Clara. I can't think what's happened to you. This thing is here – now – between Karl and me. It's no use pretending it isn't, or trying to flip it away as a joke, nor is it any use taking up a belligerent attitude over it. God knows I'm confused enough myself – utterly bewildered, but I do know that it's real, too real to be dissipated by conventional gestures—

CLARA: What is real? What are you talking about?

KARL: Love, Mrs. Bethel, we've fallen in love.

CLARA: Rubbish!

LOUISE: It's not rubbish! It's not nonsense. Be quiet!

HUBERT (*to* LOUISE): What do you want me to do?

LOUISE (*looking at* KARL): I don't know.

KARL: May I ask you a question?

HUBERT (*stiffly*): What is it?

KARL: Are you in love with Louise?

CLARA: Well really!

HUBERT: I am devoted to Louise. We have been married for many years.

KARL: I said are you in love with her?

HUBERT: I love her.

LOUISE: Don't go on evading, Hubert, you know perfectly well what he means.

HUBERT: Of course I know what he means. (*To* KARL.) I'll answer you truly. I am not in love with Louise in the way that you imagine yourself to be in love with her—

KARL: I worship her.

HUBERT: You know nothing about her.

KARL: I know that suddenly, when we were dancing, an enchantment swept over me. An enchantment that I have never known before and shall never know again. It's obvious that you should think I'm mad and that she's mad too, our behaviour looks idiotic, cheap, anything you like, but it's true, this magic that happened, it's so true that everything else, all the ordinary ways of behaviour look shabby and unreal beside it – my heart's thumping, I'm trembling like a fool, even now when I'm trying so hard, so desperately hard to be calm and explain to you reasonably, I daren't look at her, if I did, my eyes would brim over with these silly tears and I should cry like a child—

LOUISE (*making a movement towards him*): Oh, my darling—

KARL: Don't, don't speak – let him speak, let him say what's to be done.

> KARL *leaves the three of them and goes up to the veranda rail and looks out at the sea.*

CLARA: You didn't even know his name.

LOUISE: Oh, Clara! What the hell does that matter?

CLARA (*walking about*): This is really too fantastic – it's beyond belief – it's—

LOUISE (*gently*): Listen. I know you feel dreadfully upset for Hubert and for me too, but it's no use huffing and puffing and getting yourself into a state. Here it is this thing that's happened – it's terribly real – as large as life – larger than life, and we'd all better look at it clearly and as sensibly as we can.

HUBERT: You go home, Clara, you can send the car back for me.

CLARA: I shall do no such thing.

LOUISE (*hurriedly – to* HUBERT): We'd better go away – he and I – as soon as possible.

HUBERT: Where to?

LOUISE: I don't know – anywhere—

HUBERT: For God's sake be reasonable. How can you? How can I let you?

LOUISE: How much do you mind – really?

HUBERT: That obviously has nothing to do with it.

LOUISE: I want to know.

HUBERT: I want to know, too. I can't possibly tell. You've made this up, this magic that he talked about, you've conjured it out of the air and now it's smeared over everything – over me, too – none of it seems real but it has to be treated as if it were. You ask me how much I mind – you want that as well, don't you, in addition to your new love?

LOUISE: Want what? What do you mean?

HUBERT (*almost losing control*): You want me to mind – don't you – don't you?

LOUISE: Oh, Hubert – please don't look like that—

HUBERT: You want everything – everything in the world, you always have.

LOUISE: You're pitying yourself. How beastly of you to be so weak, how contemptible of you!

CLARA: Louise!

LOUISE: I've been faithful to you all these years, we stopped being in love with each other ages ago – we became a habit – a well-ordered, useful, social habit. Have you been as faithful to me as I have to you?

KARL: That's nothing to do with us – what's the use of arguing?

He joins the group again.

LOUISE: Answer me. Have you?

HUBERT: No.

CLARA: Hubert!

LOUISE: Fair's fair.

CLARA: Hubert! Louise!

LOUISE: Do stop saying Hubert and Louise, Clara, it's maddening.

KARL: What is all this? Can't you keep to the point both of you? What does it matter whether he's been faithful to you or not, or you to him either? You're not in love with each other any more, that's clear enough, and even if you were this forked lightning that has struck Louise and me would shatter it – scorch it out of existence—

CLARA: Forked lightning indeed!

KARL: Earthquake then, tidal wave, cataclysm!

HUBERT: I've never not loved you, Louise.

LOUISE (*irritably*): I know that perfectly well. I'm deeply attached to you, too. I hated it when you had your tiresome little affairs on the side—

HUBERT: With your heart?

LOUISE: Of course not. Don't be so damned sentimental. You haven't come near my heart for years.

CLARA: If Hubert doesn't strike you in a minute, I will.

IPPAGA *comes out of the dance-room with an empty tray.*

KARL: Boy, bring four whisky-and-sodas.

IPPAGA: Yes, sir.

LOUISE: They're called Stengahs here.

KARL: Four Stengahs then.

CLARA: I'd rather have lemonade.

KARL: You seem bent on complicating everything. (*To* IPPAGA.) Four Stengahs.

IPPAGA: Yes, sir.

He goes off.

LOUISE: Karl, where were we?

HUBERT: Nowhere – nowhere at all. (*He turns away.*)

KARL (*to* HUBERT): Listen, Charteris – I know you won't believe me, or even care, but I really am dreadfully sorry, about all this – not about falling in love, that's beyond being sorry about, but that it should happen to be your wife—

HUBERT: Who are you, where do you come from?

KARL: My name is Karl Sandys. I come from Hampshire. My father is Admiral Sandys—

LOUISE: Dear darling, I wouldn't mind if he were only a bosun's mate.

KARL: I know you wouldn't, sweetheart, but I must explain to your husband—

CLARA: How you can have the impertinence to be flippant, Louise, at a moment like this—

LOUISE: There's never been a moment like this, never before in the history of the world – I'm delirious.

HUBERT (*to* KARL): Please go on.

KARL: I was in the Navy myself but I was axed in 1924.

LOUISE: What's axed?

KARL: Kicked out.

LOUISE: Oh dear, whatever for?

HUBERT: Never mind that, I understand, go on.

KARL: I'm now in the shipping business. I represent the I.M.C.L.

LOUISE: What in God's name is the I.M.C.L.?

HUBERT: Imperial Malayan China Line.

KARL: Passenger and Freight.

HUBERT: I know.

KARL: I've come from Singapore, I've been interviewing our agents in Pendarla—

HUBERT: Littlejohn Thurston and Company?

KARL: Littlejohn Thurston and Company.

LOUISE (*to* CLARA): Littlejohn Thurston and Company.

KARL: I flew up here in the morning plane because I wanted to see a little of the country before I sail on Wednesday.

LOUISE: Wednesday!

HUBERT: Are you married?

KARL: I was, but we were divorced in 1927.

LOUISE: Oh, Karl. Did you love her?

KARL: Of course I did.

LOUISE: The moment's changed – I'm not delirious any more – I can't think of you ever having loved anybody else—

HUBERT: Have you any money?

KARL: Not very much – enough.

LOUISE: What was her name?

KARL: Ayleen.

LOUISE: You mean Eileen.

KARL: I do not, I mean Ayleen – A-y-l-e-e-n.

LOUISE: Very affected.

KARL: It's you I love, more than anyone in the world, past or future—

LOUISE: Oh, Karl!

HUBERT (*sharply*): Please – just a moment – both of you.

KARL: I'm sorry. That was inconsiderate.

HUBERT: I'm trying to be as detached as possible. It isn't easy.

LOUISE: I know it isn't, it's beastly for you, I do see that.

CLARA: You're all being so charming to each other it's positively nauseating.

LOUISE: My dear Clara, just because your late husband was vaguely connected with the Indian Army, there is no reason for you to be so set on blood-letting—

CLARA: I'm not – I should like to say—

LOUISE: You're no better than a Tricoteuse.

KARL: What's a Tricoteuse?

LOUISE: One of those horrid old things in the French Revolution with knitting-needles.

HUBERT: All this is beside the point.

LOUISE: Clara's been beside the point for years.

KARL: Dearest, I want you so.

LOUISE: Oh, Karl!

CLARA: This is disgusting—

HUBERT: You'd much better go home, Clara—

CLARA: I've told you before I shall do no such thing, I'm apparently the only one present with the remotest grip on sanity. I shall stay as long as you do, Hubert.

KARL: Dear Mrs. Bethel.

CLARA: I beg your pardon?

KARL: I said, 'Dear Mrs. Bethel,' because I admire your integrity enormously and I do hope when all this has blown over that we shall be close friends.

CLARA: I think you're an insufferable cad, Mr. Sandys.

LOUISE: Blown over! Oh, Karl.

KARL: Darling, I didn't mean that part of it.

HUBERT: I have something to say to you, Louise. Will everybody please be quiet for a moment?

CLARA: Hubert, I honestly think—

LOUISE: That's exactly what you don't do.

HUBERT: This man, whom you so abruptly love, is sailing on Wednesday.

KARL: On the *Euripides*.

LOUISE: But the *Euripides* goes to Australia, I know because the MacVities are going on it.

KARL: That can't be helped, I have to interview our agents in Sydney—

LOUISE: We'll have to go on another boat, I can't travel in sin with the MacVities.

HUBERT: Do you really mean to go with him?

LOUISE: Yes, Hubert.

CLARA: You're stark staring mad all of you; Hubert, for God's sake—

HUBERT: Excuse me— (*Gently.*) Louise, how true is this to you?

LOUISE: Oh, Hubert, don't be too kind.

HUBERT: Will it be worth it?

LOUISE: Oh yes, yes, of course it will – it must!

HUBERT: What has happened exactly – how do you know so surely, so soon?

SONG: 'WE WERE DANCING'

I

If you can
Imagine my embarrassment when you politely asked me to explain
Man to man
I cannot help but feel conventional apologies are all in vain.

You must see
We've stepped into a dream that's set us free
Don't think we planned it
Please understand it.

We were dancing
And the gods must have found it entrancing
For they smiled
On a moment undefiled
By the care and woe
That mortals know.
We were dancing
And the music and lights were enhancing
Our desire
When the World caught on fire
He and I were dancing.

2

Love lay in wait for us
Twisted our fate for us
No one warned us
Reason scorned us
Time stood still
In that first strange thrill.
Destiny knew of us
Guided the two of us
How could we
Refuse to see
That wrong seemed right
On this lyrical enchanted night
Logic supplies no laws for it
Only one cause for it.

We were dancing ... *etc.*

LOUISE: We were dancing – somebody introduced us, I can't remember who, we never heard each other's names – it was a waltz – and in the middle of it we looked at each other – he said just now that it was forked lightning, an earthquake, a tidal wave, cataclysm, but it was more than all those things – much more – my heart stopped, and with it the world stopped too – there was no more land or sea or sky, there wasn't even any more music – I saw in his eyes a strange infinity – only just him and me together for ever and ever – and – ever—

> *She faints.* KARL *catches her in his arms.*
> IPPAGA *enters with a tray of drinks.*

IPPAGA: Stengahs, sir.

KARL: Bring them here, quick.

> KARL *lowers* LOUISE *gently into a chair and kneels beside her with his arm under her head.* HUBERT *kneels on the other side of her.* CLARA *kneels in front of her and endeavours to make her swallow a little whisky. After a moment her eyelids flutter and she moves her head.*
>
> *The dance music that has been playing intermittently throughout the scene comes to an end, there is the sound of applause, then it strikes up the National Anthem.*

LOUISE (*weakly*): Good God! God Save the King!

> *She staggers to her feet supported by* KARL. *The others rise also and they all stand to attention as the lights fade on the scene.*

Scene II

When the lights come up on the scene, CLARA, HUBERT, LOUISE *and* KARL *are all sitting in attitudes of extreme weariness. There is a table near them on which are the remains of bacon and eggs and sandwiches.* IPPAGA *is lying on the floor on the right, fast asleep. Dawn is breaking and the stage gets lighter and lighter as the scene progresses.* LOUISE, *in a state of drooping exhaustion, is arranging her face in the mirror from her handbag which* HUBERT *is holding up for her.*

LOUISE (*petulantly*): —But surely you could interview your agents in Sydney another time—

KARL: I can't see why I should alter the whole course of my career just because of the MacVities.

LOUISE: It isn't only the MacVities, it's Australia.

KARL: What's the matter with Australia?

LOUISE: I don't know, that's what's worrying me.

HUBERT: Haven't you got any agents anywhere else?

KARL: There's Havermeyer, Turner and Price in Johannesburg but I've seen them.

LOUISE: You could see them again, couldn't you? It's not much to ask.

KARL: If I start giving in to you now, darling, we shall never have a moment's peace together.

CLARA: Well I wish you'd make up your minds where you're going and when, it's very early and I'm tired.

LOUISE: You've been wonderfully patient, both of you – I'm tired too.

HUBERT: Would you like another sandwich, dear? There are three left.

LOUISE (*patting his hand*): No thank you, Hubert, they're filthy.

KARL: I'd like to say too how grateful I am to you, you've been understanding and direct and absolutely first-rate over the whole business.

HUBERT: I'm terribly fond of Louise, I always have been.

CLARA: Fortunately Hubert's leave is almost due so we shan't have to face too much unpleasantness in the Colony.

HUBERT: What time does your plane leave?

KARL (*glancing at his watch*): Seven-thirty – it's now a quarter to six.

LOUISE: I'll come by the night train and join you in Pendarla in the morning.

HUBERT: I shall miss you dreadfully, Louise.

LOUISE: I shall miss you, too.

KARL: I'm not sure that I shan't miss you, too.

LOUISE: Oh, dear, I do wish it didn't have to be Australia.

KARL: Now then, Louise!

CLARA: Some parts of Australia can be lovely.

LOUISE: Yes, but will they?

CLARA: And there's always New Zealand.

KARL: I haven't any agents in New Zealand.

LOUISE: I shall have to write to Mother and explain. I'm afraid it will be dreadfully muddling for her.

HUBERT: Serve her right.

LOUISE: Hubert! It's not like you to be unchivalrous about Mother.

HUBERT: Now that you're leaving me the situation has changed.

LOUISE: Yes. You're quite right. I do see that.

HUBERT: Without wishing to wound you, Louise, I should like to take this opportunity of saying that she lacks charm to a remarkable degree.

LOUISE: It's funny, isn't it, when you think how attractive Father was.

KARL: This seems an ideal moment for you to give us a detailed description of where you lived as a girl.

LOUISE: I do hope you're not going to turn out to be testy.

CLARA: Never mind, come along, Hubert, we can't stay here any longer, the Fenwicks will be arriving to play golf in a minute.

HUBERT (*to* LOUISE): Do you want to come now or stay until his plane goes?

LOUISE: I'll stay for just a little while, send the car back.

HUBERT (*to* KARL): Would you care to come to the house and have a bath?

KARL: No, thanks, I can have one here.

HUBERT: Then I shan't be seeing you again.

KARL: Not unless you come and see us off on the boat.

HUBERT: I shan't be able to on Wednesday, I have to go up-country.

KARL: Well, good-bye, then.

HUBERT: Good-bye.

  They shake hands.

Try to make her happy, won't you?

KARL: I'll do my best.

HUBERT: Clara—

CLARA (*to* KARL): Good-bye.

KARL: Good-bye.

CLARA: I wish my husband were alive.

KARL: Why?

CLARA: Because he'd horsewhip you and, Tricoteuse or no Tricoteuse, I should enjoy it keenly.

KARL: Thank you very much.

> CLARA *and* HUBERT *go off.*
>> LOUISE *gets up and goes to the veranda rail, she leans on it and looks out at the sea.*

LOUISE: I feel as if I'd been run over.

KARL (*joining her*): Dearest.

LOUISE: Don't.

KARL: Don't what?

LOUISE: Don't call me dearest, just for a minute.

KARL: I love you so.

LOUISE: We ought to be able to see Sumatra really at this time of the morning.

KARL: I don't want to see Sumatra.

LOUISE: I think I will have another sandwich after all.

KARL: All right.

> *They come down from the rail and pensively take a sandwich each.*

LOUISE: Are you happy?

KARL: Wildly happy. Are you?

LOUISE: Dear Karl!

KARL: What's the matter?

LOUISE: You're doing splendidly.

KARL: Don't talk like that, my sweet, it's unkind.

LOUISE: Ayleen would be proud of you.

KARL: That was worse than unkind.

LOUISE: Where is it, our moment? What's happened to the magic?

KARL (*sadly*): I see.

LOUISE: I wonder if you do really?

KARL: Dance with me a minute.

LOUISE: Very well.

> *She hasn't quite finished her sandwich so she holds it in her left hand while they waltz solemnly round the stage.*

KARL: Of course the music makes a great difference.

LOUISE: There isn't always music.

KARL: And moonlight.

LOUISE: Moonlight doesn't last.

> *They go on dancing. The sound of a native pipe is heard a long way off in the distance.*

KARL: There's music for us.

LOUISE: It's the wrong sort.

KARL: I wish you'd finish your sandwich.

LOUISE: I have.

KARL: Kiss me.

LOUISE: My dear—

> *They kiss.*

You see!

KARL: The joke is on us.

LOUISE: It was a nice joke, while it lasted.

KARL: We've never even been lovers.

LOUISE: I don't want to now, do you?

KARL: Not much.

LOUISE: We missed our chance—

KARL: Don't talk like that, it sounds so depressing— (*They turn away from each other.*)

LOUISE: What's the name of your agents in Sydney?

KARL: Eldrich, Lincoln and Barret.

LOUISE: Give them my love.

> *She pats his face very gently and sweetly and goes quickly away. He makes a movement as if to follow her, then pauses and lights a cigarette. He hums for a moment the tune to which they were dancing and then goes up to the rail where he stands leaning against a post looking out into the morning.*
>
> GEORGE DAVIES *and* EVA BLAKE *come quietly almost furtively on from the right; they talk in whispers.*

EVA: It's awfully light.

GEORGE: There's nobody about.

EVA: Oh, George, you're so wonderful!

GEORGE: Shhh!

> *They kiss swiftly.*

I suppose it's all right about the Baileys?

EVA: Yes, Marion promised – she'll never say a word.

GEORGE: I won't take you right up to the house, I'll just drop you off at the end of the garden—

EVA: Oh, George, you think of everything—

KARL: Excuse me, is your name Eva?

EVA: Yes.

KARL: I congratulate you!

> EVA *and* GEORGE *go off.*
> KARL *comes down and kicks* IPPAGA *gently.*

Wake up – wake up, it's morning—

> IPPAGA *stretches himself as the curtain falls.*

THE ASTONISHED HEART

A Play in Six Scenes

The Astonished Heart was produced in London at the Phoenix
Theatre on 9 January 1936, with the following cast:

CHRISTIAN FABER	Mr Noël Coward
BARBARA, *his wife*	Miss Alison Leggatt
LEONORA VAIL	Miss Gertrude Lawrence
TIM VERNEY	Mr Anthony Pelissier
SUSAN BIRCH	Miss Everley Gregg
SIR REGINALD FRENCH	Mr Alan Webb
ERNEST	Mr Edward Underdown

————

The action of the entire play takes place in the drawing-room of the
FABERS' *flat in London.*

Scene I. *Late afternoon. November 1935.*
Scene II. *Late afternoon. November 1934.*
Scene III. *Midnight. January 1935.*
Scene IV. *Dawn. April 1935.*
Scene V. *Evening. November 1935.*
Scene VI. *Late afternoon. November 1935.*

Scene I

The action of the entire play takes place in the drawing-room of the
FABERS' *flat in London. The flat is on the top floor of one of the*
newly erected apartment buildings in the region of Hyde Park. The
furniture is comfortable and good without conceding too much to
prevailing fashion. On the left double doors lead to the hall, dining-
room and BARBARA's *bedroom and bathroom, etc. On the right*
other double doors lead to CHRISTIAN's *part of the flat, his*
bedroom, consulting-room and office.

When the curtain rises it is late afternoon in November 1935.
The lights are on but the curtains have not been drawn and
BARBARA *is standing looking out of the window into the foggy*
dusk. She is a tranquil, intelligent woman of about thirty-six or
seven. Her back is to the room and she is drumming her fingers on
the window pane. SUSAN BIRCH *is seated on the sofa with her*
hands clasped on her lap. Her age is somewhere between thirty and
forty and she is plainly and efficiently dressed as befits a secretary.
She is sitting very still although occasionally she bites her lip
nervously. TIM VERNEY, *a nice-looking man in the early thirties,*
is standing in front of the fireplace on the right smoking a cigarette.
There is an air of strain in the room as though any one of them
might cry out at any moment. The silence is broken by BARBARA.

BARBARA: It looks terribly dreary out, but it's like that anyhow,
at this time of year, isn't it?
TIM: Yes.
BARBARA: The traffic seems slower than usual — I expect that's
my imagination.
TIM: Don't you think you'd better come away from the window
now?
BARBARA: Yes, I suppose I had.

She comes slowly down and sits on the sofa next to SUSAN.

Don't worry, Tim, about the window I mean, it's something

we've got to get used to like everything else – part of the whole thing.

TIM: Yes, I know.

BARBARA (*to* SUSAN): She answered the telephone herself, didn't she?

SUSAN (*with an effort*): Yes.

BARBARA: She ought to be here by now.

SUSAN (*looking at her wrist-watch*): Yes – yes, she ought.

BARBARA: I suppose Ernest would be shocked if we had a cocktail, wouldn't he?

TIM: That doesn't matter.

BARBARA (*almost irritably*): I know it doesn't matter, Tim, I was only thinking how funny it is that whether Ernest should be shocked or not shocked, should come into my mind at all – will you ring for him?

TIM: All right. (*He rings the bell by the fireplace.*)

BARBARA (*impulsively patting* SUSAN's *hand*): I expect you think I'm talking too much.

SUSAN (*trying to smile*): No, I don't, dear.

BARBARA: Talking's useful, it makes a little noise but not too much, just enough to distract the attention—

SUSAN: I know. (*She gets up.*)

BARBARA: What is it?

SUSAN: I thought perhaps I'd better go into the office.

BARBARA: No, don't, sit down again, stay with us.

SUSAN: Very well. (*She sits down again.*)

ERNEST, *the butler, enters.*

ERNEST: You rang, madame?

BARBARA: Make a cocktail will you, Ernest, a dry Martini I think, don't you, Tim?

TIM (*absently*): Yes, a dry Martini.

ERNEST: Very good, madame.

BARBARA: When Mrs Vail arrives – I'm – I'm expecting her— (*Her voice breaks slightly.*)

ERNEST: Yes, madame.

He goes out.

BARBARA: That was silly of me, wasn't it? – Unnecessary – he knew perfectly well we were expecting her—

26

TIM: She's probably held up in the traffic.

BARBARA: Yes, it's bad at this time of day – I'd like a cigarette, Susan, there's a box just by you.

> SUSAN *silently hands her the box and she takes a cigarette and lights it.*

TIM: Poor woman.

BARBARA: Leonora? Yes – it's awful for her.

SUSAN (*bitterly*): She'll get over it.

BARBARA: So shall we I expect – in time.

SUSAN: It doesn't matter to her, not really, not like it matters to us – she'll cry a lot and be beautifully heartbroken—

BARBARA: Don't be unkind.

SUSAN (*violently*): I hate her.

BARBARA (*turning away*): Oh, don't, Susan – what's the use of that—

SUSAN: I don't care whether it's any use or not – I hate her, more than I've ever hated anyone in my whole life—

BARBARA: You might just as well hate a piece of notepaper, because someone's written something cruel on it.

> SIR REGINALD FRENCH *comes through the double doors on the right. He is an authoritative, elderly surgeon.*

SIR REGINALD: She hasn't arrived yet?

TIM: She's on her way.

SIR REGINALD: Good. (*He turns to go again.*)

BARBARA: There isn't much time is there?

SIR REGINALD (*gently*): No, I'm afraid not.

BARBARA: Is he – conscious?

SIR REGINALD: Only for a brief moment, every now and then.

BARBARA: It's then that he asks for her? In those brief moments?

SIR REGINALD: Yes.

BARBARA: I'll send her straight in when she comes.

SIR REGINALD: Do, my dear.

> *He goes out.*

SUSAN: Oh God! (*She breaks down and cries softly.*)

BARBARA (*putting her arm round her*): Don't, dear.

TIM: Shut up, Susan.

SUSAN: I can't help it – it would have been much better if only you'd let me go into the office when I wanted to.

BARBARA: I'd rather you cried here with us than all by yourself in there.

SUSAN (*dabbing her eyes*): I'm all right now.

BARBARA: Don't make too much of an effort, Susan, it's a dreadful strain – I'd cry if I could – tears are fine, a little relief – they let the grief out for a minute or two – I envy them—

> ERNEST *enters with a tray on which is a cocktail shaker and four glasses.*

Here are the cocktails. Put them on the small table, Ernest – Tim, you pour them out – thank you, Ernest.

> ERNEST *puts down the tray and goes out.* TIM *gives the shaker a couple of extra shakes and pours out a cocktail for each of them. They take them in silence.*

TIM (*drinking*): He's certainly made it dry enough.

BARBARA (*sipping hers and smiling faintly*): Strong enough too – oh, dear—

> *There is the sound of the front-door bell. They all jump slightly.*

TIM: Here she is – at last—

BARBARA (*suddenly*): How extraordinary – d'you see what I mean? It's the same, exactly the same as a year ago – you were there, Tim, just where you are now, with a cocktail glass in your hand – you were there, Susan, only you had your glasses on and a packet of papers in your lap – don't you remember – the first time she ever came into this room—?

> ERNEST *opens the door and announces:* 'Mrs Vail' *as the lights fade.*

Scene II

When the lights come up on the scene BARBARA, TIM, SUSAN *and* ERNEST *are all in the same position as the preceding scene.* SUSAN *is wearing glasses and has a packet of papers in her lap, her jumper is blue instead of grey.*

BARBARA *is wearing a tea gown.* TIM *is in the same suit but wearing a different tie.*

ERNEST (*announcing*): Mrs Vail.

> LEONORA VAIL *enters. She is a lovely creature of about thirty, exquisitely dressed and with great charm of manner.*

BARBARA (*greeting her*): My dear – after all these years—

LEONORA: Isn't it lovely?

> *They kiss affectionately.*

BARBARA: Bring some fresh cocktails, Ernest.

ERNEST: Yes, madame.

> *He goes out.*

BARBARA (*introducing her*): This is Susan Birch, Chris's right hand and this is Tim Verney, Chris's left hand – or perhaps it's the other way round – settle it among yourselves – Leonora Vail – Ames that was—

LEONORA: Leonora Ames, terrible at games! Do you remember?

BARBARA: Of course I do.

> *They both laugh.*

LEONORA (*shaking hands with* SUSAN): How do you do?

SUSAN: How do you do?

LEONORA (*shaking hands with* TIM): I think Barbara wrote that beastly little rhyme herself.

TIM (*smiling*): Was it true?

LEONORA: Absolutely.

BARBARA: I can't possibly say you haven't changed a bit, you've changed more thoroughly than anyone I've ever seen—

LEONORA: Having our hair up makes a great difference.

BARBARA: Your voice has changed too, but I recognised it on the telephone.

LEONORA: I'd have known yours anywhere.

TIM: Have a cocktail, it's mostly water now – perhaps you'd rather wait for a fresh one.

LEONORA: That'll do beautifully to start with.

> *He pours out a cocktail and she holds it up towards* BARBARA.

The nastiest girl in the school.

BARBARA (*laughing*): But the best King Lear.

LEONORA (*also laughing*): Oh, of course – I'd forgotten that.

BARBARA: I foresee a flood of reminiscence.

TIM: So do I – come along, Susan, we'd better go.

BARBARA: No, don't go – you can bear it, Tim, you'll probably discover a lot of useful little psychological echoes from my childhood—

SUSAN (*rising*): I must go anyhow – all these have to be dealt with. (*She indicates the papers in her hand.*)

TIM: Is there a patient in there now?

SUSAN (*glancing at her watch*): Yes, but her time's nearly up.

LEONORA (*to* BARBARA): Does he work all day long, your husband?

BARBARA: Yes, most of the night as well sometimes.

LEONORA: What's he like?

BARBARA: Horrible.

LEONORA: I sympathise, mine was an absolute darling, so much so that I divorced him after eighteen months—

SUSAN: Goodbye, Mrs Vail.

LEONORA: Goodbye.

TIM: We shall probably meet again very soon.

LEONORA: I hope so.

BARBARA: Tell Chris to come in for a second if he can when he's got rid of his patient.

TIM: All right.

He and SUSAN *go out.*

LEONORA: What a nice man.

BARBARA: Tim's a dear, he's extremely brilliant, too, Chris thinks the world of him.

LEONORA: He must be wonderful.

BARBARA: Who, Chris?

LEONORA: Yes, a little frightening though I should think.

BARBARA (*smiling*): Oh no, he's not in the least frightening – he gets a bit abstracted every now and then – when he's working too hard.

LEONORA: Dear Barbara, how nice this is – how long ago is it?—

BARBARA: Seventeen – no eighteen years – I'm thirty-five now, I left long before you did—

LEONORA: I remember missing you dreadfully.

BARBARA: It was after the war when you went to America?

LEONORA: Yes, just after. Father left Brazil in 1918 and at the beginning of 1919 we went to Washington.

BARBARA: When were you married?

LEONORA: Oh, a long while after, several years.

BARBARA: Was he really such a – a darling?

LEONORA: Oh, it was all horrid. He was much older than me, very rich – fortunately – that's all there was to it really.

BARBARA: And you never wanted to marry again?

LEONORA: I wanted to once, but it wasn't possible, everything went wrong—

> ERNEST *comes in with fresh cocktails.*

BARBARA: I'm so sorry.

LEONORA: I minded horribly at the time but I travelled a bit and got over it, it's a long while ago anyhow.

BARBARA: How long have you been in England?

LEONORA: Only two weeks – I've got a darling little house, only rented of course, I moved in on Monday – when will you come and dine?

BARBARA: Whenever you like.

LEONORA: And your husband, Chris?

BARBARA: I'm sure he'd love to but it all depends, you can never count on him—

LEONORA: I'm longing to see him.

> ERNEST *having deposited the cocktail shaker on the tray, goes out, taking with him the empty one.*

BARBARA: He'll probably come in soon for a moment.

LEONORA: Is it never more than a moment?

BARBARA: Oh, yes – not quite as bad as that – but being married to eminence requires a little forbearance, especially if the eminence is dear to you.

LEONORA: No holidays?

BARBARA: Yes – last year we got a full month – we went to Italy, Como first and then down to Venice, it was lovely. He got a bit restive during the last week, but I persuaded him to stay the course.

LEONORA: I should be jealous I think.

BARBARA: Jealous?

LEONORA: But you're better balanced than I am – less emotional – you always were—

BARBARA: It would be tiresome to go on being emotional after twelve years of marriage. (*She gives her a cocktail.*)

LEONORA: I don't really want another.

BARBARA: Come on – one more – I will too.

LEONORA: All right.

BARBARA: Old times. (*She drinks.*)

LEONORA: Old times. (*She drinks.*) What does he do exactly?

BARBARA: Chris?

LEONORA: Yes.

BARBARA (*gently*): He's only one of the most celebrated psychiatrists in the world, dear.

LEONORA (*laughing*): I know that – be patient with me – psychiatrist is only a word to me – it's nothing to do with bone-setting, is it?

BARBARA (*laughing too*): No, nothing whatever – you're thinking of osteopathy—

LEONORA: No, I'm not, it's something like psychiatrist – another word.

BARBARA: Chiropracter.

LEONORA: That's it.

BARBARA: You'd better not mention that to Chris, he doesn't approve of chiropracters at all—

LEONORA: What's a psychiatrist then?

BARBARA: Someone who cures diseases of the mind—

LEONORA: Oh, repressions and inhibitions and all that sort of thing.

BARBARA: Yes, all that sort of thing.

LEONORA: How exciting.

BARBARA: Yes, more interesting than exciting.

LEONORA: You have a superior look in your eye, Barbara, and I resent it deeply.

BARBARA: I'm sorry, dear.

LEONORA: I know I'm idiotic really, but it's most tactless of you to remind me of it. How does he start his treatments? Just a series of embarrassing questions?

BARBARA: Frightfully embarrassing.

LEONORA: I've read about it in books. You have to remember
    sinister little episodes of your childhood – falling in love with
    the cook – or being frightened by a goat – then you have to
    determine the cook or sublimate the goat or something, and
    you go away completely cured and sleep like a top.

BARBARA: I see that your ignorance was only an affectation, you
    have the whole thing in a nutshell.

LEONORA: It must be fascinating work, unearthing everybody's
    rattling little skeletons and fitting them together like Meccano.
    What about himself?

BARBARA: How do you mean?

LEONORA: Does he know all about himself right from the
    beginning? Is everything cut and dried and accounted for?

BARBARA: I expect so.

LEONORA: And you? Has he a chart of you hanging up over his
    desk?

BARBARA: He doesn't need a chart of me, Leonora.

LEONORA: Something in your manner tells me that I've gone too
    far – oh dear – I didn't mean to – don't be cross.

BARBARA (*smiling*): I'm not in the least cross.

LEONORA: I suppose he'd know all about me in a minute,
    wouldn't he? The very first second he clapped eyes on me.

BARBARA: Certainly.

LEONORA: How terrifying.

BARBARA: Don't pretend, Leonora, I'm perfectly sure you're not
    terrified of anyone.

LEONORA: Do his patients fall in love with him?

BARBARA: Practically always.

LEONORA: Don't you hate that?

BARBARA: You are funny, Leonora.

LEONORA: Am I? Nicely funny or nastily funny?

BARBARA: Charmingly funny.

LEONORA: Oh dear, I can't wait to see him, do tell someone to
    hurry him up, I shall have to go in a minute. He hasn't got a
    moustache, has he?

BARBARA: No.

LEONORA: Beard?

BARBARA: No beard.

LEONORA: Tall or short?

BARBARA: Short.

LEONORA: Fat?

BARBARA: Not exactly fat, let's say a little podgy.

LEONORA: Oh, Barbara!

BARBARA: He has very little chance of getting exercise you see, still he does his best with those things in the bathroom—

LEONORA (*horrified*): What things?

BARBARA: You know, they're attached to the wall and you gasp and strain and they snap back again – he has a rowing machine too.

LEONORA: I know, I've seen them in gymnasiums on ships.

BARBARA: He finds it very effective.

LEONORA: You're lying, aren't you?

BARBARA: Yes, Leonora.

LEONORA: I suppose he's eight feet high and absolutely bewitching.

BARBARA: If you care for long black moustaches, yes.

LEONORA: I've made up my mind to fall in love with him on sight.

BARBARA: He's quite used to that.

LEONORA: You're positively smug about him, Barbara – tell me seriously – do you really adore him?

BARBARA: I love him very much.

LEONORA: How marvellous. And does he love you?

BARBARA: Really, Leonora!

LEONORA: I know I'm behaving badly, but it seems so funny—

BARBARA: What seems so funny?

LEONORA: I know what I mean, but it's awfully difficult to explain.

BARBARA (*drily*): Don't try.

LEONORA: Darling, I think I'd like just another little sip if there's any more in the shaker—

BARBARA: It's practically full—

> BARBARA *refills her glass.* CHRISTIAN FABER *comes into the room. He is about forty years old, tall and thin. He moves quickly and decisively as though there was never quite enough time for all he had to do.*

LEONORA: At last!

CHRIS (*surprised*): What?

BARBARA: This is Mrs Vail, Chris, one of my oldest friends, we were at school together—

CHRIS (*absently*): Oh – how do you do. (*He shakes hands.*)

BARBARA: Cocktail?

CHRIS: No, I've got some more work to do.

LEONORA: I think it only fair that you should know that until Barbara disillusioned me I thought that you were a chiropracter.

CHRIS (*smiling perfunctorily*): Did you really? (*To* BARBARA.) Listen, dear, we are dining with Mary tonight, aren't we?

BARBARA: Yes.

CHRIS: Well, you go without me and tell her I'll come in for coffee—

BARBARA (*laughing*): She knows that already, darling, she told me on the telephone this morning.

CHRIS (*with a smile*): Mary is one of the most sensible women I know.

LEONORA (*with slightly forced impudence*): I also thought you had a long moustache!

CHRIS (*not quite understanding*): What—?

BARBARA (*quickly*): Moustache, dear, Leonora thought you had a moustache.

CHRIS (*with a completely empty smile*): Oh, no – I haven't a moustache.

He bows politely and goes out.

LEONORA: I'd rather he was a chiropracter.

BARBARA: Never mind.

LEONORA: He didn't even see me, I do think it's a shame.

BARBARA: He saw you all right.

LEONORA: You're being superior again, how odious of you.

BARBARA: When do you want us to come and dine?

LEONORA: I shan't even ask him, I like the other young man much better, Tim whatever his name was, bring him instead – next Wednesday?

BARBARA (*going to her book on the desk*): Wait a minute.

LEONORA: Do you want to go to a play or just sit and talk?

35

BARBARA: I don't mind a bit, whichever you like – but I'd rather make it Thursday.

LEONORA: All right – Thursday – we'll decide whether to go out or not later.

BARBARA: That'll be lovely.

LEONORA: I really must go now—

BARBARA: You're sure you wouldn't like to stay and have your bones set or anything?

LEONORA: No, I've given up the whole idea.

BARBARA: What whole idea?

LEONORA: About falling madly in love with your husband and him falling madly in love with me and then me having a lovely 'old friends together' scene with you and everyone behaving beautifully and making sacrifices all round—

BARBARA: You were always romantic, even at school, do you remember Monsieur Brachet?

LEONORA: I adored him, didn't I? But still he was rather sweet.

BARBARA: His eyes were very close together.

LEONORA: Practically two in one, darling, but charm – that's what counts, darling—

BARBARA: What's your telephone number?

LEONORA: You're not going to put me off, are you?

BARBARA: Don't be so silly, of course not.

LEONORA: Kensington 3382.

BARBARA (*scribbling it down*): Kensington 3382.

LEONORA: I'll expect you on Thursday – about eight.

BARBARA: Do you really want me to ask Tim?

LEONORA: Of course, he's an angel, and bring your old chiropodist too if he'll come—

BARBARA (*laughing, as they go out*): I'll try to persuade him—

> *Their voices are heard talking and laughing in the hall.* TIM *comes in and goes over to the desk, he rummages about on it.* BARBARA *returns.*

BARBARA: Oh, Tim, you made me jump. What are you doing?

TIM: Is there a Bible in the house?

BARBARA: I suppose there must be somewhere. Whatever do you want it for?

TIM: Chris wants a quotation to use in his lecture on Friday—
BARBARA: Does he know a special one—?
TIM: Vaguely – something in Deuteronomy—

>   ERNEST *enters.*

BARBARA: Have you got a Bible, Ernest?
ERNEST: I think the cook has one, madame.
BARBARA: Ask her if she'll lend it to me for a minute, will you?
ERNEST: Very good, madame.

>   *He goes out.*

BARBARA: Isn't she lovely?
TIM: Who? The cook?
BARBARA: No, don't be so silly, Leonora.
TIM: Very smooth and shiny.
BARBARA: Didn't you like her?
TIM: Yes, I suppose so, I only saw her for a moment.
BARBARA: She loved you at first sight, she wants you to dine
    with her on Thursday.
TIM: Good God!
BARBARA: It's all right, I shall be there to protect you.
TIM: I hate dinner parties.
BARBARA: You mustn't be disagreeable.

>   ERNEST *re-enters with a Bible.*

Ah, thank you, Ernest.
ERNEST: Have you finished with the cocktail things, madame?
BARBARA: Yes, thank you.

>   ERNEST *takes the cocktail tray away as* SUSAN *enters.*

SUSAN: Did you find one?
TIM: Yes, it's the cook's.
SUSAN: It's Moses, Deuteronomy twenty something – It starts
    with 'The Lord shall smite thee—'

>   *They look through the Bible together.*

SUSAN (*to* BARBARA): It's for his paper on the Development of
    Psychopathology starting with Hippocrates—
TIM: This must be it— (*He reads.*) 'The Lord shall smite thee
    with madness, and blindness, and astonishment of the heart.'
SUSAN: Yes, that's it.

>   *She takes the Bible and goes off as the lights fade.*

Scene III

When the lights come up on the scene, CHRIS *and* LEONORA *are discovered standing by the fireplace, his arms are round her and he is kissing her. She is wearing a diaphanous evening gown, he, a dinner jacket. About two months have passed since the preceding scene. The time is after midnight. There is a tray of sandwiches and drinks on the small table by the sofa. She detaches herself from his arms and moves away.*

LEONORA (*in a strained voice*): I must go.

CHRIS (*quietly*): Must you?

LEONORA: Of course.

CHRIS: Isn't that rather inconsistent?

LEONORA: Yes – I suppose it is.

CHRIS: What's the matter?

LEONORA: I didn't mean it to be like this—

CHRIS: Don't go away from me yet.

LEONORA: I must.

CHRIS: Do you want to?

LEONORA (*softly*): No.

CHRIS: Come back to my arms, it's cold over here by the fire.

LEONORA (*with her face turned away from him*): I lied just now when I said I didn't mean it to be like this.

CHRIS: Does it matter?

LEONORA: Yes – it matters dreadfully—

CHRIS (*moving towards her*): My dear—

LEONORA (*with panic in her voice*): Please stay there.

CHRIS (*stopping*): Very well.

LEONORA (*with a rush*): I did mean it to be like this but – but not quite like this – I mean – it was all a trick – I planned it – the first day I came, you remember, when you snubbed me – I teased you about it at dinner tonight – I made up my mind then to make you fall in love with me – now I wish I hadn't – I feel cheap – I feel frightened – I wish with all my heart I hadn't.

CHRIS (*with a smile*): I think it was rather a gay trick. Don't be upset. There's nothing to be upset about. Let's sit down quietly and have a drink.

He comes over to the sofa and pours out a drink.

Will you have one?

LEONORA: No, thank you.

CHRIS (*sitting*): Do come and sit down.

LEONORA: Now you're treating me like a patient.

CHRIS: Only because you're behaving like one.

LEONORA: I see. (*She laughs suddenly.*)

CHRIS: That's better.

LEONORA: Give me a cigarette. (*She sits down next to him.*)

CHRIS: Here. (*He lights one for her.*) You're a lovely creature.

LEONORA: I'm all right outside, but I'm not very pleased with myself inside at the moment.

CHRIS: Pangs of conscience are tiresome, Leonora, they're also exceedingly bad for you.

LEONORA: I'm feeling better now.

CHRIS: I gather that the trick is on again.

LEONORA (*sharply*): That was unkind.

CHRIS: You're very touchy.

LEONORA: What about Barbara?

CHRIS: She's very well, thank you – I had a letter from her this morning.

LEONORA: Are you in love with her?

CHRIS: What on earth did you say that for?

LEONORA: Are you in love with her?

CHRIS: You're behaving like a patient again.

LEONORA: Are you?

CHRIS: Barbara has nothing to do with this.

LEONORA: You're certainly not in love with me.

CHRIS: You have lovely eyes, but there's a little sadness in them, a little disappointment, I could tell your fortune by your eyes – shall I?

LEONORA: I'd rather you didn't.

CHRIS: And your nose—

LEONORA: I'd rather you didn't mention my nose at all.

CHRIS: It's the most unwise nose I've ever seen.

LEONORA: Do stop.

CHRIS: Then there's your mouth—

LEONORA: I must go—

CHRIS: You'd be astounded if you knew how desperately I want to kiss your mouth – again—

LEONORA: Please, Chris—

CHRIS: You're so foolish, up on your romantic high horse – how often have you ridden it wildly until it went lame and you had to walk home?

LEONORA: Often enough to teach me never to do it again.

CHRIS: That's what made the sadness in your eyes – you should never have left school, it was a grave mistake.

LEONORA: You win.

CHRIS: Do I?

LEONORA: I knew you would – quite early in the evening I knew.

CHRIS: Has it been a happy evening – for you?

LEONORA: No, not really – rather strained.

CHRIS: Were you really angry – that first time we met?

LEONORA: Yes – I think I was.

CHRIS: I didn't mean to be rude.

LEONORA: You certainly did.

CHRIS: Yes, now I come to think of it, I did.

LEONORA: Why?

CHRIS: You irritated me, you were so conscious of how absolutely beautiful you looked.

LEONORA: I never thought that.

CHRIS: Your manner demanded attention insistently, like a child banging its spoon on the table, making a clamour – yelling for more—

LEONORA: How horrid that sounds.

CHRIS: Quite natural though, I expect you've always been spoilt.

LEONORA: No, I haven't.

CHRIS: Have you had many lovers?

LEONORA (*looking down*): No – not many.

CHRIS: And the few – whoever they were – did you love them?

LEONORA: Please don't be quite so – clinical.

CHRIS (*impulsively*): Forgive me – I wanted to know.

LEONORA: I loved somebody once – very much – never so much before – and never so much since.

CHRIS: I see.

LEONORA: I know you think my conscience is tiresome and, considering how obviously I threw myself at you, a trifle ill-timed, but it's there all the same and it's making me uneasy – Please listen, I'm being really honest now – if you and I had an – an affair – how much would it hurt Barbara?

CHRIS: I don't know. If she knew, I expect it would upset her a good deal, but it would upset her just as much, if not more, if she thought we wanted to and were denying ourselves on her account. Barbara's that sort of person.

LEONORA: You have been married twelve years.

CHRIS: How naïve you are.

LEONORA: Do you love her? You never answered me before.

CHRIS: Yes, I love her deeply and truly and for ever.

LEONORA: I see.

CHRIS: I don't suppose you do, but it doesn't matter.

LEONORA: It matters a lot.

CHRIS: What do you want? Truth or lies – reality or pretence?

LEONORA: How clever of you to know, without looking, what you have in your safe.

CHRIS: Don't be unkind to me, Leonora.

LEONORA: It's you who are unkind to me.

CHRIS: Why? In what way?

LEONORA: It's my own fault of course—

CHRIS: Entirely.

LEONORA: If you feel that it would make our – our flirtation any more satisfactory, I have some X-ray plates of my teeth.

CHRIS: Stop being quarrelsome, Leonora.

LEONORA: I can't help it, you make me angry – horribly angry – I want to hit out at you.

CHRIS: Any other impulse at this particular stage of the proceedings would be abnormal.

LEONORA: You're so superbly sure of yourself, aren't you?

CHRIS (*seriously*): No, the basis of everything I've ever learned is not being sure – not being sure of anyone or anything in the world – myself least of all— (*He turns away.*)

LEONORA: Hand me my bag, it's just behind you.

CHRIS: What for?

LEONORA: I want to powder my – unwise nose.

CHRIS (*handing it to her*): Here.

LEONORA: Thank you.

She opens her bag and scrutinises herself in the glass inside it. She puts on some lipstick and powders her nose. CHRIS *watches her.*

CHRIS: There's a bit of fluff on the left.

LEONORA: I can see it.

CHRIS: You mustn't be ungracious.

LEONORA: I want to go home now. (*She rises.*)

CHRIS (*also rising*): I'll take you – there's always a taxi on the rank.

LEONORA: Please don't, I'd really rather you didn't.

CHRIS: You must be mad as a hatter.

LEONORA: Why – what do you mean?

CHRIS: To imagine – Oh, what's the use—

He suddenly crushes her in his arms and kisses her violently.

LEONORA: Don't – please, Chris – don't— (*She struggles.*)

CHRIS (*pressing her to him*): Don't be unkind – I want you dreadfully – you must know that – don't leave me – not just yet – it wasn't all a trick – it may have started as a trick, but it isn't that now, is it? Is it?

LEONORA (*breaking away from him, breathlessly*): Yes – yes it is.

CHRIS: Liar. (*He takes her hand.*) Look at me.

LEONORA (*near tears*): No. (*She turns away.*)

CHRIS: Please.

He turns her slowly and looks into her eyes.

LEONORA (*in a whisper*): Well – what's my fortune?

CHRIS: You're going to love me a little.

LEONORA (*shaking her head*): That's not enough.

CHRIS: Oh, yes – yes – more than enough.

LEONORA: Are you sure?

CHRIS: Oh, my dear – my dear—

She slips into his arms again as the lights fade on the scene.

Scene IV

*It is now April, three months having passed since the preceding
scene. The time is about five or six a.m.*

There is a greyness in the room because dawn is not far away.

BARBARA *is sitting in a chair by the fire smoking a cigarette.
She is wearing a dressing-gown, and there is an ashtray by her
side, almost filled with cigarette ends. She shivers slightly, then gets
up and pours herself a brandy and soda; she returns to her chair
and then her attention is caught by the sound of the front door
opening softly. She closes her eyes for an instant and bites her lip
as though she were trying to gather courage.*

CHRIS *comes quietly in from the left; he is wearing a light
overcoat and hat. His face is tired and strained.*

BARBARA (*in as ordinary a voice as she can manage*): Hallo, darling!
CHRIS (*startled*): Barbara!
BARBARA: I'm sorry if I made you jump.
CHRIS: What on earth—?
BARBARA: I couldn't sleep.
CHRIS (*switching on the lights*): Oh, I see—
BARBARA: Not all the lights, Chris.
CHRIS: All right. (*He switches on the desk light and turns the others off
again.*)
BARBARA: Would you like a drink?
CHRIS: No – no, thanks.
BARBARA: I'm having one – it's – it's a bit chilly.
CHRIS (*in a flat voice*): I'm awfully sorry, darling.
BARBARA: There isn't anything to be sorry for – I mean this isn't
a scene – really it isn't, only I do want to talk to you. I've
wanted to for a long while.
CHRIS: I know.
BARBARA: It's probably a bad moment, but – but during the day
it's difficult – there never seems to be any time—
CHRIS: I meant it when I said I was sorry – I am – desperately
sorry.

BARBARA: Of course you are. Don't be silly – I know that – it's all beastly – I'm sorry, too, I'm sorry for you and me and – I'm even sorry for Leonora— (*She gives a little laugh.*)

CHRIS (*noticing the ashtray*): Have you smoked all those tonight?

BARBARA: Yes – it looks awfully unattractive, doesn't it – like after a party— (*She empties the ashtray into the fireplace.*)

CHRIS (*looking away from her*): You know about me loving you all the same, don't you – more than anybody in the world?

BARBARA: Yes, of course I do, but I'd rather you didn't go on about it just at the moment. I want so very much not to be emotional.

CHRIS: Are you very unhappy?

BARBARA: Not any more than you, I don't suppose. That's the worst of the whole business, nobody's having a good time. How is Leonora?

CHRIS: She's all right, I've just left her.

BARBARA: I didn't imagine you'd been to a Masonic dinner, darling.

CHRIS (*smiling wryly*): No, I didn't think you did.

BARBARA: I hate her quite normally with all my feminine instincts; sometimes I get almost violent, all by myself – it's funny, isn't it, after so many years? – I've got over wishing to strangle her, though, now; I just wish she'd never been born.

CHRIS: I think I do, too.

BARBARA: I don't see how we can go on like this quite, do you? It really is too uncomfortable – that's why I sat up for you. I'm dreadfully worried, the personal, loving you part of the affair I could manage, I think – painful as it is – but it's everything else, too – we're all in a state, Tim and Susan – I think even Ernest's getting a bit agitated— (*She laughs again nervously.*) You're working under such tremendous pressure, and you're so terribly strained and tired – we're all frightened that you'll crack up or something.

CHRIS: Don't worry, I shan't crack up.

BARBARA: Do you want to marry her?

CHRIS: No – it isn't anything to do with marriage.

BARBARA: Does she want you to marry her?

CHRIS: No, I don't think so – no, I'm sure she doesn't.

BARBARA: I can't see why that should make me feel a bit better, but it does.

CHRIS: Oh, Baba— (*He breaks off miserably.*)

BARBARA (*brightly*): And I'll trouble you not to call me Baba just now, darling – as a psychologist you really ought to know better.

CHRIS (*trying to smile at her*): All right.

BARBARA: I have a plan, you know, otherwise I wouldn't have pounced like this, but before I tell you what it is, I want to know a little more.

CHRIS: Very well, fire away.

BARBARA: First of all, how clearly do you see the situation in your more detached moments, I mean?

CHRIS: Quite clearly, but the detached moments are getting rarer, I'm afraid.

BARBARA: Can you be detached now?

CHRIS: I'm trying with all my might.

BARBARA: Don't worry about me, please don't! I can tread water indefinitely – it would be different if I were still in love with you, but I'm not, any more than you are with me; that was all settled years ago. We are tremendously necessary to each other, though, and I hope to God we always shall be, and I want to know – I want to know— (*Her voice breaks.*)

CHRIS: How long?

BARBARA (*with control*): Yes.

CHRIS: I'm submerged now – I can't tell.

BARBARA: Very well then, you must go away.

CHRIS: Go away! How can I?

BARBARA: You must.

CHRIS: I've thought of it. I wanted to but it's quite impossible, also even if I could, even if there wasn't work or anything to prevent me, it wouldn't be any use – running away never is any use.

BARBARA: I didn't mean you to go away alone, it's too late for that now. I meant you to go away with her – take two months, three months if necessary – go to the most lovely,

45

beautiful place you can think of – relax utterly – give yourself up to loving her without any sense of strain or responsibility – don't think about work or me or any of the things that are standing in the way—

CHRIS: I can't, Baba, you know I can't.

BARBARA: I don't know anything of the sort. It's clear, cold sense. I'm not being noble and self-sacrificing and thinking only of your happiness. I'm thinking of my own happiness too, and, more important still, of your job – you can't deal wisely and successfully with twisted nerve-strained people if you're twisted and nerve-strained yourself. You must see that. It isn't your passion for Leonora alone that's undermining you, it's the fight you're putting up, you're being torn in half—

CHRIS: Darling, you're making me so dreadfully ashamed.

BARBARA: That's idiotic, unreasonable and idiotic. You said just now that you were submerged – that's true, you are; you've crushed down your emotions for years, and now you're paying for it. It's nothing to be ashamed of, with your sort of temperament it was inevitable – it had to happen, I've been waiting for it.

CHRIS: Baba!

BARBARA: Let me go on. I'm not submerged, I'm seeing the whole thing clearly – unless you put a stop to this agonising battle between your emotions and your intelligence, you'll break completely.

CHRIS (*tortured*): How can I put a stop to it? It's there – it's there all the time – every moment of the day and night – it started so easily, so gaily – little more than a joke; there were no danger signals whatever. I felt just a few conscience pangs over you, but not seriously, the whole thing was so apart from us and all we mean to each other – my intelligence lied to me – my intelligence insisted that it was nothing, just a little emotional flutter that would probably loosen me up and do me a power of good; then suddenly I felt myself being swept away and I started to struggle, but the tide was stronger than I knew; now I'm far from the land, darling – far from my life and you and safety – I'm struggling still, but the water's

46

terribly deep and I'm frightened – I'm frightened. (*He comes close to her and puts his head down on her shoulder.*)

BARBARA (*gently*): I know – I really do know—

CHRIS: It isn't Leonora, it's nothing to do with Leonora any more; it's the thing itself – her face and her body and her charm make a frame, but the picture's in me, before my eyes constantly, and I can't get it out—

BARBARA: Stop struggling.

CHRIS: I can't! If I stop struggling I shall be lost for ever. If I didn't know all the processes it would be easier, but I do – I watch myself all the time – when I'm talking to patients – in case I make a slip; it's as much as I can do sometimes to prevent myself from suddenly shrieking in their faces – 'Why are you here? What do you come to me for? How can I help you when there's a little brooch between us – a little brooch with emeralds and sapphires that someone gave to Leonora years ago – long before I ever knew her – how can I ease your poor mind when a handsome young man is burnt to death in a plane – here in the room – he was the one she really loved, you know, the only one she ever really loved—'

BARBARA: Oh, my dear – oh, my poor dear!

CHRIS (*with a great effort at control*): Tim and Susan are fine – their behaviour's almost too good. There's no reproach in their eyes, just a concentrated determination to bolster me up as much as they can. Nurse Hoskins is not so good – she ushers in the patients warily now – I think she listens outside the door, too, in case of accidents. Then there's Leonora herself – she's having a hell of a time. The ecstasy's still there – just for a few flaming moments – but in between there are bad hours. You see, I'm finding out things all the time – things about her and things about myself. We're seldom alone together – the ghosts of the people she loved before, or thought she loved, come and join us – they make me sick with jealousy, Baba – me of all people. We can laugh about that one day, can't we? I ask her questions, you see, because I can't stop myself – and out of her answers the scenes build themselves – and it's those dead moments that torture me. Can you imagine the foolishness of that? Things that happened years ago long

47

before I even knew she existed – then I lose control and say dreadful cruel things to her. I distort her memories for her, smear them with mockery, dissect them in front of her until they're spoilt and broken into little pieces. Then she cries, not false crying, but real tears for something that's lost . . . and all the time my brain's raising its eyebrows at me and sneering, and then the only thing left is to be sorry – humbly bitterly sorry – and swear never again to be unkind – never, never, never again – until the next time—

He leaves her and goes over to the window. She watches him and then takes a cigarette and lights it.

BARBARA (*quietly*): It's only the strain that makes all that, darling. I wish I could make you see. If only I could get it into your head that there is no reason in the world why you shouldn't love Leonora as much as you want to – for as long as it lasts – you'd be able to give yourself up to it and be happy – you'd probably have quarrels – one always does – but they'd be normal ones, not these dreadful twisted agonies. You must do as I say – it's your only chance. Let Tim take over everything for three months; he can manage all right with Susan. Wipe me from your mind entirely; I shall go away somewhere myself. Laura's in Paris, I can go and stay with her, and Mary's taken the Birrels' house in Kent for six months. It's absolutely lovely and I shall be so much happier than I am now, if only I know you're being sensible and giving yourself space.

CHRIS: Space?

BARBARA: Room to enjoy the best parts of it, without that horrid feeling of hours passing – without the consciousness that there's work to be done the next day and people to see and decisions to make.

CHRIS: It sounds easy, but it wouldn't be.

BARBARA: After a week or so it would, really – I know I'm right – anyhow it's worth trying.

CHRIS: It's running away all the same—

BARBARA: What on earth does that matter? It's being wise that matters. Take the car – don't stop too long in one place, forget everything but just what you're doing at the moment. You really must try it, darling – you see, I've had time to think and you haven't had any time at all.

CHRIS: You don't hate her, do you?

BARBARA (*suddenly angry*): Good God! what does it matter if I do!

CHRIS: I'm sorry.

BARBARA: I'm fighting for you. Leonora's only on the fringe of the business. It's you and me that make my world and the work you've got to do, and the happiness we've had and can have again. My jealousy is not for the desire you have for her, nor for the hours of illusion you buy from her. I'm jealous of the time in between – the waste – those bad hours you told me about just now. I sense futility in all that, and it's that futility that's nagging at you and humiliating you so. Stop trying to balance yourself – come off your tightrope, it's better to climb down than fall down, isn't it?

CHRIS: It's bitter, isn't it, to be made to put on rompers again at my age?

BARBARA: Whether you intended it or not, that remark was definitely funny.

CHRIS: I miss not being able to laugh.

BARBARA: That'll all come back.

CHRIS: Just at this moment – this now – this immediate moment I'm all right, you know – I expect it's because you're so strong.

BARBARA: Well, make the most of it.

CHRIS: You needn't tell me it won't last, I know that.

BARBARA: Hang on to it anyhow as long as you can, even when you're submerged again, try to remember it.

CHRIS: Have you ever loved anyone else, since me?

BARBARA: No, I've never happened to want to.

CHRIS: Would you have, if you had wanted to, I mean?

BARBARA (*lightly*): I expect so.

CHRIS: I wonder how much I should mind.

BARBARA: Do stop whirling about among fictions, there are enough facts to occupy us, God knows. Go away – offer yourself up – get on with it.

CHRIS: It all seems so unreal!

BARBARA: It's real enough to make us damned uncomfortable!

CHRIS (*turning*): I don't believe I really love her at all.

BARBARA: This is no moment to go into a technical argument about that, my sweet. Love is a very comprehensive term, you're certainly obsessed, by her, or by yourself through her, and that's quite enough. Oh, dear, it's more than enough— (*She gives a little laugh.*) Please, Chris—

CHRIS: All right.

BARBARA (*cheerfully*): Well, that's settled – we'll lash Tim into a frenzy of responsibility tomorrow – I mean today – you'd better try to get some sleep now.

CHRIS: Yes – I'll try.

BARBARA: Good morning, darling— (*She puts her arms round him, kisses him lightly and goes quickly out of the room.*)

CHRIS (*as the door closes on her*): Thank you, Baba.

> He leans against the window with his head in his arms as the lights fade.

Scene V

> *Seven months have passed since the preceding scene. It is midnight on the night before the first scene of the play.*
>
> *When the lights go up on the scene* LEONORA *is lying face downwards on the sofa, sobbing.* CHRIS *is leaning on the mantelpiece gazing into the fire.*

CHRIS: For the love of God stop crying. (*She continues to sob.*) I'm sorry – I've said I was sorry—

LEONORA: I can't bear any more.

CHRIS (*coming over to her*): Darling, please—

LEONORA: Don't – don't come near me.

CHRIS: You must forgive me – you must!

LEONORA (*slowly sitting up*): It isn't forgiving – it's that I can't bear any more. I mean it this time – I really can't!

CHRIS (*bitterly*): I should like to know what you propose to do then.

LEONORA: I'm going – I'm going away for good.

CHRIS: I see.

LEONORA (*rising*): I'm going now—

CHRIS (*holding her arms*): No, you're not.

LEONORA: Please, Chris—

CHRIS: You can't possibly go.

LEONORA: You're hurting me.

CHRIS (*coldly*): Why do you struggle then?

LEONORA: Don't be such a fool, what's the use of behaving like this?

CHRIS: I was under the impression that you loved me—

LEONORA: Let go of my arms.

CHRIS: More than anyone or anything in the world. How long ago was it that you said that to me – how long ago – answer me . . . (*He shakes her.*)

LEONORA (*crying again*): Oh, for God's sake, Chris—

CHRIS: You love me so much that you have to lie to me – you love me so much that you play small shabby little tricks on me – you twist me and torture me until I'm driven beyond endurance – then you sob and cry and say I'm cruel.

LEONORA (*almost screaming*): Let me go!

CHRIS: Stay still—

LEONORA (*frantically*): You're mad – don't look at me like that – you're mad—

CHRIS (*grimly*): Answer me one question, my darling – my dear darling—

LEONORA: Let me go – let me go!

CHRIS: Why did you say you hadn't been out to dine with him when you had?

LEONORA: Because I knew you'd make a dreadful scene about it.

CHRIS: Why didn't you stay the night with him then – you wanted to, didn't you? What held you back? Your love for me! Or was it fear—?

LEONORA (*wrenching herself free from him*): Oh, what's the use – what's the use—

CHRIS (*brokenly*): Do you think I like this situation? You not loving me any more, and me wanting you so—

LEONORA (*turning*): Why do you say that – you've worked it all up in your imagination. None of it's true – none of it's real.

CHRIS: Don't lie any more.

LEONORA: I'm not – I'm not.

CHRIS: How do I know? You've lied before – I've caught you out, trivial enough they were, I grant you, but they were lies all the same – little lies or big lies – what's the difference? Perhaps you forget that charming little episode in Cairo—

LEONORA: Oh, God!

CHRIS: All right – all right. I know I'm dragging things up from the past – why shouldn't I? After all, the past held portents enough – sign-posts pointing to the present – this present now – this dreary misery.

LEONORA (*with a great effort to be calm*): Listen, Chris, I want to go away for a little. I must – I've told you – I really can't bear any more.

CHRIS: You can't bear any more! What about me?

LEONORA: It's not my fault that you imagine things and torture yourself.

CHRIS: Tell me one thing – without lying or evading – tell me one thing honestly—

LEONORA (*wearily*): What is it?

CHRIS: Do you still – love me?

LEONORA: Oh, Chris! (*She turns away hopelessly.*)

CHRIS: Do you?

LEONORA (*tonelessly*): Yes.

CHRIS: As much as you did in the beginning?

LEONORA: Differently, Chris, things have changed – a year has gone by since the beginning.

CHRIS: That's an evasion.

LEONORA: It's the truth – nothing stays the same.

CHRIS: You wanted me in the beginning, didn't you? Whenever I came near you – whenever I touched you – it was more important than anything in the world, wasn't it?

LEONORA: Yes – it was.

CHRIS: And now it isn't any more?

LEONORA: Chris – what's the use of—

CHRIS: Answer me!

LEONORA (*quivering*): What do you want me to say – I'll answer – I'll say whatever you want.

CHRIS: I want the truth.

LEONORA: There isn't any truth anywhere – you've smashed everything into bits—

CHRIS: Do you love me as much as you did in the beginning?

LEONORA (*violently*): No – no – no!

CHRIS: At last!

LEONORA: That's what you wanted, isn't it? – the truth – that's the truth!

CHRIS: Then you have been lying – for weeks – for months probably—

LEONORA: Yes, I have – I have.

CHRIS: When did it die, this poor shabby love of yours?

LEONORA (*wildly*): A long while ago – you strangled it yourself with your insane jealousies and cruelties. You never trusted me – never for a minute – you've spoiled hours that could have been perfect by making scenes out of nothing. You've humiliated me and shamed me – you've dug up things that were once dear to me and made them look cheap and horrible. I can't even go back into my own memory now without finding you there jeering on every threshold – walking with me through the empty rooms – making them tawdry – shutting them off from me for ever. I hate you for that bitterly.

CHRIS: Sentiment for the dead at the expense of the living – very interesting – quite magnificent!

LEONORA: The dead at least have the sense to be quiet.

CHRIS: Long live the dead!

LEONORA (*with bitterness*): You are one of them now.

> *There is a dreadful silence for a moment. They stand quite still looking at each other.*

CHRIS (*quietly*): Did you mean that?

LEONORA (*hesitantly*): Yes – I think I did.

CHRIS: Oh – please – please don't mean that!

LEONORA: Let me go away now.

CHRIS: Couldn't you wait another minute?

LEONORA: It isn't any use – you know it isn't.

CHRIS: Very well.

LEONORA: Goodbye, Chris.

CHRIS: I love you, my darling.

LEONORA: No, it's not love, it hasn't anything to do with love.

CHRIS: I know it's over now – I really do – I won't make any more scenes.

LEONORA: Goodbye.

She goes to him slowly and kisses him – he crushes her in his arms.

CHRIS (*hoarsely*): Is it quite dead – quite dead?

LEONORA (*struggling*): Don't, Chris – please!

CHRIS: All passion spent – everything tidied up and put back in the box.

LEONORA: Let me go.

CHRIS: The last time I shall kiss you – the last time I shall feel you in my arms – the very last time of all—

LEONORA (*trying to twist away from him*): Chris—

CHRIS: Stay still!

LEONORA: Let me go!

CHRIS: God damn you, stay still!

He kisses her again violently and throws her away from him. She staggers and falls.

How does it feel to be so desirable – to be wanted so much – tell me, please – I want to know – I want to know what your heart's doing now, your loving female heart! How enviable to be able to walk away into the future, free of love, free of longing, a new life before you and the dead behind you – not quite the dead, though, let's say the dying – the dying aren't as sensibly quiet as the dead – they can't help crying a little – you must walk swiftly out of earshot and don't – don't, I implore you, look back, it would make too dreary a picture for your neat, sentimental memory book. There's little charm in dying – it's only clinically interesting – the process of defeat, but your viewpoint is far from clinical, my sweet – you're a sane, thrilling animal without complications, and the fact that my life has been broken on your loveliness isn't your fault. I don't believe it's even mine – it's an act of God, darling, like fire and wind and pestilence. You're in on a grand tragedy, the best tragedy of all, and the best joke, the triumphant, inevitable defeat of mind by matter! Just for a minute I'm seeing it all clearly, myself and you and the world around us – but it's only a last flare, like a Verey light shooting through the sky, it'll splutter out in a second leaving everything darker than before, for me too dark to bear. You see, I had a life to live and work to do and people to love, and now I haven't any more. They're eager to help, those people I loved and who love me. I can see them still, gentle and wise and understanding, trying to get to me, straining to clutch my hand, but it's too late – they can't reach me. . . . Get up and go – it doesn't matter any more to me whether you're here or in the moon. Get up and go—

> LEONORA *rises to her feet. She is trembling.* CHRIS *goes over to the window and stands there with his back to her.*
>
> *She takes her bag from the table, and goes quietly out of the room, closing the door behind her.*
>
> CHRIS *turns at the sound of the door closing and stands tense and quivering waiting for the front door to slam. When it does he starts to walk about the room. He goes to the table and pours out a tumbler of neat whisky. He drinks it down in one gulp and chokes a little. He pours himself another and drinks it, then he sits down for a moment, waiting for it to have some effect. Suddenly he stands up, then the tension of his muscles relaxes and with infinite weariness he goes to the window, opens it wide, climbs on to the sill and drops.*
>
> *The lights fade on the scene.*

Scene VI

This scene is the continuation of Scene I.

> BARBARA, TIM *and* SUSAN *are in the same places and* ERNEST *is standing by the door.*

ERNEST (*announcing*): Mrs Vail.

> LEONORA *comes in. Her eyes are red from crying. She is obviously trying with all her will to control herself.*

BARBARA: Leonora— (*She takes her hand.*) I'm so glad you came—
LEONORA: Is he – is he—?
BARBARA: He asked for you.
TIM (*brusquely*): You'd better go in – at once.

BARBARA: Here, drink this— (*She hands her her cocktail.*) It's important that you don't break down.

LEONORA: I'll be all right.

BARBARA: Please drink it.

LEONORA: Very well. (*She gulps it down.*)

BARBARA: Tim, will you please take her—

TIM: Come this way, will you?

> TIM *goes to the doors on the right and holds one open for* LEONORA. *She says* 'Thank you' *huskily as she goes through.* TIM *follows her and returns in a moment.*

BARBARA: It wasn't so foggy.

SUSAN: What?

BARBARA: Last year, I mean, when she came for the first time – it wasn't so foggy.

SUSAN: No – I remember – it wasn't.

> BARBARA *wanders about the room.*

BARBARA: I wish – I do wish this moment hadn't had to happen too.

TIM (*gently*): Do sit down, my dear.

BARBARA: No – I'm all right – I like wandering—

TIM (*at cocktail shaker*): Do you want some more, Susan?

SUSAN: No, thank you.

BARBARA (*with a tremulous smile*): It's too much of a good thing – it really is— (*She breaks off and turns her head away.*)

> TIM *and* SUSAN *look at her miserably. She recovers herself quickly and comes back to the sofa again.*

I have a dreadful feeling that I'm making it all much horrider for you— ˙

TIM: Don't be so foolish!

BARBARA: I know what you mean, though – I'm behaving well, almost consciously well; that's always much more agonising for other people.

SUSAN: No, it isn't – it's ever so much better.

BARBARA (*blowing her nose*): I'm not at all sure. If I broke down, collapsed completely, there'd be something to do – something for us all to do – smelling salts and brandy and all that.

TIM: Burnt feathers.

BARBARA: Yes, burnt feathers. (*She gives a polite little laugh.*)

SUSAN (*looking at the door*): I wonder—

TIM (*quickly*): Don't wonder anything – it's better not.

BARBARA: You mustn't snap at Susan, Tim, it's beastly of you.

TIM: Sorry, Susan, I didn't mean to snap.

SUSAN (*trying to smile at him*): I didn't even hear—

BARBARA (*suddenly*): I wish she'd come out now – I wish to God she'd come out now.

TIM: She will – in a minute—

> *They wait in silence. Presently* LEONORA *comes quietly back into the room. She goes to* BARBARA.

BARBARA: Is it all over? Is he—?

LEONORA: Yes.

BARBARA: Oh – oh, dear— (*She sinks back again on to the sofa.*)

LEONORA: He didn't know me, he thought I was you, he said – 'Baba – I'm not submerged any more' – and then he said 'Baba' again – and then – then he died.

> LEONORA *goes out of the room very quickly as the curtain falls.*

57

'RED PEPPERS'

An Interlude with Music

'*Red Peppers*' was produced in London at the Phoenix Theatre on 9 January 1936, with the following cast:

GEORGE PEPPER	Mr Noël Coward
LILY PEPPER	Miss Gertrude Lawrence
BERT BENTLEY	Mr Anthony Pelissier
MR EDWARDS	Mr Alan Webb
MABEL GRACE	Miss Alison Leggatt
ALF	Mr Kenneth Carten

———————

The action of the play takes place on the stage, a dressing-room, and the stage again of the Palace of Varieties in one of the smaller English provincial towns.

TIME: Saturday night, the present day.

The interlude occurs in the Palace Theatre of Varieties in one of the smaller English provincial towns on a Saturday night.

GEORGE *and* LILY PEPPER *are a singing and dancing comedy act. They are both somewhere in the thirties. They have been married for many years and in the Profession since they were children. Their act consists of a 'Man-About-Town' Dude number for which they wear smooth red wigs, tails, silk hats and canes, and a 'Sailor' number for which they wear curly red wigs, sailor clothes with exaggerated bell-bottomed trousers and carry telescopes. They are first discovered performing 'in one' before a backcloth on which is painted an ordinary street scene.*

'HAS ANYBODY SEEN OUR SHIP?'
(Sailor Number)

VERSE I

What shall we do with the drunken sailor?
So the saying goes.
We're not tight but we're none too bright
Great Scott! I don't suppose!
We've lost our way
And we've lost our pay,
And to make the thing complete,
We've been and gone and lost the bloomin' fleet!

REFRAIN I

Has anybody seen our ship?
The H.M.S. Peculiar.
We've been on shore
For a month or more,
And when we see the Captain we shall get 'what for'.
Heave ho, me hearties,
Sing Glory Halleluiah,

A lady bold as she could be
Pinched our whistles at 'The Golden Key'.
Now we're in between the devil and the deep blue sea
Has anybody seen our ship?

Ad lib. from orchestra.

GEORGE (*singing*): La la la la – la la la la—
LILY: Here, what are you singing about?
GEORGE: What am I singing about?
LILY: Yes, what are you singing about?
GEORGE: What's the matter with my singing?
LILY: What isn't the matter with it!
GEORGE: Don't you think I could ever do anything with my voice?
LILY: Well, it might be useful in case of fire!
GEORGE: Oi! Skip it.
LILY: Who was that lady I saw you walking down the street with the other morning?
GEORGE: That wasn't a lady, that was my wife!
LILY: Keep it clean. Keep it fresh. Keep it fragrant!
GEORGE: Was that your dog I saw you with in the High Street?
LILY: Yes, that was my dog.
GEORGE: What's his name?
LILY: Fruit Salts.
GEORGE: Fruit Salts?
LILY: Yes, Fruit Salts.
GEORGE: Why?
LILY: Ask him – Eno's.
GEORGE: Keep it clean. Keep it fresh. Keep it fragrant!
BOTH: La la la la – la la la la.
GEORGE: Why did you leave school?
LILY: Appendicitis.
GEORGE: Appendicitis?
LILY: Yes, appendicitis.
GEORGE: What do you mean, appendicitis?
LILY: Couldn't spell it!
GEORGE: I heard you had adenoids.

LILY: Adenoids?

GEORGE: Yes, adenoids.

LILY: Don't speak of it.

GEORGE: Why not?

LILY: Adenoids me!

GEORGE: Oi! Skip it! Skip it!

BOTH: La la la la – la la la la.

GEORGE: I saw a very strange thing the other day.

LILY: What was it?

GEORGE: Twelve men standing under one umbrella and they didn't get wet.

LILY: How's that?

GEORGE: It wasn't raining! (Wait for it – wait for it.)

LILY: Do you know what a skeleton is?

GEORGE: Do I know what a skeleton is?

LILY: Do you know what a skeleton is?

GEORGE: Yes.

LILY: Well, what is it?

GEORGE: A lot of bones with the people scraped off!

LILY: Keep it clean. Keep it fresh. Keep it fragrant.

GEORGE: Why is twelve midnight like the roof of a house?

LILY: Why is twelve midnight like the roof of a house?

GEORGE: Yes, why is twelve midnight like the roof of a house?

LILY: S'late!

BOTH: La la la la – la la la la.

LILY: Where did you go last night?

GEORGE: The cemetery.

LILY: Anyone dead?

GEORGE: All of 'em.

LILY: Are we going fishing?

GEORGE: Yes, we're going fishing.

LILY: We're not taking the dog with us, are we?

GEORGE: Of course we're taking the dog with us.

LILY: Why?

GEORGE: He's got the worms!

REFRAIN 2

Has anybody seen our ship?
The H.M.S. Disgusting.
We've three guns aft
And another one fore
And they've promised us a funnel for the next world war.
Heave ho, me hearties,
The quarter-deck needs dusting.
We had a binge last Christmas year,
Nice plum puddings and a round of beer,
But the captain pulled his cracker and we cried 'Oh dear!
Has anybody seen our ship?'

REFRAIN 3

Has anybody seen our ship?
The H.M.S. Suggestive.
She sailed away
Across the bay,
And we haven't had a smell of her since New Year's Day.
Heave ho, me hearties,
We're getting rather restive,
We pooled our money, spent the lot,
The world forgetting by the world forgot.
Now we haven't got a penny for the you know what!
Has anybody seen our ship?

VERSE 2 (*if necessary*)

What's to be done with the girls on shore
Who lead our tars astray?
What's to be done with the drinks galore
That make them pass away?
We got wet ears
From our first five beers—
After that we lost control,
And now we find we're up the blinking pole!

Their exit consists of a neat walk off together, one behind the other,
with their telescopes under their arms. Unfortunately, in course of

this snappy finale, LILY, *who is behind* GEORGE, *drops her telescope and hurriedly retrieves it thereby ruining the whole effect.* GEORGE *shoots her a look of fury and mutters something to her out of the corner of his mouth. The curtain falls and they take a call before it breathless and smiling, but with a certain quality of foreboding behind their smiles.*

The curtain rises on the interior of their dressing-room. It is a fairly squalid room, for although they are comparatively well-known in the provinces, they have never, to date, achieved the dignity of the star dressing-room or the pride of topping the bill. The room is three sides of a square. There is a wooden shelf all the way round it, above it, mirrors and lights at set intervals.

Down stage on the right there is a door leading to the passage. Down stage on the left there is a lavatory basin with a screen round it. In the centre is a wooden hanging arrangement for clothes.

GEORGE'*s dressing place is on the right and* LILY'*s is on the left.*

As the curtain rises on the scene they both enter in silence but wearing expressions of set rage. They are still breathless and extremely hot. GEORGE *goes to his dressing place and* LILY *goes to hers. They both take off their wigs and fling them down, then, still in silence, they proceed to rip off their sailor clothes. These are made with zippers in order to facilitate their quick change.* LILY *is wearing a brassiere and silk knickers, and* GEORGE *a vest and drawers. They both have black shoes with taps on them and black socks and sock suspenders.*

GEORGE: Now then.

LILY: Now then what?

GEORGE (*contemptuously*): Now then what!

LILY: I don't know what you're talking about.

GEORGE: Oh, you don't, don't you?

LILY: No I don't, so shut up.

GEORGE: I suppose you don't know you mucked up the whole exit!

LILY: It wasn't my fault.

GEORGE: Whose fault was it then, Mussolini's?

LILY (*with sarcasm*): Funny, hey?

GEORGE (*witheringly*): I suppose you didn't drop your prop, did you? And having dropped it, you didn't have to go back for it, leaving me to prance off all by meself – who d'you think you are, Rebla?

LILY: The exit was too quick.

GEORGE: It was the same as it's always been.

LILY: It was too quick, I tell you, it's been too quick the whole week, the whole number's too quick—

GEORGE: Bert Bentley takes that number at the same tempo as he's always done.

LILY: You and your Bert Bentley, just because he stands you a Welsh rarebit at the Queen's you think he's God Almighty.

GEORGE: Bert Bentley's the best conductor in the North of England and don't you make any mistake about it.

LILY: Best conductor my foot! I suppose he thinks it's funny to see us leaping up and down the stage like a couple of greyhounds.

GEORGE: If you're a greyhound I'm Fred Astaire.

LILY: Oh, you're Fred Astaire all right, with a bit of Pavlova thrown in – you're wonderful, you are – there's nothing you can't do, except behave like a gentleman.

GEORGE: Oh, so you expect me to behave like a gentleman, do you? That's a good one, coming from you.

LILY: Oh, shut up, you make me tired.

GEORGE: I make *you* tired! I suppose it was me that mucked up the exit – I suppose it was me that dropped me bloody telescope!

LILY (*heated*): Now look here, George Pepper—

GEORGE: Stop George Peppering me – why can't you admit it when you're in the wrong? – You mucked up the exit – nobody else did – you did!

LILY: Well, what if I did? It was an accident, wasn't it? I didn't do it on purpose.

GEORGE: It doesn't matter how you did it or why you did it, you did it.

LILY (*screaming*): All right, I did it!

GEORGE (*triumphantly*): Well, don't do it again.

There is a knock on the door.

LILY: Who is it?

ALF (*outside*): Me, Alf.

LILY: All right, come in.

ALF, *the callboy, enters. He is laden with the* PEPPERS' *discarded evening suits, silk hats and canes. He plumps them down.*

ALF: There!

GEORGE: Thanks. (*He gets some money out of his coat pocket.*) Here, tell Fred to pop out and get me twenty Players and a large Guinness.

LILY: Why can't you wait and have it with your steak?

GEORGE: You mind yours and I'll mind mine.

ALF: You'll have to wait until Mabel Grace is finished.

LILY: She's been finished for years as far as I'm concerned.

GEORGE: What's the matter with Mabel Grace?

LILY: Ask the public, dear, just ask the public.

ALF (*about to leave*): Same as usual, I suppose, between the houses?

GEORGE: Yes, and tell 'em not to forget the salt, like they did last night.

ALF: Righto.

> ALF *goes out.*
> LILY *starts to pack various things into a large hamper which has emblazoned on it in large black letters: 'The Red Peppers'.*

GEORGE: What did you want to say that about Mabel Grace for in front of him?

LILY (*grandly*): It happens to be my opinion.

GEORGE: Well, in future you'd better keep your opinions to yourself in front of strangers.

LILY (*mumbling*): If you're so fond of Mabel Grace I wonder you don't go and ask her for her autograph – she'd drop dead if you did – I bet nobody's asked her for one since *Trelawny of the Wells.*

GEORGE: Mabel Grace is an artist and don't you forget it – she may be a bit long in the tooth now but she's a bigger star than you'll ever be, so there!

LILY: You make me sick, sucking up to the topliners.

GEORGE: Who sucks up to the topliners?

LILY: You do – look at Irene Baker!

GEORGE: What's the matter with Irene Baker?

LILY: When last heard from she was falling down drunk at the Empire, Hartlepool.

GEORGE: That's a dirty lie, Irene never touches a drop till after the show and well you know it.

LILY (*contemptuously*): Irene! It was Miss Baker this and Miss Baker that, the last time you saw her.

GEORGE: That's all you know.

LILY: Trying to make me think you got off with her, eh? What a chance!

GEORGE: Oh, shut up nagging!

LILY (*muttering*): Irene—!

GEORGE: If a day ever dawns when you can time your laugh like Irene Baker does, I'll give you a nice red apple!

LILY: Time my laughs! That's funny. Fat lot of laughs I get when you write the gags.

GEORGE (*grandly*): If you're dissatisfied with your material you know what you can do with it.

LILY: I know what I'd like to do with it.

GEORGE: You can't even do a straight walk off without balling it up.

LILY: Oh, we're back at that again, are we?

GEORGE: Yes we are, so there!

LILY (*coming over to him*): Now look here, just you listen to me for a minute. . . .

GEORGE: I've been listening to you for fifteen years, one more minute won't hurt.

LILY: I've had about enough of this. I'm sick of you and the whole act. It's lousy, anyway.

GEORGE: The act was good enough for my mum and dad and it's good enough for you.

LILY (*with heavy sarcasm*): Times have changed a bit since your mum and dad's day, you know. There's electric light now and telephones and a little invention called Moving Pictures. Nobody wants to see the 'Red Peppers' for three bob when they can see Garbo for ninepence!

GEORGE: That's just where you're wrong, see! We're flesh and blood we are – the public would rather see flesh and blood any day than a cheesy photograph. Put Garbo on on a Saturday night in Devonport, and see what would happen to her!

LILY: Yes, look what happened to us!

GEORGE: That wasn't Devonport, it was Southsea.

LILY: Well, wherever it was, the Fleet was in.

GEORGE: If you think the act's so lousy it's a pity you don't rewrite some of it.

LILY: Ever tried going into St Paul's and offering to rewrite the Bible?

GEORGE: Very funny! Oh, very funny indeed! You're wasted in the Show Business, you ought to write for *Comic Cuts* you ought.

LILY: At that I could think up better gags than you do – 'That wasn't a lady, that was my wife!' – 'D'you mind if I smoke?' 'I don't care if you burn!' – hoary old chestnuts – they were has-beens when your grandmother fell off the high wire.

GEORGE: What's my grandmother got to do with it?

LILY: She didn't fall soon enough, that's all.

GEORGE (*furiously*): You shut your mouth and stop hurling insults at my family. What were you when I married you, I should like to know! One of the six Moonlight Maids – dainty songs and dances, and no bookings!

LILY (*hotly*): When we did get bookings we got number one towns which is more than your mum and dad ever did!

GEORGE: Who wants the number one towns, anyway? You can't get a public all the year round like my mum and dad by doing a parasol dance twice a year at the Hippodrome Manchester!

LILY: The Moonlight Maids was just as good an act as the 'Red Peppers' any day, and a bloody sight more refined at that!

GEORGE: You've said it. That's just what it was – refined. It was so refined it simpered itself out of the bill—

LILY: A bit of refinement wouldn't do you any harm—

GEORGE: Perhaps you'd like to change the act to 'Musical Moments' with me playing a flute and you sitting under a standard lamp with a 'cello?

There is a knock at the door.

LILY: Who is it?

BERT (*outside*): Me – Bert Bentley.

GEORGE: Come in, old man.

LILY (*under her breath*): Old man—

BERT BENTLEY *enters. He is the musical director, a flashy little man wearing a tail suit and a white waistcoat that is none too clean.*

BERT (*cheerfully*): Well, well, well, how's tricks?

GEORGE: Mustn't grumble.

BERT: Anybody got a Gold Flake?

GEORGE: Here's a Players, that do?

BERT (*taking one*): It's your last?

GEORGE: I've sent Fred out for some more.

BERT: Okay – thanks.

GEORGE: Sketch on?

BERT: Yes, the old cow's tearing herself to shreds.

GEORGE: It's a pretty strong situation she's got in that sketch – I watched it from the side first house on Wednesday—

BERT: She nearly got the bird second house.

LILY: Too refined, I expect. For this date.

BERT: Well, they're liable to get a bit restless, you know, when she stabs herself – she takes such a hell of a time about it – that's legits all over – we had Robert Haversham here a couple of months ago – what a make-up – stuck together with stamp paper he was – Robert Haversham the famous tragedian and company! You should have seen the company: a couple of old tats got up as Elizabethan pages with him doing a death scene in the middle of them – he died all right.

GEORGE: Did he buy it?

BERT: He bought it – three and eightpence in coppers and a bottle of Kola.

LILY: Poor old man, what a shame!

BERT: Well, what did he want to do it for? That sort of stuff's no good. They're all alike – a few seasons in the West End and they think they're set.

LILY: Lot of hooligans birding the poor old man.

BERT (*with slight asperity*): This is as good a date as you can get, you know!

LILY: I've played better.

GEORGE: Oh, dry up, Lil, for heaven's sake! (*To* BERT.) Sorry I can't offer you a drink, old man, Fred hasn't brought it yet.

BERT: That's all right, George – I'll have one with you in

70

between the houses. By the way, don't you think that exit of yours is dragging a bit?

LILY (*explosively*): Dragging?

GEORGE: Lil thinks it was a bit too quick.

BERT: Whatever you say, it's all the same to me.

GEORGE: Maybe you could pep it up a little.

LILY: Maybe it would be better if we did the whole act on skates!

GEORGE (*conciliatorily*): Bert's quite right, you know, Lil.

LILY: I don't know any such thing.

BERT: All right, all right, all right – there's no need to get nasty.

GEORGE: Oh, don't take any notice of her, she don't know what she's talking about.

LILY (*with overpowering sweetness*): My husband's quite right, Mr Bentley, my husband is always quite right. You don't have to pay any attention to me, I don't count – I'm only a feed.

GEORGE: Oh, dry up.

LILY (*continuing*): But I should just like to say one thing, Mr Bentley, if you'll forgive me for stepping out of my place for a minute, and that is, that if you take that exit any quicker at the second house, I shall not drop my telescope — Oh no – I shall sock you in the chops with it!

BERT: Who the hell d'you think you are, talking to me like that!

GEORGE: You ought to be ashamed of yourself.

LILY: You and your orchestra – orchestra! More like a hurdy-gurdy and flat at that!

BERT: What's wrong with my orchestra?

LILY: Nothing, apart from the instruments and the men what play 'em.

BERT: My orchestra's played for the best artists in the business—

LILY: Yes, but not until they were too old to care.

BERT: I didn't come up here to be insulted by a cheap little comedy act.

GEORGE (*incensed*): What's that! What's that? What's that?

BERT: You heard. You're damned lucky to get this date at all!

GEORGE: Lucky! My God, it's a fill-in – that's all – a fill-in!

BERT: I suppose Nervo and Knox use it as a fill-in, and Lily Morris and Flanagan and Allen?

LILY: They probably have friends living near.

BERT (*making a movement to go*): Before you start saucing me just take a look at your place on the bill – that's all – just take a look at it.

GEORGE: We're in the second half, anyway.

BERT: Only because the acrobats can't make their change.

LILY: It's in our contract – after the interval's in our contract.

BERT: Well, make the most of it while you've got it.

GEORGE: Get the hell out of here, you twopenny-halfpenny little squirt – lucky for you we've got another show to play.

BERT: Not so damned lucky – I've got to look at it.

LILY: Well, it'll be the first time – maybe we'll get the tempos right for a change!

BERT: You set your tempos Monday morning and they haven't been changed since.

LILY: That's your story, but don't forget you were sober on Monday morning.

BERT: Are you insinuating that I drink during the show?

LILY: Insinuating! That's a laugh. I'm not insinuating, I'm stating a fact. I can smell it a mile off.

BERT: What a lady! And what an artist, too – I don't suppose!

GEORGE: Don't you talk in that tone to my wife.

LILY: Send for the manager, George. Send for Mr Edwards.

BERT: I'm the one that's going to send for Mr Edwards—

GEORGE: Get out of here before I crack you one—

> ALF *knocks at the door.*

LILY: Come in.

> ALF *pushes open the door with his foot and comes in carrying a tray on which are two plates of steak and chips with other plates over them to keep them hot, a bottle of A.I. Sauce and three bottles of Guinness.*

ALF: You're wanted, Mr Bentley, the sketch is nearly over.

BERT (*grimly to the* PEPPERS): I'll be seeing you later.

> *He goes out, slamming the door after him.*

GEORGE (*after him*): Lousy son of a—Lounge Lizard.

LILY (*to* ALF): Here, put it down on the hamper.

ALF (*doing so*): I've got the Players in me pocket.

LILY (*feeling for them*): All right.

GEORGE: Come back later for the tray.

ALF: Righto.

He goes out.

GEORGE: Mr Edwards – I'll have something to say to Mr Edwards.

LILY: Lucky to play this date, are we? We'll see about that.

GEORGE: You were right, old girl.

LILY: What about – him?

GEORGE: Yes – dirty little rat.

LILY (*dragging up two chairs to the hamper*): Well, we all make mistakes sometimes – open the Guinness, there's a dear—

GEORGE: He's a little man, that's his trouble, never trust a man with short legs – brains too near their bottoms.

LILY: Come and sit down.

GEORGE (*opening a bottle of Guinness*): 'Alf a mo'—

LILY: That exit was too quick, you know!

GEORGE: All right – all right—

They both sit down and begin to eat.

They've forgotten the salt again—

LILY: No, here it is in a bit of paper—

GEORGE: Well, thank God for that anyway—

The lights fade on the scene.

When the lights come up on the scene, GEORGE *and* LILY *are sitting at the dressing places freshening their make-ups. They both have a glass of Guinness within reach, and they are both wearing the rather frowsy dressing-gowns that they had put on during the preceding scene. The tray, with the remains of their dinner on it, is on the floor beside the hamper.*

GEORGE *gets up, opens the door and listens.*

LILY: What's on?

GEORGE: The Five Farthings.

LILY: That's the end of the first half – we'd better get a move on—

GEORGE (*returning to his place*): Fancy putting an act like that on at the end of the first half – you'd think they'd know better, wouldn't you?

LILY: I wouldn't think they'd know better about anything in this hole.

GEORGE: It's a badly run house and it always has been.

He proceeds to put on his dress shirt, collar and tie, which are all in one with a zipper up the back. LILY *is doing the same on her side of the room. They stuff wads of Kleenex paper in between their collars and their necks to prevent the make-up soiling their ties.*

There is a knock at the door.

LILY: Who is it?

MR EDWARDS (*outside*): Mr Edwards.

LILY (*pulling on her trousers*): Just a minute—

GEORGE (*under his breath*): Go easy – Bert Bentley's been at him.

LILY: I'll have something to say about that.

GEORGE: You leave it to me – I'll do the talking.

LILY: That'll be nice – Come in!

MR EDWARDS *enters. He is the house manager and very resplendent. He is smoking a large cigar.*

GEORGE (*rising and offering him a chair*): Good evening, Mr Edwards.

MR EDWARDS (*disdaining it*): Good evening.

LILY (*amiably*): How's the house?

MR EDWARDS: Same as usual – full.

GEORGE: That's fine, isn't it?

MR EDWARDS (*grimly*): I watched your act tonight, first house.

GEORGE (*gaily*): There you are, Lil, what did I tell you – I had a sort of hunch you was out there – I said to my wife – what's the betting Mr Edwards is out front? – you know – you have a sort of feeling—

LILY: Went well, didn't it?

MR EDWARDS: I've seen things go better.

GEORGE: We follow Betley Delavine, you know – a ballad singer – they always take a bit of warming up after a ballad singer.

LILY: I'd defy Billy Bennett to get away with it in our place on the bill – I'd defy him – see?

MR EDWARDS: There isn't anything wrong with your place on the bill.

GEORGE: Well, I'd be willing to make a little bet with you – put the Five Farthings on before us and change Betley Delavine to the end of the first half and see what happens!

LILY: You'd send them out to the bars and they'd stay there.

MR EDWARDS: I did not come here to discuss the running of my theatre.

GEORGE: Oh – sorry, I'm sure.

MR EDWARDS: That exit of yours killed the whole act.

GEORGE: A little mishap that's all – anybody might drop a telescope—

LILY: Even a sailor.

MR EDWARDS: It looked terrible.

GEORGE: The tempo was all wrong, Mr Edwards.

MR EDWARDS: Sounded all right to me.

GEORGE: Maybe it did, but we know our own numbers, you know.

MR EDWARDS: It didn't look like it from the front.

GEORGE: We've never had any trouble before – that exit's stopped the show in every town we've played.

LILY: A musical director can make or mar an act, you know – make or mar it.

MR EDWARDS: Mr Bentley is one of the finest musical directors in the business.

LILY: Then he's wasted here, that's all I can say.

GEORGE (*warningly*): Lily!

LILY: Well, if he's so wonderful, why isn't he at the Albert Hall – doing *Hiawatha*—

MR EDWARDS: I understand you had words with Mr Bentley.

GEORGE: We did, and we will again if he starts any of his funny business.

MR EDWARDS: I understand that you accused him of drinking during the show.

LILY: Getting quite bright, aren't you?

GEORGE: Shut up, Lil, leave this to me.

MR EDWARDS: Did you or did you not?

GEORGE: Look here, who d'you think you are – coming talking to us like this?

MR EDWARDS: Did you or did you not accuse Mr Bentley of drinking during the show?

LILY (*heatedly*): Yes, we did, because he does, so there!

MR EDWARDS: That's serious, you know – it's slander!

LILY: I don't care if it's arson, it's true!

MR EDWARDS: Now look here, Mrs Pepper, I think it only fair to warn you—

LILY: And I think it's only fair to warn you that unless you get a better staff in this theatre and a better orchestra and a better musical director, you'll find yourself a cinema inside six months!

MR EDWARDS: You won't gain anything by losing your temper.

GEORGE: And you won't gain anything by coming round backstage and throwing your weight about – your place is in the front of the house – my theatre this and my theatre that – it's no more your theatre than what it is ours – you're on a salary same as us, and I'll bet it's a damn sight less, too, and don't you forget it—

MR EDWARDS (*losing his temper*): I'm not going to stand any more of this—

LILY: Oh, go and play with yourself and shut up—

MR EDWARDS: I'll guarantee one thing, anyhow, you'll never play this date again as long as I'm in charge—

GEORGE: In charge of what, the Fire Brigade!

LILY: Play this date – anybody'd think it was the Palladium to hear you talk—

GEORGE: You'd better be careful, Mr Edwards – you don't want a scandal like this to get round the profession—

MR EDWARDS: What are you talking about?

GEORGE: I'm talking about the way this house is run.

MR EDWARDS (*working up*): You mind your own business.

LILY: More than one act's been mucked up here, you know, by that orchestra of yours – it's beginning to get a name—

MR EDWARDS: Oh, it is, is it?

GEORGE: They're all over the shop – no discipline.

LILY: What can you expect with a drunk in charge of it!

MR EDWARDS (*raising his voice*): Look here – you stop talking like that or it'll be the worse for you.

GEORGE: His tempos are wrong and he hasn't got any authority over his men—

LILY: This date's only a fill-in for us, you know—

GEORGE: You ask our agents.

MR EDWARDS: I shall report this conversation.

LILY: Do – report it to the Lord Mayor – if you're sober enough to remember the lyrics.

GEORGE: Shut up, Lil.

MR EDWARDS: I will not stay here and argue—

GEORGE: You're dead right, you won't—

MR EDWARDS: You were a flop last time you played here and you've been a flop this time and that's enough for me—

LILY (*screaming*): Flop! What d'you mean flop! We're a bigger draw than anybody on the bill—

There is a knock on the door.

GEORGE (*loudly*): Come in—

MISS MABEL GRACE *enters. She is a faded ex-West End actress wearing a towel round her head to keep her hair in place, and an elaborate dressing-gown.*

MABEL GRACE (*acidly*): Good evening – I'm sorry to intrude – but you're making such a dreadful noise I'm quite unable to rest—

MR EDWARDS: I'm very sorry, Miss Grace—

MABEL GRACE: I find it hard enough to play a big emotional scene twice a night in any case—

LILY: Oh, that's an emotional scene, is it? I wondered what it was—

MABEL GRACE: I am not accustomed to being spoken to in that tone, Mrs Whatever your name is—

LILY: Pepper's the name – Pepper – P E P P E R – same as what you put in your soup.

MABEL GRACE (*coldly*): Very interesting.

MR EDWARDS: I apologise, Miss Grace.

MABEL GRACE (*grandly*): Thank you, Mr Edwards.

GEORGE (*in an affected voice*): What you must think of us, Miss Grace – so common – we're mortified, we are really – and you fresh from His Majesty's.

LILY: Fairly fresh.

MABEL GRACE: Mr Edwards, I'm really not used to dressing-room brawls – I'll leave it to you to see that there is no further noise—

LILY: Except for the raspberries at the end of your sketch – even Mr God Almighty Edwards can't control those—

MABEL GRACE: You're almost as vulgar off the stage as you are on, I congratulate you.

LILY (*very loudly*): Vulgar, are we! I'd like to ask you something. If you're so bloody West End why the hell did you leave it?

GEORGE: There'll be an answer to that in next Sunday's edition.

LILY: Thank you, George.

MR EDWARDS: Look here, you two, I've had about enough of this—

GEORGE: You've had about enough, have you? What about us?

The conversation becomes simultaneous.

LILY: You and your cigar and your shirt-front and your Woolworth studs! Alfred Butt with knobs on—

GEORGE: You get out of here, you fat fool, before I throw you out!—

MABEL GRACE: Thank you for your courtesy, Mr Edwards—

MR EDWARDS: I'll see you don't play this date any more or any other date either—

GEORGE: Oh, put it where the monkey put the nuts—

LILY: – Play this date again – thank you for the rabbit – I'd sooner play Ryde Pier in November—

In the middle of the pandemonium ALF *puts his head round the door.*

ALF (*yelling*): Red Peppers – three minutes—

GEORGE: Good God! We're off—

LILY (*wildly*): Get out, all of you – get out—

> GEORGE *takes* MR EDWARDS *by the shoulders, and shoves him out of the room.* MABEL GRACE, *laughing affectedly, follows him.*
>
> LILY *and* GEORGE *put on their wigs, powder their make-up, tweak their ties into place, grab their hats and canes – then, muttering curses under their breaths, they collect their sailor clothes and sailor wigs and telescopes and rush out of the room as the lights fade.*
>
> *The lights come up on the curtain as the orchestra is playing their introduction music. The curtain rises on the street scene again. They make their entrance for the 'dude' number, 'Men About Town'.*

ROUTINE

'MEN ABOUT TOWN'
(*Dude Number*)

VERSE

We're two chaps who
Find it thrilling
To do the killing
We're always willing
To give the girls a treat.
Just a drink at the Ritz
Call it double or quits
Then we feel the world is at our feet.
Top hats white spats
Look divine on us,
There's a shine on us
Get a line on us
When we come your way.
Gad! Eleven o'clock!
Let's pop into the Troc:
Ere we start the business of the day.

REFRAIN I

As we stroll down Picc – Piccadilly
In the bright morning air,
All the girls turn and stare
We're so nonchalant and frightfully debonair.
When we chat to Rose, Maud or Lily
You should see the way their boy friends frown,
For they know without a doubt
That their luck's right out,
Up against a couple of men about town.

REFRAIN 2

As we stroll down Picc – Piccadilly
All the girl say 'Who's here?
Put your hat straight, my dear,
For it's Marmaduke and Percy Vere de Vere.'
As we doff hats, each pretty filly
Gives a wink at us and then looks down
For they long with all their might
For a red-hot night
When they see a couple of men about town.

They proceed to execute a complicated tap dance, during which BERT
BENTLEY *vengefully takes the music faster and faster. They try vainly
to keep up with it, finally* GEORGE *slips and falls, whereupon* LILY
loses her temper and flings her hat at BERT BENTLEY.

LILY (*screaming*): You great drunken fool!

THE CURTAIN FALLS AMID DISCORD

HANDS ACROSS THE SEA

A Light Comedy in One Scene

Hands Across the Sea was produced in London at the Phoenix Theatre on 13 January 1936, with the following cast:

LADY MAUREEN GILPIN (Piggie)	Miss Gertrude Lawrence
COMMANDER PETER GILPIN, R.N., *her husband*	Mr Noël Coward
THE HON. CLARE WEDDERBURN	Miss Everley Gregg
LIEUT. COMMANDER ALASTAIR CORBETT, R.N.	Mr Edward Underdown
MAJOR GOSLING (Bogey)	Mr Anthony Pelissier
MR WADHURST	Mr Alan Webb
MRS WADHURST	Miss Alison Leggatt
MR BURNHAM	Mr Kenneth Carten
WALTERS	Miss Moya Nugent

The action of the play takes place in the drawing-room of the GILPINS' *flat in London.*

TIME: The present day.

The Scene is the drawing-room of the GILPINS' *flat in London. The room is nicely furnished and rather untidy. There is a portable gramophone on one small table and a tray of cocktail things on another; apart from these, the furnishing can be left to the discretion of the producer.*

When the Curtain rises the telephone is ringing. WALTERS, *a neat parlourmaid, enters and answers it. The time is about six p.m.*

WALTERS (*at telephone*): Hallo – yes – no, her ladyship's not back yet – she said she'd be in at five, so she ought to be here at any minute now – what name, please? – Rawlingson – Mr and Mrs Rawlingson — (*She scribbles on the pad.*) Yes – I'll tell her —

She hangs up the receiver and goes out. There is the sound of voices in the hall and LADY MAUREEN GILPIN *enters, followed at a more leisurely pace by her husband,* PETER GILPIN. MAUREEN, *nicknamed* PIGGIE *by her intimates, is a smart, attractive woman in the thirties.* PETER *is tall and sunburned and reeks of the Navy.*

PIGGIE (*as she comes in*): – and you can send the car back for me at eleven-thirty – it's quite simple, darling, I wish you wouldn't be so awfully complicated about everything —

PETER: What happens if my damned dinner goes on longer than that and I get stuck?

PIGGIE: You just get stuck, darling, and then you get unstuck and get a taxi

PETER (*grumbling*): I shall be in uniform, clinking with medals —

PIGGIE: If you take my advice you'll faint dead away at eleven o'clock and then you can come home in the car and change and have time for everything —

PETER: I can't faint dead away under the nose of the C.-in-C.

PIGGIE: You can feel a little poorly, can't you – anybody has the right to feel a little poorly — (*She sees the telephone pad.*) My God!

PETER: What is it?

PIGGIE: The Rawlingsons.

PETER: Who the hell are they?

PIGGIE: I'd forgotten all about them – I must get Maud at once — (*She sits at the telephone and dials a number.*)

PETER: Who are the Rawlingsons?

PIGGIE: Maud and I stayed with them in Samolo, I told you about it, that time when we had to make a forced landing – they practically saved our lives — (*At telephone.*) Hullo – Maud – darling, the Rawlingsons are on us – what – the RAWLING-SONS – yes – I asked them today and forgot all about it – you must come at once – but, darling, you *must* – Oh, dear – no, no, that was the Frobishers, these are the ones we stayed with – mother and father and daughter – you must remember – pretty girl with bad legs — No – they didn't have a son – we swore we'd give them a lovely time when they came home on leave – I know they didn't have a son, that was those other people in Penang — Oh, all right – you'll have to do something about them, though – let me ask them to lunch with you tomorrow – all right – one-thirty – I'll tell them — (*She hangs up.*) – she can't come —

PETER: You might have warned me that a lot of Colonial strangers were coming trumpeting into the house —

PIGGIE: I tell you I'd forgotten —

PETER: That world trip was a grave mistake —

PIGGIE: Who can I get that's celebrated – to give them a thrill?

PETER: Why do they have to have a thrill?

PIGGIE: I'll get Clare, anyway — (*She dials another number.*)

PETER: She'll frighten them to death.

PIGGIE: Couldn't you change early and come in your uniform? That would be better than nothing —

PETER: Perhaps they'd like to watch me having my bath!

PIGGIE (*at telephone*): I want to speak to Mrs Wedderburn, please – yes — (*To* PETER.) I do wish you'd be a little helpful — (*At telephone.*) Clare? – this is Piggie – I want you to come round at once and help me with the Rawlingsons – no, I know you haven't, but that doesn't matter — Mother, father and daughter – very sweet – they were divine to us in the East – I'm repaying hospitality – Maud's having them to lunch to-morrow and Peter's going to take them round the dockyard —

PETER: I'm not going to do any such thing —

PIGGIE: Shut up, I just thought of that and it's a *very* good idea — (*At telephone.*) All right, darling – as soon as you can — (*She hangs up.*) – I must go and change —

PETER: You know perfectly well I haven't time to take mothers and fathers and daughters with bad legs round the dockyard —

PIGGIE: It wouldn't take a minute, they took us all over their rubber plantation.

PETER: It probably served you right.

PIGGIE: You're so disobliging, darling, you really should try to conquer it – it's something to do with being English, I think – as a race I'm ashamed of us – no sense of hospitality – the least we can do when people are kind to us in far-off places is to be a little gracious in return.

PETER: They weren't kind to me in far-off places.

PIGGIE: You know there's a certain grudging, sullen streak in your character – I've been very worried about it lately – it's spreading like a forest fire —

PETER: Why don't you have them down for the week-end?

PIGGIE: Don't be so idiotic, how can I possibly? There's no room to start with and even if there were they'd be utterly wretched —

PETER: I don't see why.

PIGGIE: They wouldn't know anybody – they probably wouldn't have the right clothes – they'd keep on huddling about in uneasy little groups —

PETER: The amount of uneasy little groups that three people can huddle about in is negligible.

> ALASTAIR CORBETT *saunters into the room. He is good-looking and also distinctly Naval in tone.*

ALLY: Hallo, chaps.

PIGGIE: Ally, darling – how lovely – we're in trouble – Peter'll tell you all about it —

> *The telephone rings and she goes to it. The following conversations occur simultaneously.*

ALLY: What trouble?

PETER: More of Piggie's beach friends.

ALLY: Let's have a drink.

PETER: Cocktail?

ALLY: No, a long one, whisky and soda.

PETER (*going to drink table*): All right.

ALLY: What beach friends?

PETER: People Maud and Piggie picked up in the East.

PIGGIE (*at phone*): Hullo! – Yes – Robert, dear – how lovely! (*To others.*) It's Robert.

ALLY: Piggie ought to stay at home more.

PIGGIE (*on phone*): Where are you?

PETER: That's what I say!

PIGGIE (*on phone*): Oh, what a shame! – No – Peter's going to sea on Thursday – I'm going down on Saturday.

ALLY: Rubber, I expect – everybody in the East's rubber.

PIGGIE (*on phone*): No – nobody particular – just Clare and Bogey and I think Pops; but he thinks he's got an ulcer or something and might not be able to come.

PETER: We thought you might be a real friend and take them over the dockyard.

ALLY: What on earth for?

PETER: Give them a thrill.

PIGGIE (*on phone*): All right – I'll expect you – no, I don't think it can be a very big one – he looks as bright as a button.

ALLY: Why don't you take them over the dockyards?

PETER: I shall be at sea, Thursday onwards – exercises!

PIGGIE (*on phone*): No, darling, what is the use of having her – she only depresses you – oh – all right! (*Hangs up.*) Oh, dear —

PETER: It's quite easy for you – you can give them lunch on board.

ALLY: We're in dry dock.

PETER: They won't mind. (*To* PIGGIE.) What is it?

PIGGIE: Robert – plunged in gloom – he's got to do a course at Greenwich – he ran into a tram in Devonport – and he's had a row with Molly – he wants me to have her for the week-end so that they can make it up all over everybody. Have you told Ally about the Rawlingsons?

PETER: Yes, he's taking them over the dockyard, lunching them on board and then he's going to show them a submarine —

86

PIGGIE: Marvellous! You're an angel, Ally – I must take off these clothes, I'm going mad —

> *She goes out of the room at a run.*
> *There is the sound of the front-door bell.*

PETER: Let's go into my room – I can show you the plans —

ALLY: Already? They've been pretty quick with them.

PETER: I made a few alterations – there wasn't enough deck space – she ought to be ready by October, I shall have her sent straight out to Malta —

ALLY: Come on, we shall be caught —

> *They go off on the left as* WALTERS *ushers in* MR *and* MRS WADHURST *on the right.*
> *The* WADHURSTS *are pleasant, middle-aged people, their manner is a trifle timorous.*

WALTERS: Her ladyship is changing, I'll tell her you are here.

MRS WADHURST: Thank you.

MR WADHURST: Thank you very much.

> WALTERS *goes out.*
> *The* WADHURSTS *look round the room.*

MRS WADHURST: It's a very nice flat.

MR WADHURST: Yes – yes, it is.

MRS WADHURST (*scrutinising a photograph*): That must be him.

MR WADHURST: Who?

MRS WADHURST: The Commander.

MR WADHURST: Yes – I expect it is.

MRS WADHURST: Sailors always have such nice open faces, don't they?

MR WADHURST: Yes, I suppose so.

MRS WADHURST: Clean-cut and look you straight in the eye – I like men who look you straight in the eye.

MR WADHURST: Yes, it's very nice.

MRS WADHURST (*at another photograph*): This must be her sister – I recognise her from the *Tatler* – look – she was Lady Hurstley, you know, then she was Lady Macfadden and I don't know who she is now.

MR WADHURST: Neither do I.

MRS WADHURST: What a dear little boy – such a sturdy little fellow – look at the way he's holding his engine.

MR WADHURST: Is that his engine?

MRS WADHURST: He has rather a look of Donald Hotchkiss, don't you think?

MR WADHURST: Yes, dear.

MRS WADHURST: I must say they have very nice things – oh, dear, how lovely to be well off – I must write to the Brostows by the next mail and tell them all about it.

MR WADHURST: Yes, you must.

MRS WADHURST: Don't you think we'd better sit down?

MR WADHURST: Why not?

MRS WADHURST: You sit in that chair and I'll sit on the sofa.

She sits on the sofa. He sits on the chair.

MR WADHURST: Yes, dear.

MRS WADHURST: I wish you wouldn't look quite so uncomfortable, Fred, there's nothing to be uncomfortable about.

MR WADHURST: She does expect us, doesn't she?

MRS WADHURST: Of course, I talked to her myself on the telephone last Wednesday, she was perfectly charming and said that we were to come without fail and that it would be divine.

MR WADHURST: I still feel we should have telephoned again just to remind her. People are always awfully busy in London.

MRS WADHURST: I do hope Lady Dalborough will be here, too – I should like to see her again – she was so nice.

MR WADHURST: She was the other one, wasn't she?

MRS WADHURST (*irritably*): What do you mean, the other one?

MR WADHURST: I mean not this one.

MRS WADHURST: She's the niece of the Duke of Frensham, her mother was Lady Merrit, she was a great traveller too – I believe she went right across the Sahara dressed as an Arab. In those days that was a very dangerous thing to do.

MR WADHURST: I shouldn't think it was any too safe now.

WALTERS *enters and ushers in* MR BURNHAM, *a nondescript young man carrying a longish roll of cardboard.*

WALTERS: I'll tell the Commander you're here.

MR BURNHAM: Thanks – thanks very much.

WALTERS *goes out.*

MRS WADHURST (*after a slightly awkward silence*): How do you do?

MR BURNHAM: How do you do?

MRS WADHURST (*with poise*): This is my husband.

MR BURNHAM: How do you do?

MR WADHURST: How do you do?

They shake hands.

MRS WADHURST (*vivaciously*): Isn't this a charming room – so – so lived in.

MR BURNHAM: Yes.

MR WADHURST: Are you in the Navy, too?

MR BURNHAM: No.

MRS WADHURST (*persevering*): It's so nice to be home again – we come from Malaya, you know.

MR BURNHAM: Oh – Malaya.

MRS WADHURST: Yes, Lady Maureen and Lady Dalborough visited us there – my husband has a rubber plantation up-country – there's been a terrible slump, of course, but we're trying to keep our heads above water – aren't we, Fred?

MR WADHURST: Yes, dear, we certainly are.

MRS WADHURST: Have you ever been to the East?

MR BURNHAM: No.

MRS WADHURST: It's very interesting really, although the climate's rather trying until you get used to it, and of course the one thing we do miss is the theatre —

MR BURNHAM: Yes – of course.

MRS WADHURST: There's nothing my husband and I enjoy so much as a good play, is there, Fred?

MR WADHURST: Nothing.

MRS WADHURST: And all we get is films, and they're generally pretty old by the time they come out to us — (*She laughs gaily.*)

MR WADHURST: Do you go to the theatre much?

MR BURNHAM: No.

There is silence which is broken by the telephone ringing. Everybody jumps.

MRS WADHURST: Oh, dear – do you think we ought to answer it?

MR WADHURST: I don't know.

The telephone continues to ring. CLARE WEDDERBURN *comes in.*

89

She is middle-aged, well-dressed and rather gruff. She is followed by
'BOGEY' GOSLING, *a Major in the Marines, a good-looking man in
the thirties.*

CLARE: Hallo – where's the old girl?

MRS WADHURST (*nervously*): I – er, I'm afraid I —

CLARE (*going to the telephone*): Mix a cocktail, Bogey – I'm a
stretcher case — (*At telephone.*) Hallo – no, it's me – Clare —
God knows, dear – shall I tell her to call you back? – all right –
no, it was bloody, darling – a gloomy dinner at the Embassy,
then the worst play I've ever sat through and then the Café de
Paris and that awful man who does things with a duck – I've
already seen him six times, darling – oh, you know, he pinches
its behind and it quacks 'Land of Hope and Glory' – I don't
know whether it hurts it or not – I minded at first but I'm past
caring now, after all, it's not like performing dogs, I mind
about the performing dogs terribly – all right – good-bye —
(*She hangs up and turns to* MRS WADHURST.) Ducks are pretty
bloody anyway, don't you think?

MRS WADHURST: I don't know very much about them.

CLARE: The man swears it's genuine talent, but I think it's the
little nip that does it.

MRS WADHURST: It sounds rather cruel.

CLARE: It's a gloomy form of entertainment anyhow, particularly
as I've always hated 'Land of Hope and Glory' —

BOGEY: Cocktail?

CLARE (*taking off her hat*): Thank God!

BOGEY *hands round cocktails, the* WADHURSTS *and* MR BURNHAM
accept them and sip them in silence.

BOGEY: I suppose Piggie's in the bath.

CLARE: Go and rout her out.

BOGEY: Wait till I've had a drink.

CLARE (*to* MRS WADHURST): Is Peter home or is he still darting
about the Solent?

MRS WADHURST: I'm afraid I couldn't say – you see —

BOGEY: I saw him last night with Janet —

CLARE: Hasn't she had her baby yet?

BOGEY: She hadn't last night.

CLARE: That damned baby's been hanging over us all for months —

The telephone rings – CLARE answers it.

(*At telephone.*) Hallo – yes – hallo, darling – no, it's Clare – yes, he's here — No, I really couldn't face it – yes, if I were likely to go to India I'd come, but I'm not likely to go to India — I think Rajahs bumble up a house-party so terribly – yes, I know *he's* different, but the other one's awful – Angela had an agonising time with him – all the dining-room chairs had to be changed because they were leather and his religion prevented him sitting on them – all the dogs had to be kept out of the house because they were unclean, which God knows was true of the Bedlington, but the other ones were clean as whistles – and then to round everything off he took Laura Merstham in his car and made passes at her all the way to Newmarket – all right, darling – here he is — (*To* BOGEY.) It's Nina, she wants to talk to you —

She hands the telephone to BOGEY, *who reaches for it and lifts the wire so that it just misses* MRS WADHURST'S *hat. It isn't quite long enough so he has to bend down to speak with his face practically touching her.*

BOGEY (*at telephone*): Hallo, Nin — I can't on Wednesday, I've got a Guest Night – it's a hell of a long way, it'd take hours —

PIGGIE *comes in with a rush.*

PIGGIE: I am so sorry —

CLARE: Shhh!

BOGEY: Shut up, I can't hear —

PIGGIE (*in a shrill whisper*): Who is it?

CLARE: Nina.

BOGEY (*at telephone*): Well, you can tell George to leave it for me – and I can pick it up.

PIGGIE: How lovely to see you again!

BOGEY (*at telephone*): No, I shan't be leaving till about ten, so if he leaves it by nine-thirty I'll get it all right —

PIGGIE: My husband will be here in a minute – he has to go to sea on Thursday, but he's arranged for you to be taken over the dockyard at Portsmouth —

BOGEY (*at telephone*): Give the old boy a crack on the jaw.

PIGGIE: It's the most thrilling thing in the world. You see how the torpedoes are made – millions of little wheels inside, all clicking away like mad – and they cost thousands of pounds each —

BOGEY (*at telephone*): No, I saw her last night – not yet, but at any moment now – I should think — All right — Call me at Chatham – if I can get away I shall have to bring Mickie, too —

PIGGIE: How much do torpedoes cost each, Clare?

CLARE: God knows, darling – something fantastic – ask Bogey —

PIGGIE: Bogey —

BOGEY: What?

PIGGIE: How much do torpedoes cost each?

BOGEY: What? – (*At telephone.*) – wait a minute, Piggie's yelling at me —

PIGGIE: Torpedoes — (*She makes a descriptive gesture.*)

BOGEY: Oh, thousands and thousands – terribly expensive things – ask Peter — (*At telephone.*) – If I do bring him you'll have to be frightfully nice to him, he's been on the verge of suicide for weeks —

PIGGIE: Don't let her go, I must talk to her —

BOGEY (*at telephone*): Hold on a minute, Piggie wants to talk to you – all right – I'll let you know – here she is —

> PIGGIE *leans over the sofa and takes the telephone from* BOGEY, *who steps over the wire and stumbles over* MRS WADHURST.

BOGEY: I'm most awfully sorry —

MRS WADHURST: Not at all —

PIGGIE (*to* MRS WADHURST): It's so lovely you being in England — (*At telephone.*) Darling – what was the meaning of that sinister little invitation you sent me?

BOGEY: You know what Mickie is.

PIGGIE (*at telephone*): No, dear, I really can't – I always get so agitated —

CLARE: Why does he go on like that? It's so tiresome.

PIGGIE (*at telephone*): I'll come if Clare will — (*To* CLARE.) Are you going to Nina's Indian ding-dong?

CLARE: Not without an anæsthetic.

PIGGIE (*at telephone*): She's moaning a bit, but I'll persuade her –

what happens after dinner? – the man with the duck from the
Café de Paris — (*To the room in general.*) She's got that sweet
duck from the Café de Paris —

CLARE: Give me another cocktail, Bogey, I want to get so drunk
that I just can't hear any more —

PIGGIE (*at telephone*): But, darling, do you think it's quite *wise* – I
mean Maharajahs are terribly touchy and there's probably
something in their religion about ducks being mortal sin or
something – you know how difficult they are about cows and
pigs – just a minute – (*To the* WADHURSTS.) You can tell us, of
course —

MR WADHURST: I beg your pardon?

PIGGIE: Do Indians mind ducks?

MR WADHURST: I – I don't think so —

BOGEY: Do you come from India?

MRS WADHURST: No, Malaya.

PIGGIE: It's the same sort of thing, though, isn't it? – if they don't
mind them in Malaya it's unlikely that they'd mind them in
India — (*At telephone.*) It'll probably be all right, but you'd
better get Douglas Byng as a standby.

CLARE: There might be something in their religion about
Douglas Byng.

PIGGIE: Shh! (*At telephone.*) Everyone's making such a noise! The
room's full of the most frightful people. Darling, it definitely *is*
Waterloo Station — No, I'm almost sure he can't – he's going
to sea on Thursday – don't be silly, dear, you can't be in the
Navy without going to sea *sometimes* —

PETER *enters, followed by* ALLY.

(*At telephone.*) Here he is now, you can ask him yourself — (*To*
PETER.) Peter, it's Nina, she wants to talk to you — (*To the*
WADHURSTS.) This is my husband and Commander Corbett – he's
been longing to meet you and thank you for being so sweet to us
– I told him all about your heavenly house and the plantation —

MRS WADHURST (*bridling – to* ALLY): It was most delightful, I
assure you, to have Lady Maureen with us —

PIGGIE: Not him, him – that's the wrong one —

MRS WADHURST: Oh, I'm so sorry —

PETER (*shaking hands with* MRS WADHURST): It was so kind of you – my wife has talked of nothing else —

PIGGIE (*grabbing him*): Here – Nina's yelling like a banshee —

PETER: Excuse me. (*He takes the telephone.*) Hallo, Nin – what for? — No, I can't, but Piggie probably can — (*To* PIGGIE.) Can you go to Nina's party for the Rajahs?

PIGGIE: We've been through all that —

PETER: All right – I didn't know — (*At telephone.*) No, I shall be at sea for about three days – it isn't tiresome at all, I like it —

PIGGIE (*to* MRS WADHURST): How's your daughter?

MRS WADHURST (*surprised*): She's a little better, thank you.

PIGGIE: Oh, has she been ill? I'm so sorry.

MR WADHURST (*gently*): She's been ill for five years.

PIGGIE (*puzzled*): How dreadful for you – are you happy with that cocktail, or would you rather have tea?

MRS WADHURST: This is delicious, thank you.

PETER (*at telephone*): I honestly can't do anything about that, Nina, you might be able to find out from the Admiral – well, if his mother was mad too that is an extenuating circumstance – he'll probably be sent home — (*To* CLARE.) Did you know that Freda Bathurst had once been in an asylum?

CLARE: No, but it explains a lot.

PIGGIE: Why?

PETER: Her son went mad in Hong Kong.

CLARE: What did he do?

PETER: I don't know, but Nina's in a state about it.

PIGGIE: I don't see what it's got to do with Nina —

PETER: He's a relation of some sort — (*At telephone.*) What did he do, Nina? — Oh — Oh, I see — Oh – well, he'll certainly be sent home and a good job too, we can't have that sort of thing in the Service — If I were you I'd keep well out of it – all right — Good-bye. (*He hangs up.*)

PIGGIE: What was it?

PETER: I couldn't possibly tell you.

PIGGIE: Poor boy, I expect the climate had something to do with it – the climate's awful in Hong Kong – look at poor old Wally Smythe —

ALLY (*to the* WADHURSTS): Did you ever know Wally Smythe?

MRS WADHURST: No, I'm afraid not.

CLARE: You didn't miss much.

PIGGIE: I adored Wally, he was a darling.

CLARE: He kept on having fights all the time – I do hate people hitting people — (*To* MRS WADHURST.) Don't you?

MRS WADHURST: Yes.

There is suddenly complete silence – PIGGIE *breaks it with an effort.*

PIGGIE (*vivaciously to the* WADHURSTS): Maud was so frightfully sorry that she couldn't come today – she's pining to see you again and she asked me to ask you if you'd lunch there to-morrow?

MRS WADHURST: How very kind of her.

PIGGIE: She's got a divine little house hidden away in a mews, it's frightfully difficult to find — (*The telephone rings.*) I've got millions of questions I want to ask you, what happened to that darling old native who did a dance with a sword? — (*At telephone.*) Hallo – (*Continuing to everyone in general.*) It was the most exciting thing I've ever seen, all the villagers sat round in torchlight and they beat — (*At telephone.*) Hallo – yes, speaking — (*Continuing.*) beat drums and the — (*At telephone.*) hallo – darling, I'd no idea you were back — (*To everybody.*) and the old man tore himself to shreds in the middle, it was marvellous — (*At telephone.*) I can't believe it, where are you speaking from? — My dear, you're *not!* — (*To everybody.*) It's Boodie, she's got back last night and she's staying with Norman —

CLARE: Is Phyllis there?

PIGGIE (*at telephone*): Is Phyllis there? — She's away? — (*To* CLARE.) She's away.

PETER (*to* MR WADHURST): That's the best joke I ever heard.

CLARE: It's made my entire season that's all, it's just made it.

PIGGIE (*at telephone*): You'd better come and dine tonight – I'm on a diet, so there's only spinach, but we can talk — Yes, she's here – absolutely worn out – we all are — Oh yes, it was pretty grim, it started all right and everything was going beautifully when Vera arrived, unasked, my dear, and more determined than Hitler – of course there was the most awful scene – Alice flounced upstairs with tears cascading down her

95

face and locked herself in the cook's bedroom — Clare tried to save the situation by dragging Lady Borrowdale on to the terrace —

CLARE (*sibilantly*): That was *afterwards!* —

PIGGIE (*at telephone*): Anyhow hell broke loose – you can imagine – Janet was there, of course, and we were all worried about her – no, it hasn't arrived yet, but the odds were mounting — (*To everybody.*) She hasn't had it yet, has she, Peter?

PETER: If she has it was born in the gramophone department at Harrods – I left her there at four-thirty —

PIGGIE (*at telephone*): No, it's still what's known as on the way – I'll expect you about eight-thirty – I've got to do my feet and then I'm going to relax – all right – yes, she's here — (*To* CLARE.) Here, Clare, she wants to talk to you —

> CLARE *in order to reach the telephone comfortably has to kneel on the sofa.*

CLARE: Excuse me.

MRS WADHURST: I'm so sorry.

CLARE (*at telephone*): Darling – I'm dead with surprise —

PIGGIE (*to* MRS WADHURST): Now you must tell me some more —

MRS WADHURST: Well, really, I don't —

CLARE: Shhh! – I can't hear a word — (*At telephone.*) He what? – when? — He must be raving —

PIGGIE (*in a harsh whisper*): Have you still got that sweet dog?

MRS WADHURST (*also whispering*): Yes, we've still got Rudolph.

PIGGIE (*to everybody*): Rudolph's an angel, I can never tell you how divine he was – he used to come in every morning with my breakfast tray and jump on to the bed —

MRS WADHURST (*horrified*): Oh, you never told me that, how very naughty of him – he's very seldom allowed in the house at all —

PIGGIE (*puzzled*): But – but —

MR WADHURST: Perhaps you're thinking of some other dog, Lady Maureen – Rudoph is a Great Dane —

PIGGIE (*bewildered*): Oh, yes, of course, how idiotic of me —

CLARE (*at telephone*): – Well, all I can say is she ought to be deported – you can't go about making scenes like that, it's so lacking in everything – all right, darling – call me in the morning – I've got a hairdresser in the afternoon, why don't you make an appointment at the same time? – lovely — Good-bye. (*She hangs up.*)

PIGGIE: Do sit down, Clare, and stop climbing about over everybody. (*To* MRS WADHURST.) You must forgive me – this is a mad-house – it's always like this – I can't think why —

CLARE (*in a whisper to* PETER, *having noticed* MR BURNHAM): Why's that man got a roll of music, is he going to sing?

PETER (*also in a whisper*): I don't know – he ought by rights to be a lovely girl of sixteen —

MRS WADHURST: Have you been in London for the whole season?

PIGGIE: Yes, it's been absolutely frightful, but my husband is getting leave soon, so we shall be able to pop off somewhere —

ALLY (*to* MR WADHURST): I suppose you've never run across a chap in Burma called Beckwith?

MR WADHURST: No, I've never been to Burma.

ALLY: He's in rubber, too, I believe – or tea – he's very amusing.

MRS WADHURST (*to* PIGGIE): We did hope you'd come and lunch with us one day – but I expect you're terribly busy —

PIGGIE: My dear, I'd worship it — (*The telephone rings.*) Oh really, this telephone never stops for one minute — (*At telephone.*) Hallo – yes, speaking — Who? – Mrs Rawlingson — Oh, yes, yes, yes — (*She hands the telephone to* MRS WADHURST.) Here – it's for you —

MRS WADHURST (*astonished*): For me? How very curious —

PIGGIE: Give me a cocktail, Bogey – I haven't had one at all yet and I'm exhausted —

MRS WADHURST (*at telephone*): Hallo – what – who? – I'm afraid I don't quite understand —

BOGEY (*giving* PIGGIE *a cocktail*): Here you are – it's a bit weak —

MRS WADHURST (*still floundering*): I think there must be some mistake – just a moment — (*To* PIGGIE.) It's for you, Lady Maureen – a Mrs Rawlingson —

PIGGIE (*laughing*): Now isn't that the most extraordinary coincidence — (*She takes the telephone.*) – Hallo – yes – speaking — (*She listens and her face changes.*) – Oh yes, of course, how stupid

of me — (*She looks hurriedly at the* WADHURSTS, *then at* PETER.)
I'm so awfully sorry, I only just came in — Oh, what a shame
– no, no, no, it doesn't matter a bit — No – indeed you must
call me up the first moment he gets over it — Yes – I expect it
was – yes — Good-bye.

> *She slowly hangs up the receiver, looking at the* WADHURSTS *in
> complete bewilderment. She makes a sign to* PETER *over* MRS
> WADHURST'S *shoulder, but he only shakes his head.*

PIGGIE (*brightly, but with intense meaning*): That was Mrs Rawlingson.

PETER: Good God!

PIGGIE (*with purpose, sitting next to* MRS WADHURST): Did you ever
meet the Rawlingsons out East?

MRS WADHURST: No – I don't know them.

PIGGIE: Maud and I stayed with them too, you know.

MRS WADHURST: Where?

PIGGIE: It was in Malaya somewhere, I think – I do get so
muddled.

MRS WADHURST: I think we should have heard of them if they
lived in Malaya.

> PETER *meanwhile has gone to the piano and started to strum idly –
> he begins to hum lightly at the same time.*

PETER (*humming to a waltz refrain, slightly indistinctly, but clearly
enough for* PIGGIE *to hear*): If these are not them who are they?
Who are they? Who are they?

> PIGGIE *rises and saunters over to the piano.*

PIGGIE: Play the other bit, dear, out of the act — (*She hums.*) –
you know – 'I haven't the faintest idea — Oh no – I haven't
the faintest idea'.

PETER (*changing tempo*): 'Under the light of the moon, dear –
you'd better find out pretty soon, dear'.

CLARE: What on earth's that out of?

PIGGIE: Don't be *silly*, Clare – all I ask is that you shouldn't be
silly!

CLARE (*understanding*): Oh yes – I see.

> *There is silence except for* PETER'S *playing – everyone looks covertly
> at the* WADHURSTS. PIGGIE *goes over to* MR WADHURST.

PIGGIE (*with determination*): What ship did you come home in?

MR WADHURST: The *Naldera*.

ALLY: P & O?

MRS WADHURST: Yes.

PIGGIE: I suppose you got on at Singapore?

MR WADHURST: No, Penang.

PIGGIE (*the light breaking*): Penang! Of course, Penang.

MRS WADHURST: Yes, we have some friends there, so we went by train from Singapore and stayed with them for a couple of days before catching the boat.

PIGGIE (*sunk again*): Oh yes – yes, I see.

PETER (*at piano, humming to march time*): 'When you hear those drums rat-a-plan – rat-a-plan – find out the name of the place if you can – la la la la la la la la —'

PIGGIE (*persevering*): How far is your house from the sea? Maud and I were arguing about it for hours the other day —

MR WADHURST: It's right on the sea.

PIGGIE: That's exactly what I said, but you know Maud's so vague – she never remembers a thing —

CLARE: I suppose it's hell hot all the year round where you are?

MRS WADHURST: Yes, the climate is a little trying, but one gets used to it.

BOGEY: Are you far from Kuala Lumpur.

MRS WADHURST: Yes, a long way.

BOGEY: Oh, I knew some people in Kuala Lumpur once.

MR WADHURST: What were their names?

BOGEY: Damn it, I've forgotten – something like Harrison —

PIGGIE (*helpfully*): Morrison?

ALLY: Williamson?

PETER: Lightfoot?

BOGEY: No, it's gone —

PIGGIE (*irritably*): Never mind – it couldn't matter less really, could it?

MRS WADHURST (*rising*): I'm afraid we must really go now, Lady Maureen —

PIGGIE: Oh no – please —

MRS WADHURST: We have to dress because we're dining and

going to the theatre – that's the one thing we do miss dreadfully in Pendarla – the theatre —

CLARE: We miss it a good deal here, too.

PIGGIE (*remembering everything*): Pendarla – oh dear, what a long way away it seems – dear Mrs Wadhurst – (*She shoots a triumphant glance at* PETER.) – it's been so lovely having this little peep at you – you and Mr Wadhurst must come and dine quietly one night and we'll go to another theatre —

MRS WADHURST: That would be delightful – Fred —

MR WADHURST: Good-bye.

PIGGIE: Peter – come and say good-bye to Mr and Mrs Wadhurst.

PETER (*coming over and shaking hands*): Good-bye – I can never tell you how grateful I am to you for having been so kind and hospitable to my wife —

MRS WADHURST: Next time, I hope you'll come and call on us too.

PETER: I should love to.

MRS WADHURST: Good-bye.

CLARE: Good-bye —

> *Everybody says good-bye and shakes hands,* PETER *opens the door for the* WADHURSTS *and they go out on a wave of popularity. He goes out into the hall with them closing the door after him.* PIGGIE *collapses on to the sofa.*

PIGGIE (*hysterically*): Oh, my God, that was the most awful half an hour I've ever spent —

CLARE: I thought it all went down like a dinner.

PIGGIE: I remember it all now, we stayed one night with them on our way from Siam – a man in Bangkok had wired to them or something —

ALLY: That was a nice bit you did about the old native dancing with the sword —

PIGGIE: Oh dear, they must have thought I was drunk.

> PETER *re-enters.*

PETER: Next time you travel, my darling, I suggest you keep a diary.

PIGGIE: Wasn't it frightful – poor angels – I must ring up Maud — (*She dials a number.*) I think they had a heavenly time though, don't you – I mean they couldn't have noticed a thing —

PETER: Oh no, the whole affair was managed with the utmost subtlety – I congratulate you —

PIGGIE: Don't be sour – Peter — (*At telephone.*) Hallo – Maud? – darling, it's not the Rawlingsons at all, it's the Wadhursts — (*To everybody.*) Good heavens, I never gave them Maud's address. (*At telephone.*) I forgot to give them your address – how can you be so unkind, Maud, you ought to be ashamed of yourself – they're absolute pets, both of them —

PETER: Come on, Ally, I've got to dress —

ALLY: All right —

CLARE: Shall I see you on Sunday?

ALLY: Yes – I'll be over —

PIGGIE (*at telephone*): – they had a lovely time and everybody was divine to them —

CLARE: Come on, Bogey, we must go, too —

PIGGIE: Wait a minute, don't leave me – I've got to do my feet — (*At telephone.*) – no, I was talking to Clare — My dear, I know, she rang me up too – she's staying with Norman – Phyllis will be as sour as a quince —

> PETER *and* ALLY *go off talking.*

CLARE: Darling, I really *must* go —

PIGGIE (*at telephone*): – all right – I'll try to get hold of them in the morning and put them off – I do think it's horrid of you though, after all, they were frightfully sweet to us – I've done all I can – well, there's no need to get into a rage, I'm the one to get into a rage – yes, you are, I can hear you – your teeth are chattering like dice in a box — Oh, all right! (*She hangs up.*) Maud's impossible —

CLARE: Listen, Piggie —

PIGGIE: Wait just one minute, I've got to get the things to do my feet —

> She rushes out of the room.

CLARE: I really don't see why we should all wait about — (*She suddenly sees* MR BURNHAM.) Oh – hallo.

MR BURNHAM (*nervously*): Hallo.

CLARE: I thought you'd left with your mother and father.

MR BURNHAM: They weren't my mother and father – I'm from Freeman's. I've brought the designs for the Commander's speed boat – Mr Driscoll couldn't come —

CLARE: Well, you'd better wait – he'll be back soon —

MR BURNHAM: I'm afraid I can't wait much longer – I have to get back to the shop —

CLARE: You should have piped up before —

BOGEY: Listen, Clare, we must push off —

CLARE: All right.

> MR BURNHAM *retires again into the shadows as* PIGGIE *returns with several bottles, a towel and a pair of scissors. She sits on the sofa and takes her shoes and stockings off.*

PIGGIE: The trouble with Maud is, she's too insular —

CLARE: Are you driving down on Saturday?

PIGGIE: Yes – I promised to stop off at Godalming and have a cutlet with Freda on the way – do you want to come?

CLARE: You know perfectly well I hate Freda's guts.

PIGGIE (*beginning on her feet*): All right, darling – I'll expect you in the afternoon —

> *The telephone rings –* PIGGIE *reaches for it with one hand and goes on painting her toe nails with the other – at telephone:*

Hallo – yes. Oh, David, I'm *so* sorry – I completely forgot —

> CLARE *and* BOGEY *hiss good-bye at her, she waves to them, and they go out.*

I couldn't help it, I had to be sweet to some people that Maud and I stayed with in Malaya — Oh! David darling, don't be so soured-up – yes, of course I do, don't be so silly — No, I'm quite alone doing my feet – well, I can't help that, I happen to *like* them red – well, after all they are my feet, I suppose I can paint them blue if I want to —

> MR BURNHAM *begins to tiptoe out of the room, he leaves his roll of designs on the table.* PIGGIE *catches sight of him just as he is gingerly opening the door.*

(*To* MR BURNHAM.): Oh, good-bye – it's been absolutely lovely, you're the sweetest family I've ever met in my life —

CURTAIN

FUMED OAK

An Unpleasant Comedy in Two Scenes

Fumed Oak was produced in London at the Phoenix Theatre on 13 January 1936, with the following cast:

HENRY GOW	Mr Noël Coward
DORIS, *his wife*	Miss Gertrude Lawrence
ELSIE, *his daughter*	Miss Moya Nugent
MRS ROCKETT, *his mother-in-law*	Miss Alison Leggatt

Scene I. *Morning.*
Scene II. *Evening.*

The action of the play passes in the sitting-room of the GOWS' *house in South London.*

TIME: The present day.

Scene I

The GOWS' *sitting-room is indistinguishable from several thousand other suburban sitting-rooms. The dominant note is refinement. There are french windows at the back opening to a narrow lane of garden. These are veiled discreetly by lace curtains set off by a pelmet and side pieces of rather faded blue casement cloth. There is a tiled fireplace on the right; an upright piano between it and the window; a fumed oak sideboard on the left and, below it, a door leading to the hall, the stairs and the front door. There is a fumed oak dining-room suite consisting of a table, and six chairs; a sofa; an arm-chair in front of the fire; a radio, and a plentiful sprinkling over the entire room of ornaments and framed photographs.*

When the Curtain rises it is about eight-thirty on a spring morning. Rain is trickling down the windows and breakfast is laid on the table.

MRS ROCKETT *is seated in the arm-chair by the fire; on a small table next to her is a cup of tea, and a work-basket. She is a fattish, grey-looking woman dressed in a blouse and skirt and a pepper and salt jumper of artificial silk. Her pince-nez snap in and out of a little clip on her bosom and her feet are bad which necessitates the wearing of large quilted slippers in the house.*

DORIS, *aged about thirty-five, is seated at the table reading a newspaper propped up against the cruet. She is thin and anæmic and whatever traces of past prettiness she might have had are obscured by the pursed-up, rather sour gentility of her expression. She wears a nondescript coat-frock, a slave bangle and a necklace of amber glass beads.* ELSIE, *her daughter aged about fourteen, is sitting opposite to her, cutting her toast into strips in order to dip them into her boiled egg. She is a straight-haired ordinary-looking girl dressed in a navy blue school dress with a glacé red leather waist belt.*

There is a complete silence broken only by the occasional rattle of a spoon in a cup or a sniffle from ELSIE *who has a slight head cold.*

    HENRY GOW *comes into the room. He is tall and spare, neatly dressed in a blue serge suit. He wears rimless glasses and his hair is going grey at the sides and thin on the top. He sits down at the table without a word.* DORIS *automatically rises and goes out, returning in a moment with a plate of haddock which she places in front of him and resumes her place.* HENRY *pours himself out some tea.* DORIS, *without looking at him, being re-immersed in the paper, passes him the milk and sugar. The silence continues until* ELSIE *breaks it.*

ELSIE: Mum?

DORIS: What?

ELSIE: When can I put my hair up?

DORIS (*snappily*): When you're old enough.

ELSIE: Gladys Pierce is the same age as me and she's got hers up.

DORIS: Never you mind about Gladys Pierce, get on with your breakfast.

ELSIE: I don't see why I can't have it cut. That would be better than nothing.

    This remark is ignored.

Maisie Blake had hers cut last week and it looks lovely.

DORIS: Never you mind about Maisie Blake neither. She's common.

ELSIE: Miss Pritchard doesn't think so. Miss Pritchard likes Maisie Blake a lot, she said it looked ever so nice.

DORIS (*irritably*): What?

ELSIE: Her hair.

DORIS: Get on with your breakfast. You'll be late.

ELSIE (*petulantly*): Oh, Mum —

DORIS: And stop sniffling. Sniffle sniffle sniffle! Haven't you got a handkerchief?

ELSIE: Yes, but it's a clean one.

DORIS: Never mind, use it.

MRS ROCKETT: The child can't help having a cold.

DORIS: She can blow her nose, can't she, even if she has got a cold?

ELSIE (*conversationally*): Dodie Watson's got a terrible cold, she's had it for weeks. It went to her chest and then it went back to her head again.

MRS ROCKETT: That's the worst of schools, you're always catching something.

ELSIE: Miss Pritchard's awful mean to Dodie Watson, she said she'd had enough of it.

DORIS: Enough of what?

ELSIE: Her cold.

> *There is silence again which is presently shattered by the wailing of a baby in the house next door.*

MRS ROCKETT: There's that child again. It kept me awake all night.

DORIS: I'm very sorry, I'm sure.

MRS ROCKETT (*fiddling in her work-basket*): I wasn't blaming you.

DORIS: The night before last it was the hot-water pipes.

MRS ROCKETT: You ought to have them seen to.

DORIS: You know as well as I do you can't stop them making that noise every now and then.

MRS ROCKETT (*threading a needle*): I'm sure I don't know why you don't get a plumber in.

DORIS (*grandly*): Because I do not consider it necessary.

MRS ROCKETT: You would if you slept in my room – gurgle gurgle gurgle all night long – it's all very fine for you, you're at the end of the passage.

DORIS (*with meaning*): You don't have to sleep there.

MRS ROCKETT: What do you mean by that?

DORIS: You know perfectly well what I mean.

MRS ROCKETT (*with spirit*): Listen to me, Doris Gow. I've got a perfect right to complain if I want to and well you know it. It isn't as if I was staying here for nothing.

DORIS: I really don't know what's the matter with you lately, Mother, you do nothing but grumble.

MRS ROCKETT: Me, grumble! I like that, I'm sure. That's rich, that is.

DORIS: Well, you do. It gives me a headache.

MRS ROCKETT: You ought to do something about those headaches of yours. They seem to pop on and off at the least thing.

DORIS: And I wish you wouldn't keep passing remarks about not staying here for nothing.

MRS ROCKETT: Well, it's true, I don't.

DORIS: Anyone would think we was taking advantage of you.

MRS ROCKETT: Well, they wouldn't be far wrong.

DORIS: Mother, how can you! You're not paying a penny more than you can afford.

MRS ROCKETT: I never said I was. It isn't the money, it's the lack of consideration.

DORIS: Pity you don't go and live with Nora for a change.

MRS ROCKETT: Nora hasn't got a spare room.

DORIS: Phyllis has, a lovely one, looking out over the railway. I'm sure her hot-water pipes wouldn't annoy you, there isn't hot water in them.

MRS ROCKETT: Of course, if I'm not wanted here, I can always go to a boarding-house or a private hotel.

DORIS: Catch you!

MRS ROCKETT: I'm not the sort to outstay my welcome anywhere —

DORIS: Oh, for heaven's sake don't start that again —

MRS ROCKETT (*addressing the air*): It seems as though some of us had got out of bed the wrong side this morning.

ELSIE: Mum, can I have some more toast?

DORIS: No.

ELSIE: I could make it myself over the kitchen fire.

DORIS: No, I tell you. Can't you understand plain English? You've had quite enough and you'll be late for school.

MRS ROCKETT: Never mind, Elsie, here's twopence, you can buy yourself a sponge-cake at Barret's.

ELSIE (*taking the twopence*): Thanks, Grandma.

DORIS: You'll do no such thing, Elsie. I'm not going to have a child of mine stuffing herself with cake in the middle of the High Street.

MRS ROCKETT (*sweetly*): Eat it in the shop, dear.

DORIS: Go on, you'll be late.

ELSIE: Oh, Mum, it's only ten to.

DORIS: Do as I tell you.

ELSIE: Oh, all right.

She goes sullenly out of the room and can be heard scampering noisily up the stairs.

MRS ROCKETT (*irritatingly*): Poor little soul.

DORIS: I'll trouble you not to spoil Elsie, Mother.

MRS ROCKETT: Spoil her! I like that. Better than half starving her.

DORIS (*hotly*): Are you insinuating —

MRS ROCKETT: I'm not insinuating anything. Elsie's getting a big girl, she only had one bit of toast for her breakfast and she used that for her egg, I saw her.

DORIS: It's none of your business and in future I'd be much obliged if you'd keep your twopences to yourself.

MRS ROCKETT (*hurt*): Very well, of course if I'm to be abused every time I try to bring a little happiness into the child's life —

DORIS: Anyone would think I ill-treated her the way you talk.

MRS ROCKETT: You certainly nag her enough.

DORIS: I don't do any such thing and I wish you'd be quiet.

She flounces up from the table and goes over to the window, where she stands drumming her fingers on the pane. HENRY *quietly appropriates the newspaper she has flung down.*

MRS ROCKETT (*unctuously*): There's no need to lose your temper.

DORIS: I am not losing my temper.

MRS ROCKETT: If I'd known when you were Elsie's age what you were going to turn out like I'd have given you what for, I can tell you.

DORIS: Pity you didn't, I'm sure.

MRS ROCKETT: One thing, I never stinted any of my children.

DORIS: I wish you'd leave me to bring up my own child in my own way.

MRS ROCKETT: That cold's been hanging over her for weeks and a fat lot you care —

DORIS: I've dosed her for it, haven't I? The whole house stinks of Vapex. What more can I do?

MRS ROCKETT: She ought to have had Doctor Bristow last Saturday when it was so bad. He'd have cleared it up in no time.

DORIS: You and your Doctor Bristow.

MRS ROCKETT: Nice thing if it turned to bronchitis. Mrs

Henderson's Muriel got bronchitis, all through neglecting a cold; the poor child couldn't breathe, they had to have two kettles going night and day —

DORIS: I suppose your precious Doctor Bristow told you that.

MRS ROCKETT: Yes, he did, and what's more he saved the girl's life, you ask Mrs Henderson.

DORIS: Catch me ask Mrs Henderson anything, not likely, stuck up thing —

MRS ROCKETT: Mrs Henderson's a very nice ladylike woman, just because she's quiet and a bit reserved you say she's stuck up —

DORIS: Who does she think she is anyway, Lady Mountbatten?

MRS ROCKETT: Really, Doris, you make me tired sometimes, you do really.

DORIS: If you're so fond of Mrs Henderson it's a pity you don't see more of her. I notice you don't go there often.

MRS ROCKETT (*with dignity*): I go when I am invited.

DORIS (*triumphantly*): Exactly.

MRS ROCKETT: She's not the kind of woman that likes people dropping in and out all the time. We can't all be Amy Fawcetts.

DORIS: What's the matter with Amy Fawcett?

> ELSIE *comes into the room wearing a mackintosh and a tam-o'-shanter. She stamps over to the piano and begins to search untidily through the pile of music on it.*

MRS ROCKETT: Well, she's common for one thing, she dyes her hair for another, and she's a bit too free and easy all round for my taste.

DORIS: She doesn't put on airs, anyway.

MRS ROCKETT: I should think not, after the sort of life she's led.

DORIS: How do you know what sort of a life she's led?

MRS ROCKETT: Everybody knows, you only have to look at her; I'm a woman of the world, I am, you can't pull the wool over my eyes —

DORIS: Don't untidy everything like that, what are you looking for?

ELSIE: *The Pixie's Parade*, I had it last night.

DORIS: If it's the one with the blue cover it's at the bottom.

ELSIE: It isn't – oh dear, Miss Pritchard will be mad at me if I can't find it.

MRS ROCKETT: Perhaps you put it in your satchel, dear, here, let me look — (*She opens* ELSIE'S *satchel, which is hanging over the back of a chair and fumbles in it.*) Is this it?

ELSIE: Oh yes, thanks, Grandma.

DORIS: Go along now, for heaven's sake, you'll be late.

ELSIE: Oh, all right, Mum. Good-bye, Mum, good-bye, Grandma, good-bye, Dad.

HENRY: Good-bye.

MRS ROCKETT: Good-bye, dear, give Grandma a kiss.

> ELSIE *does so.*

DORIS: Don't dawdle on the way home.

ELSIE: Oh, all right, Mum.

> *She goes out. The slam of the front door shakes the house.*

DORIS (*irritably*): There now.

MRS ROCKETT (*with studied politeness*): If you are going down to the shops this morning, would it be troubling you too much to get me a reel of white cotton?

DORIS: I thought you were coming with me.

MRS ROCKETT: I really don't feel up to it.

DORIS: I'll put it on my list.

> *She takes a piece of paper out of the sideboard drawer and scribbles on it.*

MRS ROCKETT: If it's out of your way, please don't trouble, it'll do another time.

DORIS: Henry, it's past nine.

HENRY (*without looking up*): I know.

DORIS: You'll be late.

HENRY: Never mind.

DORIS: That's a nice way to talk, I must say.

MRS ROCKETT: I'm sure if my Robert had ever lazed about like that in the mornings, I'd have thought the world had come to an end.

DORIS: Henry'll do it once too often, mark my words.

MRS ROCKETT (*biting off her thread*): Well, that corner's finished.

DORIS (*to* HENRY): You'll have to move now, I've got to clear.

HENRY (*rising – absently*): All right.

MRS ROCKETT: Where's Ethel?

DORIS: Doing the bedroom.

> *She takes a tray which is leaning against the wall by the sideboard and proceeds to stack the breakfast things on to it.*
>
> HENRY *quietly goes out of the room.*

DORIS: Look at that wicked waste. (*Throws more scraps in fire.*)

MRS ROCKETT: What's the matter with him?

DORIS: Don't ask me, I'm sure I couldn't tell you.

MRS ROCKETT: He came in very late last night, I heard him go into the bathroom. (*There is a pause.*) That cistern makes a terrible noise.

DORIS: Does it indeed!

MRS ROCKETT: Yes, it does.

DORIS (*slamming the teapot on to the tray*): Very sorry, I'm sure.

MRS ROCKETT: Where'd he been?

DORIS: How do I know?

MRS ROCKETT: Didn't you ask him?

DORIS: I wouldn't demean myself.

MRS ROCKETT: Been drinking?

DORIS: No.

MRS ROCKETT: Sounded very like it to me, all that banging about.

DORIS: You know Henry never touches a drop.

MRS ROCKETT: I know he says he doesn't.

DORIS: Oh, do shut up, Mother, we're not all like father.

MRS ROCKETT: You watch your tongue, Doris Gow, don't let me hear you saying anything against the memory of your poor father.

DORIS: I wasn't.

MRS ROCKETT (*belligerently*): Oh yes, you were, you were insinuating again.

DORIS (*hoisting up the tray*): Father drank and you know it – everybody knew it.

MRS ROCKETT: You're a wicked woman.

DORIS: It's true.

MRS ROCKETT: Your father was a gentleman, which is more than your husband will ever be, with all his night-classes and his book reading – night-classes indeed!

DORIS: Who's insinuating now?

MRS ROCKETT (*angrily*): I am, and I'm not afraid to say so.

DORIS: What of it?

MRS ROCKETT (*with heavy sarcasm*): I suppose he was at a night-class last night?

DORIS (*loudly*): Mind your own business.

> HENRY *comes in wearing his mackintosh and a bowler hat.*

HENRY: What's up?

DORIS: Where were you last night?

HENRY: Why?

DORIS: Mother wants to know and so do I.

HENRY: I was kept late at the shop and I had a bit of dinner in town.

DORIS: Who with?

HENRY: Charlie Henderson.

> *He picks up the paper off the table and goes out. After a moment the front door slams.*
>
> *The baby next door bursts into fresh wails.*

MRS ROCKETT: There goes that child again. It's my belief it's hungry.

DORIS: Wonder you don't go and give it twopence to buy sponge-cake.

> *She pulls the door open with her foot and goes out with the tray as the lights fade on the scene.*

Scene II

It is about seven-thirty in the evening. ELSIE *is sitting at the piano practising with the loud pedal firmly down all the time.*

MRS ROCKETT *is sitting in her chair by the fire, but she is dressed in her street things and wearing a black hat with a veil.*

DORIS, *also in street clothes, is clearing some paper patterns and pieces of material from the table.*

There is a cloth across the end of the table on which is set a loaf, a plate of cold ham, a saucer with two tomatoes in it, a bottle of A.1 sauce and a teapot, teacup, sugar basin and milk jug.

HENRY *comes in, taking off his mackintosh. He gives one look round the room and goes out into the hall again to hang up his things.* ELSIE *stops playing and comes over to* DORIS.

ELSIE: Can we go now?

DORIS: In a minute.

ELSIE: We'll miss the Mickey.

DORIS: Put on your hat and don't worry.

ELSIE (*grabbing her hat from the sideboard*): Oh, all right.

> HENRY *re-enters.*

DORIS: Your supper's all ready, the kettle's on the gas stove when you want it. We've had ours.

HENRY: Oh!

DORIS: And you needn't look injured either.

HENRY: Very well.

DORIS: If you managed to get home a bit earlier it'd save a lot of trouble all round.

HENRY (*amiably*): Sorry, dear.

DORIS: It's all very fine to be sorry, you've been getting later and later these last few weeks, they can't keep you overtime every night.

HENRY: All right, dear, I'll tell them.

DORIS: Here, Elsie, put these away in the cupboard.

> *She hands her a pile of material and pieces of paper.* ELSIE *obediently takes them and puts them in the left-hand cupboard of the sideboard.*

HENRY (*sitting at the table*): Cold ham, what a surprise!

DORIS (*looking at him sharply*): What's the matter with it?

HENRY: I don't know, yet.

DORIS: It's perfectly fresh, if that's what you mean?

HENRY: Why are you all so dressed up?

ELSIE: We're going to the pictures.

HENRY: Oh, I see.

DORIS: You can put everything on the tray when you've finished and leave it in the kitchen for Ethel.

HENRY: Good old Ethel.

DORIS (*surprised*): What?

HENRY: I said good old Ethel.

DORIS: Well, it sounded very silly, I'm sure.

MRS ROCKETT (*scrutinising him*): What's the matter with you?

HENRY: Nothing, why?

MRS ROCKETT: You look funny.

HENRY: I feel funny.

MRS ROCKETT: Have you been drinking?

HENRY: Yes.

DORIS: Henry!

MRS ROCKETT: I knew it.

HENRY: I had a whisky and soda in town and another one at the Plough.

DORIS (*astounded*): What for?

HENRY: Because I felt like it.

DORIS: You ought to be ashamed of yourself.

HENRY: I'm going to have another one too, a bit later on.

DORIS: You'll do no such thing.

HENRY: That hat looks awful.

DORIS (*furiously*): Don't you speak to me like that.

HENRY: Why not?

DORIS (*slightly nonplussed*): Because I won't have it, so there.

HENRY: It's a common little hat and it looks awful.

DORIS (*with an admirable effort at control*): Now listen to me, Henry Gow, the next time I catch you drinking and coming home here and insulting me, I'll —

HENRY (*interrupting her gently*): What will you do, Dorrie?

DORIS (*hotly*): I'll give you a piece of my mind, that's what I'll do.

HENRY: It'll have to be a very little piece, Dorrie, you can't afford much! (*He laughs delighted at his own joke.*)

DORIS: I'd be very much obliged if you'd kindly tell me what this means?

HENRY: I'm celebrating.

DORIS: What do you mean, celebrating? What are you talking about?

HENRY: Tonight's our anniversary.

DORIS: Don't talk so soft, our anniversary's not until November.

HENRY: I don't mean that one. Tonight's the anniversary of the first time I had an affair with you and you got in the family way.

DORIS (*shrieking*): Henry!

HENRY (*delighted with his carefully calculated effect*): Hurray!

DORIS (*beside herself*): How dare you say such a dreadful thing, in front of the child, too.

HENRY (*in romantic tones*): Three years and a bit after that wonderful night our child was born! (*Lapsing into his normal voice.*) Considering all the time you took forming yourself, Elsie, I'm surprised you're not a nicer little girl than you are.

DORIS: Go upstairs, Elsie.

HENRY: Stay here, Elsie.

DORIS: Do as I tell you.

ELSIE: But, Mum —

DORIS: Mother, take her for God's sake! There's going to be a row.

HENRY (*firmly*): Leave her alone and sit down.

     MRS ROCKETT *hesitates.*

Sit down, I tell you.

MRS ROCKETT (*subsiding into a chair*): Well, I never, I —

HENRY (*happily*): See? It works like a charm.

DORIS: A fine exhibition you're making of yourself, I must say.

HENRY: Not bad, is it? As a matter of fact I'm rather pleased with it myself.

DORIS: Go to bed!

HENRY: Stop ordering me about. What right have you got to nag at me and boss me? No right at all. I'm the one that pays the rent and works for you and keeps you. What do you give me in return, I'd like to know! Nothing! I sit through breakfast while you and mother wrangle. You're too busy being snappy and bad-tempered even to say good morning. I come home tired after working all day and ten to one there isn't even a hot dinner for me; here, see this ham? This is what I think of it! (*He throws it at her feet.*) And the tomatoes and the A.1 bloody sauce! (*He throws them too.*)

DORIS (*screaming*): Henry! All over the carpet.

HENRY (*throwing the butter-dish face downwards on the floor*): And that's what I think of the carpet, now then!

DORIS: That I should live to see this! That I should live to see the man I married make such a beast of himself!

HENRY: Stop working yourself up into a state, you'll need all your control when you've heard what I'm going to say to you.

DORIS: Look here —

HENRY: Sit down. We'll all sit down, I'm afraid you'll have to miss the pictures for once.

DORIS: Elsie, you come with me.

MRS ROCKETT: Yes, go on, Ducks.

> *She makes a movement towards the door, but* HENRY *is too quick for her. He locks the door and slips the key into his pocket.*

HENRY: I've been dreaming of this moment for many years, and believe me it's not going to be spoilt for me by you running away.

DORIS (*on the verge of tears*): Let me out of this room.

HENRY: You'll stay where you are until I've had my say.

DORIS (*bursting into tears and sinking down at the table*): Oh! Oh! Oh! —

ELSIE (*starting to cry too*): Mum – oh, Mum —

HENRY: Here you, shut up, go and get the port out of the sideboard and give some to your mother – go on, do as I tell you.

> ELSIE, *terrified and hypnotised into submission, goes to the sideboard cupboard and brings out a bottle of invalid port and some glasses, snivelling as she does so.* DORIS *continues to sob.*

That's right.

MRS ROCKETT (*quietly*): You drunken brute, you!

HENRY (*cheerfully*): Worse than that, Mother, far worse. Just you wait and see.

MRS ROCKETT (*ignoring him*): Take some port, Dorrie, it'll do you good.

DORIS: I don't want any – it'd choke me —

HENRY (*pouring some out*): Come on – here —

DORIS: Keep away from me.

HENRY: Drink it and stop snivelling.

DORIS: I'll never forgive you for this, never, never, never as long as I live! (*She gulps down some port.*)

HENRY (*noting her gesture*): That's better.

MRS ROCKETT: Pay no attention, Dorrie, he's drunk.

HENRY: I'm not drunk. I've only had two whiskies and sodas, just to give me enough guts to take the first plunge. You'd never believe how scared I was, thinking it over in cold blood. I'm not scared any more though, it's much easier than I thought it was going to be. My only regret is that I didn't come to the boil a long time ago, and tell you to your face, Dorrie, what I think of you, what I've been thinking of you for years, and this horrid little kid, and that old bitch of a mother of yours.

MRS ROCKETT (*shrilly*): Henry Gow!

HENRY: You heard me, old bitch was what I said, and old bitch was what I meant.

MRS ROCKETT: Let me out of this room, I'm not going to stay here and be insulted – I'm not —

HENRY: You're going to stay here just as long as I want you to.

MRS ROCKETT: Oh, am I? We'll see about that —

With astonishing quickness she darts over to the window and manages to drag one open. HENRY *grabs her by the arm.*

HENRY: No, you don't.

MRS ROCKETT: Let go of me.

DORIS: Oh, Mother, don't let the neighbours know all your business.

HENRY: Not on your life!

MRS ROCKETT (*suddenly screaming powerfully*): Help! Help! Police! Help! Mrs Harrison – help! —

HENRY *drags her away from the window, turns her round and gives her a light slap on the face, she staggers against the piano, meanwhile he shuts the window again, locks it and pockets the key.*

DORIS (*looking at him in horror*): Oh, God! Oh, my God!

ELSIE (*bursting into tears again*): Oh, Mum, Mum, he hit Grandma! Oh, Mum —

She runs to DORIS *who puts her arm round her protectively.*

MRS ROCKETT (*gasping*): Oh – my heart! I think I'm going to faint – oh – my heart —

HENRY: Don't worry, I'll bring you round if you faint —

MRS ROCKETT: Oh – oh – oh, dear —

MRS ROCKETT *slides on to the floor, perceptibly breaking her fall by clinging on to the piano stool.*

DORIS *jumps up from the table.*

DORIS: Mother!

HENRY: Stay where you are.

HENRY *goes to the sideboard and pours out a glass of water.* DORIS, *disobeying him, runs over to her mother.* ELSIE *wails.*

HENRY: Stand out of the way, Doris, we don't all want to get wet.

He approaches with the glass of water. MRS ROCKETT *sits up weakly.*

MRS ROCKETT (*in a far-away voice*): Where am I?

HENRY: Number Seventeen Cranworth Road, Clapham.

MRS ROCKETT: Oh – oh, dear!

HENRY: Look here, Mother, I don't want there to be any misunderstanding about this. I liked slapping you just now, see? It was lovely, and if you don't behave yourself and keep quiet I shall slap you again. Go and sit in your chair and remember if you feel faint the water's all ready for you.

He helps her up and escorts her to her chair by the fire. She collapses into it and looks at him balefully.

Now then. Sit down, Dorrie, you look silly standing about.

DORIS (*with a great effort at control*): Henry —

HENRY (*slowly, but very firmly*): Sit down! And keep Elsie quiet or I'll fetch her one, too.

DORIS (*with dignity*): Come here, Elsie. Shut up, will you!

She sits at the table, with ELSIE.

HENRY: That's right.

He walks round the room slowly and in silence, looking at them with an expression of the greatest satisfaction on his face. Finally he goes over to the fireplace; MRS ROCKETT *jumps slightly as he approaches her, but he smiles at her reassuringly and lights a cigarette. Meanwhile* DORIS, *recovering from her fear, is beginning to simmer with rage, she remains still, however, watching.*

Now then. I'm going to start, quite quietly, explaining a few things to you.

DORIS: Enjoying yourself, aren't you?

HENRY: You've said it.

DORIS (*gaining courage*): You'll grin on the other side of your face before I've done with you.

HENRY (*politely*): Very likely, Dorrie, very likely indeed!

DORIS: And don't you Dorrie me, either! Coming home here drunk, hitting poor mother and frightening Elsie out of her wits.

HENRY: Maybe it'll do her good, do 'em both good, a little excitement in the home. God knows, it's dull enough as a rule.

DORIS (*with biting sarcasm*): Very clever, oh, very clever, I'm sure.

HENRY: Fifteen, no sixteen years ago tonight, Dorrie, you and me had a little rough and tumble in your Aunt Daisy's house in Stansfield Road, do you remember?

DORIS: Henry —

HENRY (*ignoring her*): We had the house to ourselves, it being a Sunday, your aunt had popped over to the Golden Calf with Mr Simmonds, the lodger, which, as the writers say, was her wont —

MRS ROCKETT: This is disgusting, I won't listen to another word.

HENRY (*rounding on her*): You will! Shut up!

DORIS: Pay no attention, Mother, he's gone mad.

HENRY: Let me see now, where was I? Oh yes, Stansfield Road. You'd been after me for a long while, Dorrie, I didn't know it then, but I realised it soon after. You had to have a husband, what with Nora married and Phyllis engaged, both of them younger than you, you had to have a husband, and quick, so you fixed on me. You were pretty enough and I fell for it hook, line and sinker; then, a couple of months later you'd told me you'd clicked, you cried a hell of a lot, I remember, said the disgrace would kill your mother if she ever found out. I didn't know then that it'd take a sight more than that to kill that leathery old mare —

MRS ROCKETT (*bursting into tears*): I won't stand it, I won't! I won't!

HENRY (*rising above her sobs*): I expect you were in on the whole business, in a refined way of course, you knew what was going on all right, you knew that Dorrie was no more in the family way than I was, but we got married; you both saw to that, and

I chucked up all the plans I had for getting on, perhaps being a steward in a ship and seeing a bit of the world. Oh yes, all that had to go and we settled down in rooms and I went into Ferguson's Hosiery.

DORIS: I've given you the best years of my life and don't you forget it.

HENRY: You've never given me the best of anything, not even yourself. You didn't even have Elsie willingly.

DORIS (*wildly*): It's not true – stop up your ears, Elsie, don't listen to him, he's wicked – he's wicked —

HENRY (*grimly*): It's true all right, and you know it as well as I do.

DORIS (*shrilly*): It was only right that you married me. It was only fair! You took advantage of me, didn't you? You took away my innocence. It was only right that you paid for it.

HENRY: Come off it, Dorrie, don't talk so silly. I was the innocent one, not you. I found out you'd cheated me a long, long time ago, and when I found out, realised it for certain, I started cheating you. Prepare yourself, Dorrie, my girl, you're going to be really upset this time. I've been saving! Every week for over ten years I've been earning a little bit more than you thought I was. I've managed, by hook and by crook, to put by five hundred and seventy-two pounds – d'you hear me? – five hundred and seventy-two pounds!

MRS ROCKETT (*jumping to her feet*): Henry! You never have – it's not true —

DORIS (*also jumping up*): You couldn't have – you'd have given it away – I should have found out —

HENRY: I thought that'd rouse you, but don't get excited, don't get worked up. I haven't got it on me, it's in the bank. And it's not for you, it's for me – all but fifty pounds of it, that much is for you, just fifty pounds, the last you'll ever get from me —

DORIS: Henry! You couldn't be so cruel! You couldn't be so mean!

HENRY: I've done what I think's fair and what I think's fair is damn sight more than you deserve. I've transferred the freehold of this house into your name, so you'll always have a roof over your head – you can take in lodgers at a pinch, though God help the poor bastards if you do!

DORIS: Five hundred and seventy-two pounds! You've got all that and you're going to leave me to starve!

HENRY: Cut out the drama, Dorrie, and have a look at your mother's savings bank book – I bet you'll find she's got enough to keep you in comfort till the day you die. She soaked her old man plenty, I'm sure – before he took to soaking himself!

MRS ROCKETT: It's a lie!

HENRY: Now listen to me, Mother Machree – you've 'ad one sock in the jaw this evening and you're not just asking for another, you're sitting up and begging for it.

MRS ROCKETT: I'll have you up for assault. I'll have the police on you, my fine fellow!

HENRY: They'll have to be pretty nippy – my boat sails first thing in the morning.

DORIS (*horrified*): Boat!

HENRY: I'm going away. I've got my ticket here in my pocket, and my passport. My passport photo's a fair scream, I wish I could show it to you, but I don't want you to see the nice new name I've got.

DORIS: You can't do it, I can have you stopped by law. It's desertion.

HENRY: That's right, Dorrie, you've said it. Desertion's just exactly what it is.

DORIS (*breathlessly*): Where are you going, you've got to tell me. Where are you going?

HENRY: Wouldn't you like to know? Maybe Africa, maybe China, maybe Australia. There are lots of places in the world you know nothing about, Dorrie. You've often laughed at me for reading books, but I've found out a hell of a lot from books. There are islands in the South Seas for instance with cocoa palms and turtles and sunshine all the year round – you can live there for practically nothing, then there's Australia or New Zealand, with a little bit of capital I might start in a small way sheep-farming. Think of it; miles and miles of open country stretching as far as the eye can see – good food and fresh air – that might be very nice, that might suit me beautifully. Then there's South America. There are coffee plantations, there, and sugar plantations, and banana plantations. If I go to South America I'll send you a whole crate. 'Ave a banana, Dorrie! 'Ave a banana!

DORIS: Henry, listen to me, you can't do this dreadful thing, you can't! If you don't love me any more, think of Elsie.

HENRY (*still in his dream*): Then there's the sea, not the sea we know at Worthing with the tide going in and out regular and the band playing on the pier. The real sea's what I mean. The sea that Joseph Conrad wrote about, and Rudyard Kipling and lots of other people, too, a sea with whacking great waves and water spouts and typhoons and flying-fish and phosphorus making the foam look as if it was lit up. Those people knew a thing or two I can tell you. They knew what life could be like if you give it a chance. They knew there was a bit more to it than refinement and fumed oak and lace curtains and getting old and miserable with nothing to show for it. I'm a middle-aged man, but my health's not too bad taken all round. There's still time for me to see a little bit of real life before I conk out. I'm still fit enough to do a job of work – real work, mind you – not bowing and scraping and wearing meself out showing fussy old cows the way to the lace and the china ware and the bargain basement.

DORIS (*hysterically*): God will punish you, you just see if He doesn't, you just see —

HENRY: God's been punishing me for fifteen years, it's high time He laid off me now. He's been punishing me good and proper for being damn fool enough to let you get your claws into me in the first place —

DORIS (*changing tactics*): Henry, have pity, please don't be so cruel, please – please —

HENRY: And don't start weeping and wailing either, that won't cut any ice with me, I know what you're like, I know you through and through. You're frightened now, scared out of your wits, but give you half a chance and you'd be worse than ever you were. You're a bad lot, Dorrie, not what the world

would call a bad lot, but what I call a bad lot. Mean and cold
and respectable. Good-bye, Dorrie —

DORIS (*flinging her arms round him and bursting into tears*): Listen to
me, Henry, you've got to listen – you must. You can't leave us
to starve, you can't throw us on to the streets – if I've been a
bad wife to you, I'm sorry – I'll try to be better, really I will, I
swear to God I will — You can't do this, if you won't forgive
me, think of Elsie, think of poor little Elsie —

HENRY: Poor little Elsie, my eye! I think Elsie's awful. I always
have ever since she was little. She's never done anything but
whine and snivel and try to get something for nothing —

ELSIE (*wailing*): Oh, Mum, did you hear what he said? Oh, Dad,
oh dear —

MRS ROCKETT (*comforting her*): There, there, dear, don't listen to
him —

HENRY: Elsie can go to work in a year or so, in the meantime,
Dorrie, you can go to work yourself, you're quite a young
woman still and strong as an ox. – Here's your fifty pounds —

*He takes an envelope out of his pocket and throws it on to the table.
Then he goes towards the door.* DORIS *rushes after him and hangs on
to his arm.*

DORIS: Henry, Henry, you shan't go, you shan't —

HENRY (*struggling with her*): Leave hold of me.

DORIS: Mother, Mother – help – help me, don't let him go —

HENRY *frees himself from her and, taking her by the shoulders, forces
her back into a chair, then he unlocks the door and opens it.*

HENRY: I'm taking my last look at you, Dorrie. I shall never see
you again as long as I live —

DORIS: Mother! Oh God! – oh, my God! —

She buries her head in her arms and starts to sob loudly. ELSIE *runs
and joins her, yelling.* MRS ROCKETT *sits transfixed staring at him
murderously.*

HENRY (*quietly*): Three generations. Grandmother, Mother and
Kid. Made of the same bones and sinews and muscles and
glands, millions of you, millions just like you. You're past it
now, Mother, you're past the thick of the fray, you're nothing
but a music-hall joke, a mother-in-law with a bit of money put
by. Dorrie, the next few years will show whether you've got

guts or not. Maybe what I'm doing to you will save your immortal soul in the long run, that'd be a bit of all right, wouldn't it? I doubt it, though, your immortal soul's too measly. You're a natural bully and a cheat, and I'm sick of the sight of you; I should also like to take this opportunity of saying that I hate that bloody awful slave bangle and I always have. As for you, Elsie, you've got a chance, it's a slim one, I grant you, but still it's a chance. If you learn to work and be independent and, when the time comes, give what you have to give freely and without demanding life-long payment for it, there's just a bit of hope that you'll turn into a decent human being. At all events, if you'll take one parting piece of advice from your cruel ungrateful father, you'll spend the first money you ever earn on having your adenoids out. Good-bye, one and all. Nice to have known you!

The wails of DORIS *and* ELSIE *rise in volume as he goes jauntily out, slamming the door behind him.*

CURTAIN

SHADOW PLAY

A Musical Fantasy

Shadow Play was produced in London at the Phoenix Theatre on 13 January 1936, with the following cast:

VICTORIA GAYFORTH	Miss Gertrude Lawrence
SIMON GAYFORTH	Mr. Noël Coward
MARTHA CUNNINGHAM	Miss Everley Gregg
GEORGE CUNNINGHAM	Mr. Alan Webb
LENA	Miss Moya Nugent
SIBYL HESTON	Miss Alison Leggatt
MICHAEL DOYLE	Mr. Edward Underdown
A YOUNG MAN	Mr. Anthony Pelissier
HODGE, *dresser*	Mr. Kenneth Carten

TIME: The Present.

The scene is a well-furnished, rather luxurious bedroom in the
GAYFORTHS' *house in Mayfair. There is a bed on the right with a
table by the side of it on which are various bottles, books and a
telephone.*

*Below the bed there is a door which leads to the bathroom. On
the left there is a door leading to the passage and the rest of the
house. Above this is a dressing-table. At the foot of the bed there is
a small sofa.*

When the curtain rises LENA, VICTORIA'S *maid, is bustling
about the room. It is about midnight and she is laying out a
dressing-gown or negligee on the bed and generally arranging the
room for the night.*

VICTORIA *and* MARTHA *come in from the left.* VICTORIA *is
about thirty; beautifully gowned. Her manner is bored and
irritable.* MARTHA *is slightly older, also well dressed but more
tranquil.*

VICKY: —It couldn't matter less whether I go to Alice's or not –
   in fact it would be infinitely more comfortable for everybody
   concerned if I didn't.

MARTHA: What nonsense!

VICKY: Alice's parties are always dreary, and I don't feel in the
   mood even for a good party to-night.

MARTHA: What's the matter?

VICKY: I've told you – I've got a headache.

MARTHA: I think you're unwise.

VICKY: What do you mean, darling?

MARTHA: You know perfectly well what I mean.

VICKY (*sitting down at the dressing-table*): Of course I do, but I'm
   getting tired of everybody being subtle and hiding behind the
   furniture – I know that Simon will go without me and I know
   that Sibyl will be there and I know that if I don't go he will
   leave with her and if I do go he will leave with me and wish he
   was leaving with her. I also know that I'm bored stiff with the
   whole situation – let it rip—

MARTHA: Line of least resistance.

VICKY: Exactly – I have a headache – I feel thoroughly disagreeable – all I want is sleep – no more resisting – just sleep – Lena – give me three Anytal—

LENA: Three, madame?

VICKY: Yes, three – and you can go to bed.

LENA: Yes, madame.

MARTHA: Is the extra tablet a gesture of defiance?

VICKY: Don't be tiresome, Martha.

> LENA *brings her three tablets from a bottle by the bed and a glass of water.*

MARTHA: Do you take those things every night?

VICKY (*swallowing the tablets*): No, darling, I don't. And even if I did it wouldn't matter a bit – they're perfectly harmless.

LENA: Are you sure that's all, madame?

VICKY: Yes, thank you, Lena – good-night.

LENA: Good-night, madame.

> *She goes out.*

MARTHA: I don't like seeing people unhappy.

VICKY: I'm not in the least unhappy – just tired.

MARTHA: How much do you mind?

VICKY: Mind what?

> *She takes the dressing-gown off the bed and goes into the bathroom, leaving the door open.*

MARTHA (*firmly*): About Simon and Sibyl.

VICKY: Heart-broken, dear— (*She laughs.*) You mustn't be deceived by my gay frivolity, it's really only masking agony and defeat and despair—

MARTHA (*helping herself to a cigarette*): You're extremely irritating.

VICKY: That's what you wanted, isn't it?

MARTHA: You needn't be suspicious of me, you know – I have no axe to grind – I merely wanted to help—

VICKY: You're a noble, understanding old friend, darling, that's what you are, and I must say I should like to crack you over the head with a bottle.

MARTHA: Thank you, dear.

> *The telephone rings.*

VICKY: Answer that, will you? – it's probably Michael – I'll be out in a minute—

MARTHA: All right. (*She goes to the telephone.*) Hallo – No, it's Martha – She's in the bathroom, she'll be out in a minute – No, she's not – We've been to a play and it was so good that it gave her a headache – Hold on, here she is—

> VICKY *comes in in a dressing-gown, flings herself on to the bed and takes the telephone.*

VICKY: Hallo, Michael – No, I'm not – Yes, I've doped myself to the eyes and I'm about to go off into a coma – Of course you can't, don't be so idiotic – What are you in such a state about? – I thought we'd settled all that – It's no use dropping your voice like that – Martha can hear perfectly well, she's got ears like a hawk—

MARTHA: Perhaps you'd like me to go?

VICKY (*to* MARTHA): Be quiet, darling— (*At telephone.*) —I'm tired, Michael, and I've got a headache and so will you kindly shut up – Yes, all right – tomorrow – Good God, no, I shall be sound asleep – Go away, Michael, I can't bear any more— (*She hangs up.*) It's lovely being loved, isn't it?

> *She rolls over on the bed face downwards.*

MARTHA: You'd better get into bed—

VICKY: Perhaps you'd like to fill a hot-water bottle and take my temperature?

MARTHA (*patiently*): Have you got a book to read?

VICKY: Yes, but it's unreadable.

MARTHA: Do get into bed.

VICKY: Go to hell, darling, and don't fuss—

MARTHA (*seriously*): I really wish I could do something—

VICKY (*violently*): Stop it, I tell you— I don't want your sympathy —I don't want anybody's sympathy – whatever happens, happens – let it – what does it matter—

MARTHA: Very well. (*She turns to go.*)

VICKY (*jumping off the bed and coming to her*): I'm sorry – I know I'm beastly, but you see it's no use discussing things – the Anytal will begin to work soon and I shall have a nice long sleep and feel much better in the morning – It was the play that upset me, I think – you were quite right – everybody seemed to be having such a good time, didn't they? – it's a bit tantalising to see everybody having quite such a good time – it would be so much easier, wouldn't it, if we had music when things go wrong – music and a little dancing and the certainty of 'Happy ever after' – I hope you didn't miss the ironic twist at the end when they were married – crashing chords and complete tidiness – very convenient – Go away, darling – go and collect George and Simon and go on to Alice's – I shall go to sleep in a minute – really I will—

MARTHA: All right – I'll telephone you in the morning—

> *She kisses her and is about to go, when* SIMON *comes into the room. He is wearing a dressing-gown over his evening clothes.*

VICKY (*surprised*): Simon!

SIMON (*to* MARTHA): George is waiting for you, Martha – he's getting a bit restive.

VICKY: Aren't you going to Alice's?

SIMON: No, I didn't feel that I could face it.

VICKY: Oh, I see.

MARTHA: Do you want me to make excuses for you both, or just not say anything about it?

VICKY: Say that you haven't seen us, and why aren't we there, and is there any truth in the rumour that we're not getting on very well— (*She laughs.*)

SIMON: Don't be silly, Vicky.

VICKY: Say that I've gone to Ostend with Michael and that Simon's shot himself – but only in the leg.

SIMON (*bitterly*): Say that it's definitely true that we're not getting on very well – say that it's due to incompatibility of humour.

MARTHA: I shall say that I don't know you at all – any more.

> *She goes out.*

VICKY (*calling after her*): Give my love to Sibyl!

SIMON: That was a bit cheap, wasn't it?

VICKY: I thought it was only kind – Sibyl can't live without love – like the woman in the play to-night – don't you remember—? (*She hums.*) 'Nobody can live without loving somebody, nobody can love without leaving somebody!'

SIMON: You mustn't forget to sing that to Michael.

VICKY: Are we going to bicker? There's nothing like a nice bicker to round off a jolly evening.

SIMON: I'm getting a little tired of bickering.

VICKY: Let's not then, let's be absolutely divine to each other – let's pretend.

SIMON: I didn't go to Alice's party on purpose—

VICKY: I didn't think it was a sudden attack of amnesia.

SIMON: I want to talk to you.

VICKY: Do you, Simon? What about?

SIMON: Lots of things.

VICKY: Name fifteen.

SIMON: Seriously.

VICKY: There you are, you see – our moods are clashing again – it really is most unfortunate.

SIMON: I failed to notice during the evening that your spirits were so abnormally high.

VICKY: A sudden change for the better, dear, let's make the most of it.

SIMON: There's something I want to say to you – I've been wanting to say it for quite a while.

VICKY: Take the plunge, my darling – we're alone in the swimming bath.

SIMON: Would you consider divorcing me?

VICKY: Oh, Simon!

SIMON: If I made everything easy—

VICKY: Naming Sibyl?

SIMON: Of course not.

VICKY: You mean you'd prefer to be implicated with a professional homebreaker as opposed to an amateur one?

SIMON: I would like, if possible, to keep this conversation impersonal.

VICKY: We might put on fancy dress for it.

SIMON: I'm serious, Vicky.

VICKY: I'm told that all really funny comedians are serious.

SIMON: You haven't answered my question yet.

VICKY: I thought perhaps I hadn't heard it quite clearly.

SIMON: I want you to divorce me.

VICKY: Yes, now I hear – it's a beastly question, isn't it?

SIMON: Not so very beastly if you analyse it – quite sensible really.

VICKY: It oughtn't to be such a shock – but somehow it is – it makes me feel a little sick.

SIMON: I'm sorry.

VICKY: Don't worry about being sorry – feeling a little sick doesn't matter that much.

SIMON: I've thought it all over very carefully.

VICKY: Oh, Simon, have you? Have you really?

SIMON: Of course I have. It's been on my mind for a long time.

VICKY: How sinister that sounds – surely not for a very long time?

SIMON: Long enough.

VICKY: You're cruelly definite.

SIMON: It's less cruel to be definite – in the long run.

VICKY: It's been an awfully short run – really.

SIMON: You haven't answered me yet.

VICKY: An amicable divorce – everything below board?

SIMON: Yes.

VICKY: Where will you go with your temporary light of love? The South of France, or just good old Brighton?

SIMON: I don't think we need discuss that.

VICKY: It's a nasty business, isn't it – a very nasty business.

SIMON: Not necessarily, if it can be arranged discreetly and without fuss.

VICKY: Do you love her so much? Sibyl, I mean.

SIMON: I'd rather not discuss that either.

VICKY: Perhaps you'd prefer to conduct the whole thing by signs – sort of Dumb Crambo.

SIMON: You're unbelievably irritating.

VICKY: When did you first begin to hate me? – When did I first begin to get on your nerves? – What did I say? – What did I do? – Was it a dress I wore – the way I laughed at somebody's joke? – Was I suddenly gay when you were sad? – Was I insensitive? – Was I dull? When did it start – tell me if you can remember – please tell me.

SIMON: Don't be so foolish.

VICKY: I won't be irritating any more, Simon – I'll try to be sensible – really I will – but I must know why – why things change – I wish to God I hadn't taken those sleeping tablets – my head's going round – I would so love to be clear, just at this moment, but nothing's clear at all.

SIMON: I didn't know you'd taken anything.

VICKY: Don't be alarmed – I'm not becoming a drug fiend – it's an amiable, gentle prescription, just to make me sleep when I have a headache, or when I'm overtired or unhappy—

SIMON: There's the overture – we shall be late.

VICKY: What did you say?

SIMON: —You really ought not to get into the habit of taking things to make you sleep – however harmless they are—

VICKY: We've only been married five years – it seems longer at moments – then it seems no time at all—

The music begins, and, after a few chords, stops again.

SIMON: There it is again – listen.

VICKY: If you really love Sibyl, deeply and truly, it's different, but I have an awful feeling that you don't – anyhow, not enough—

SIMON: 'We will wander on together—
        Through the sunny summer weather—
        To our cosy little château
        Like a pastoral by Watteau.

TOGETHER: To our cosy little château on the Rhine.'

SIMON: —It isn't that I don't love you – I always shall love you— but this is something else – I don't know what started it, but I do know that it's terribly strong – and then there's Michael – I've been awfully angry about Michael—

VICKY: That's idiotic – Michael doesn't mean a thing to me – you know perfectly well he doesn't—

The music begins again, this time more loudly.

SIMON: There it is again – do hurry. (*He dances a few steps.*)

VICKY (*calling*): Lena – Lena – hurry up – I was miserable anyhow to-night – all the time we were in the theatre – everybody was having such a good time – and then they were married in the end – that was funny, wasn't it? – about them being married in the end. . . .

SIMON: —It isn't that I want to make you unhappy, but you

must admit we haven't been hitting it off particularly well
during the last year – if we're not comfortable together surely
it would be much more sensible to separate—

*The scene darkens. The side flats move off and upstage away from
the centre flat.*

VICKY: I feel so sad inside about it – I wish I could make you
understand – it was so lovely in the beginning—

SIMON: Things never stay the same – you can't expect what was
lovely then to be lovely now—

VICKY (*almost crying*): Why not – why not? – Then we were
happy—

SIMON: But, darling, you must see—

'THEN'

SIMON: Here in the light of this unkind familiar now
    Every gesture is clear and cold for us,
    Even yesterday's growing old for us,
        Everything changed somehow.
        If some forgotten lover's vow
    Could wake a memory in my heart again,
    Perhaps the joys that we knew would start again.
        Can't we reclaim an hour or so
        The past is not so long ago.
VICKY: Then, love was complete for us
    Then, the days were sweet for us
    Life rose to its feet for us
        And stepped aside
        Before our pride.
        Then, we knew the best of it
        Then, our hearts stood the test of it.
        Now, the magic has flown
        We face the unknown
        Apart and alone.

SIMON: Hodge – where's Hodge? – I must change – quick –
we're going back.

The orchestra swells. FLORRIE (LENA) *comes hurrying in with an evening gown over her arm and a pair of shoes, a mirror, a powder-puff, etc., in her hands.* VICKY *sinks on to the bed.*

SIMON: You can't sit there – we're going back—

FLORRIE: Here, dear – here's a chair.

VICKY: I'm not sure that I want to – I'm not at all sure – maybe it won't be as lovely as I think it was—

SIMON: Don't be such a fool – grab it while you can – grab every scrap of happiness while you can – Hodge – come on—

HODGE, *a dresser, comes in with a dinner-jacket.* SIMON *takes off his dressing-gown and puts on the dinner-jacket.* VICKY *is changing on the opposite side of the stage. Meanwhile the whole scene is changing. The lights in the foreground fade except for the two spotlights on* SIMON *and* VICKY.

VICKY (*breathlessly*): Play – go on playing – we must have music—

SIMON *comes down to the footlights and begins to sing to the conductor. He sings*

'PLAY, ORCHESTRA, PLAY'

SIMON: Listen to the strain it plays once more for us,
　　　There it is again, the past in store for us.
　　　　Wake in memory some forgotten song
　　　　To break the rhythm – driving us along
　　　And make harmony again a last encore for us.

　　　　Play, orchestra, play
　　　　Play something light and sweet and gay
　　　　　For we must have music
　　　　　We must have music
　　　　To drive our fears away.
　　　While our illusions swiftly fade for us,
　　　　Let's have an orchestra score.
　　　In the confusions the years have made for us
　　　　Serenade for us, just once more.
　　　Life needn't be grey,
　　　Although it's changing day by day,

Though a few old dreams may decay,
Play, orchestra, play.

VICKY joins him and they finish it together. Meanwhile all the lights fade entirely except for two pin-spots on the two of them. The spot on SIMON *goes out and* VICKY *is left singing almost hysterically 'We Must Have Music'. The orchestra rises to a crescendo and there is a complete black-out.*

To measured music and in a pool of light, SIBYL HESTON *appears. She lights a cigarette and glances at her wrist-watch.* SIMON *appears from the opposite side of the stage. He stands a little apart from her. The music stops.*

SIBYL: I'm waiting – I'm waiting – why don't you tell her?

SIMON: It will hurt her, you know.

SIBYL: She can weep on Michael's shoulder – it's a very attractive shoulder.

SIMON: I don't want to hurt her.

SIBYL: She'll have to know sooner or later. Nobody can live without loving somebody, nobody can love without leaving somebody.

SIMON: I saw you in the theatre to-night – you looked marvellous.

SIBYL: Sweet Simon.

SIMON: Very cool and green and wise.

SIBYL: Not wise – oh, my dear, not wise at all. I happen to love you.

SIMON: Is that so unwise?

SIBYL: Let's say – indefinite!

SIMON: It's less cruel to be indefinite in the long run.

SIBYL: Tell her the truth – you must tell her the truth.

SIMON: I have been awfully angry about Michael.

SIBYL: Why be angry, darling? It's such waste of energy.

SIMON: I don't like Vicky making a fool of herself.

SIBYL: I don't like Vicky making a fool of you.

SIMON: I didn't know she took things to make her sleep.

SIBYL: You must tell her the truth – sleep or no sleep.

The music starts again. MICHAEL *walks on. He passes* SIBYL *and*

SIMON, *stops, lights a cigarette and glances at his wrist-watch. The music stops.*

MICHAEL: I'm waiting – I'm waiting – why don't you tell her?

SIMON: I don't want to hurt her.

MICHAEL: Give her my love.

SIMON: That was a bit cheap, wasn't it?

SIBYL (*laughing*): When did she first begin to get on your nerves, Simon? What started it? Was it a dress she wore? Was it the way she laughed at somebody's joke? Was she suddenly gay when you were sad? Was she insensitive? Was she dull?

MICHAEL: Was she dull?

SIBYL: Was she dull?

SIMON: It was so lovely in the beginning.

SIBYL: Things never stay the same – you can't expect what was lovely then to be lovely now.

SIMON: We're going back all the same – it's our only chance—

SIBYL: Was she dull?

MICHAEL: Was she dull?

SIMON: Shut up – shut up both of you – we're going back—

He begins to sing and as he sings the lights fade on SIBYL *and* MICHAEL.

Life needn't be grey
Though it is changing day by day.
Though a few old dreams may decay
Play Orchestra – Play Orchestra – Play – Orchestra—
Play—

Blackout.

The lights come up on a moonlit garden. There is a stone seat on the left of the stage. VICKY *and a* YOUNG MAN *are sitting on it.*

VICKY: It's nice and cool in the garden.

YOUNG MAN: It's nice and cool in the garden.

VICKY: Country house dances can be lovely when the weather's good, can't they?

YOUNG MAN: Rather – rather – yes, of course – rather.

VICKY: I'm waiting for something.

YOUNG MAN: Country house dances can be lovely when the weather's good, can't they?

VICKY: This is where it all began.

YOUNG MAN: It's nice and cool in the garden.

VICKY: Please hurry, my darling, I can't wait to see you for the first time.

YOUNG MAN: Do you know this part of the country?

VICKY: Intimately. I'm staying here with my aunt, you know.

YOUNG MAN: Does she ride to hounds?

VICKY: Incessantly.

YOUNG MAN: That's ripping, isn't it? – I mean it really is ripping.

VICKY: Yes. She's a big woman and she kills little foxes – she's kind *au fond*, but she dearly loves killing little foxes.

YOUNG MAN: We're getting on awfully well – it's awfully nice out here – I think you're awfully pretty.

VICKY: This is waste of time – he should be here by now – walking through the trees – coming towards me.

YOUNG MAN: I think you're an absolute fizzer.

VICKY: Yes, I remember you saying that – it made me want to giggle – but I controlled myself beautifully.

YOUNG MAN: I think you know my sister – she's in pink.

VICKY: I remember her clearly – a beastly girl.

YOUNG MAN: In pink.

VICKY (*suddenly*): 'In pink – in pink—
　　　　　　　　Your sister's dressed in pink
　　　　　　　　It wasn't very wise I think
　　　　　　　　To choose that unbecoming shade
　　　　　　　　Of pink—'

YOUNG MAN: I'm so glad you like her – you must come and stay with us – my mother's an absolute fizzer – you'd love her.

VICKY: God forbid!

YOUNG MAN: That's absolutely ripping of you.

VICKY: Now – now – at last – you're walking through the trees—hurry—

　　　SIMON *comes through the trees. He is smoking a cigarette.*

VICKY: I thought you'd missed your entrance.

SIMON: Are you engaged for this dance?

140

VICKY: I was, but I'll cut it if you'll promise to love me always and never let anything or anybody spoil it – never—

SIMON: But of course – that's understood.

YOUNG MAN: Will you excuse me – I have to dance with Lady Dukes.

VICKY: Certainly.

YOUNG MAN: Good hunting.

VICKY: Thank you so much – it's been so boring.

YOUNG MAN: Not at all – later perhaps.

He goes.

SIMON: Well – here we are.

VICKY: The first time – we knew at once, didn't we? Don't you remember how we discussed it afterwards?

SIMON: I saw you in the ballroom – I wondered who you were.

VICKY: My name's Victoria – Victoria Marden.

SIMON: Mine's Simon Gayforth.

VICKY: How do you do?

SIMON: Quite well, thank you.

VICKY: I suppose you came down from London for the dance?

SIMON: Yes, I'm staying with the Bursbys—

VICKY: What do you do?

SIMON: I'm in a bank.

VICKY: High up in the bank? Or just sitting in a cage totting up things?

SIMON: Oh, quite high up really – it's a very good bank.

VICKY: I'm so glad.

SIMON: How lovely you are.

VICKY: No, no, that came later – you've skipped some.

SIMON: Sorry.

VICKY: You're nice and thin – your eyes are funny – you move easily – I'm afraid you're terribly attractive—

SIMON: You never said that.

VICKY: No, but I thought it.

SIMON: Stick to the script.

VICKY: Small talk – a lot of small talk with quite different thoughts going on behind it – this garden's really beautiful – are you good at gardens?—

SIMON: No, but I'm persevering – I'm all right on the more

straightforward blooms – you know – Snapdragons, sweet william, cornflowers and tobacco plant – and I can tell a Dorothy Perkins a mile off.

VICKY: That hedge over there is called Cupressus Macrocapa.

SIMON: Do you swear it?

VICKY: It grows terrifically quickly but they do say that it goes a bit thin underneath in about twenty years—

SIMON: How beastly of them to say that – it's slander.

VICKY: Did you know about Valerian smelling of cats?

SIMON: You're showing off again.

VICKY: It's true.

SIMON: I can go one better than that – Lotuses smell of pineapple.

VICKY (*sadly*): Everything smells of something else – it's dreadfully confusing—

SIMON: Never mind, darling – I love you desperately – I knew it the first second I saw you—

VICKY: You're skipping again.

They sing a light duet: 'You Were There', after which they dance.

'YOU WERE THERE'

I

SIMON: Was it in the real world or was it in a dream?
Was it just a note from some eternal theme?
Was it accidental or accurately planned?
   How could I hesitate
   Knowing that my fate
Led me by the hand?

REFRAIN

  You were there
I saw you and my heart stopped beating
  You were there
And in that first enchanted meeting

Life changed its tune, the stars, the moon came
    near to me.
Dreams that I dreamed, like magic seemed to be
    clear to me, dear to me.
    You were there.
Your eyes looked into mine and faltered.
    Everywhere
The colour of the whole world altered.
    False became true
    My universe tumbled in two
The earth became heaven, for you were there.

2

VICKY: How can we explain it – the spark, and then the fire?
How add up the total of our hearts' desire?
Maybe some magician, a thousand years ago—
Wove us a subtle spell – so that we could tell – so that
    we could know—
    You were there—(etc.)

*During the dance the lights fade on the scene and they finish in each
other's arms in a spotlight. The spotlight fades and in the darkness a
voice is heard singing 'Then they knew the best of it – then their
hearts stood the test of it', etc.*

A spotlight picks up LENA *– singing, holding the tablets and a
glass of water. After song fade again.*

Then love was complete for them
Then the days were sweet for them
Life rose to its feet for them
And stepped aside
Before their pride.
Then they knew the best of it
Then their hearts stood the test of it.
Now the magic has flown
They face the unknown
Apart and alone.

The lights go up again on the interior of a limousine. MARTHA *and* GEORGE CUNNINGHAM *are sitting in it.*

GEORGE: On the whole this has been one of the most uncomfortable evenings I've ever spent.

MARTHA: There, there, dear, I know, but for heaven's sake don't go on about it.

GEORGE (*petulantly*): Why, if they had to take us to dinner and a play, should they have chosen that particular dinner and that particular play?

MARTHA: What was wrong with the dinner?

GEORGE: Gastronomically speaking it was excellent, but the atmosphere reeked with conjugal infelicity – when people are at loggerheads they should refrain from entertaining – it's bad for the digestive tract.

MARTHA: For an elderly barrister you're unduly sensitive.

GEORGE: I expected the grouse to sit up on its plate and offer me a brief.

MARTHA: Never mind, when we get to Alice's you'll be able to have a nice drink and talk to some lovely young things and feel much better.

GEORGE: And why that play? Sentimental twaddle.

MARTHA: The music was lovely.

GEORGE: That's no good to me. You know perfectly well I can't distinguish 'Abide with me' from 'God Save the King'.

MARTHA: Concentrate on 'God Save the King'.

GEORGE: I couldn't even go to sleep with those idiotic people loving each other for ever all over the stage.

MARTHA: Well we'll go to a nice soothing gangster picture to-morrow night and you can watch people killing each other all over the screen.

GEORGE: What's wrong with them, anyway?

MARTHA: Who, Simon and Vicky?

GEORGE: Yes.

MARTHA: They're unhappy.

GEORGE: Well, they oughtn't to be – they've got everything they want.

MARTHA: Sibyl Heston's got hold of Simon and Vicky's trying to pretend that she doesn't mind a bit and everything's in a dreary muddle – women like Sibyl Heston ought to be shot.

GEORGE: Sometimes they are.

MARTHA: Not often enough.

GEORGE: I suppose Vicky's got a young man hanging around, hasn't she?

MARTHA: No, not really – she's been encouraging Michael Doyle a bit but it doesn't mean anything – it's just part of the pretending.

GEORGE: Damn fools – they're all damn fools—

VICKY *runs on from the side of the stage. She is picked up by a blue spotlight.*

VICKY: Go away, you're spoiling it all – I know what you're saying – I know what everybody's saying—

MARTHA: I was only trying to help.

VICKY: I know – I know – you're very kind – but it isn't any use—

GEORGE: People were so much more sensible twenty years ago – take my sister, for instance – look how brilliantly she managed her life – you ought to have known my sister—

VICKY: In pink.

GEORGE: In brilliant pink.

VICKY (*singing*): 'In pink – in pink
                    Your sister's dressed in pink,
                    It wasn't very wise I think
                    To choose that unbecoming shade
                    Of pink—!'

SIMON *enters and is picked up in a blue spot.*

SIMON: This compartment is reserved – we're going back.

GEORGE: I'm most awfully sorry.

VICKY: There are probably some empty ones farther along the train.

MARTHA: But of course – we quite understand – George, help me with my dressing-case—

SIMON: Allow me—

He helps them to remove imaginary luggage from the rack.

GEORGE: I suppose you don't happen to know what time we reach Milan?

SIMON: I know we arrive in Venice at about six-thirty – I think there's about four hours' difference.

VICKY: It's really charming of you to be so considerate – you see we are on our honeymoon.

MARTHA: Grab every scrap of happiness while you can.

GEORGE: We shall meet later.

SIMON: I hope so.

> MARTHA *and* GEORGE *step out of the car and walk off.*
> SIMON *and* VICKY *climb in. The spotlights follow them into the cab.*

SIMON: Well, here we are.

VICKY: My name's Victoria.

SIMON: Victoria what?

VICKY: Victoria Gayforth.

SIMON: What a silly name.

VICKY: I adore it.

SIMON: That's because you're sentimental.

VICKY: Fiercely sentimental – over-romantic too.

SIMON: Dearest darling.

VICKY: The wedding went off beautifully, didn't it?

SIMON: Brief, to the point, and not unduly musical.

VICKY: Didn't Mother look nice?

SIMON: Not particularly.

VICKY: Oh, Simon!

SIMON: It was her hat, I think – it looked as though it were in a hurry and couldn't stay very long.

VICKY: Was that man who slapped you on the back your uncle?

SIMON: Yes, dear – that was my uncle.

VICKY: I'm so sorry.

SIMON: He ran away to sea, you know, when he was very young, and then, unfortunately, he ran back again.

VICKY: Your sister looked charming.

SIMON: In pink.

VICKY: In pink – in pink—

SIMON: Stop it – stop it – you'll wake yourself up.

146

VICKY: It was that rhyme in the play to-night – it keeps coming into my mind.

SIMON: Do concentrate – we're on our honeymoon.

VICKY: Happy ever after.

SIMON: That's right.

VICKY: Do you think that those people we turned out of the carriage ever loved each other as much as we do?

SIMON: Nobody ever loved each other as much as we do with the possible exception of Romeo and Juliet, Héloïse and Abélard, Paolo and Francesca, Dante and Beatrice—

VICKY: I wish she hadn't been called Beatrice – it's such a smug name.

SIMON: Antony and Cleopatra, Pelléas and Mélisande—

VICKY: I've always felt that Mélisande was rather a silly girl – so vague.

SIMON: All right – wash out Mélisande.

VICKY (*looking out of the window*): Look at all those little houses flashing by – think of all the millions of people living in them – eating and drinking – dressing and undressing – getting up and going to bed – having babies—

SIMON: When I was a young bride I never mentioned such things on my honeymoon.

VICKY: Things never stay the same.

SIMON: It was considered immodest to do anything but weep gently and ask for glasses of water.

VICKY: I'm abandoned, darling – I can't wait to be in your arms—

SIMON: Dear heart—

He takes her in his arms.

VICKY (*struggling*): No no – this isn't right – my clothes are all wrong – I must go—

SIMON: Don't go.

VICKY: I must – this dressing-gown's all wrong I tell you – when we arrived in Venice I was wearing a blue tailor-made – and then later we dined – and I was in grey—

SIMON: In grey – in grey
       Your dress was soft and grey
       It seems a million years away

The ending of that sweet and happy day.

VICKY: Oh darling—

SIMON: Don't go—

VICKY: I must – I must—

> *She steps out of the carriage and disappears into the darkness.*
>
> SIMON *left alone, sings a reprise of 'You Were There', and the lights fade completely.*
>
> *When the lights go up* SIMON *and* VICKY *are sitting at a little table with a shaded light on it. They are just finishing dinner.*

SIMON: We can sit on the piazza for a little and then we can drift . . .

VICKY: Let's call the gondola right away and cut out the piazza – I'm a big drifting girl.

SIMON: I think the band on the piazza will be awfully disappointed.

VICKY: It's funny, isn't it, to be so frightfully in love that you feel as if you were going mad?

SIMON: Ever so funny.

VICKY: Do you think our front gondolier is nicer than our back one?

SIMON: Not altogether – he has better teeth, of course, but then he's about fifty years younger.

VICKY: Let's come here again in fifty years' time.

SIMON: All right.

VICKY: We can arrange to be carried on to the train – it will be quite simple.

SIMON: It won't be a train, darling – it will be a pointed silver bullet leaving Croydon at four and arriving here at twenty-past three.

VICKY: Oh dear!

SIMON: What's the matter?

VICKY: We haven't quarrelled yet.

SIMON: Never mind.

VICKY: We'll have a nice quarrel when we get back to London, won't we?

SIMON: I shall sulk for the first few days, anyhow – I'm the sulky type, you know.

VICKY: That's why I married you.

SIMON: Oh, darling – I'm going to be terribly serious for a minute – will you bear with me?

VICKY: Of course.

SIMON: There's something I want to say to you – I've been wanting to say it for quite a while—

VICKY (*with panic in her voice*): Oh, Simon, don't – what is it? What is it?

SIMON: I love you.

VICKY (*putting her head down on the table*): You mustn't make people cry on their honeymoons – it's not cricket.

SIMON (*tenderly*): Dearest – everything's cricket if only you have faith.

VICKY: When did you know you loved me – the very first minute, I mean?

SIMON: In the garden – during the dance – I saw you and my heart stopped beating—

VICKY: It was a most enchanted meeting.

SIMON: Life changed its tune – the stars and moon came near to me—

VICKY: Dreams that I'd dreamed, like magic seemed to be clear to me – dear to me—

SIMON: False became true – my universe tumbled in two – the earth became heaven – for you were there—

VICKY: Stop it – stop it – it's that damned musical comedy again – going round and round in my head – listen – before the dream breaks say what you said that night in Venice – say it from your heart as you said it then – say it, please – please—

SIMON: I'm not sure that I can remember – it's a long while ago—

VICKY: Please, Simon – please—

SIMON: It's this, darling – we're here together close as close and it's the beginning – but we're going to be together for a long time – probably all our lives, so we must be careful – I want to reassure you now about later on – about any tricks the future might play on us – I know I love you with all my heart – with every bit of me – it's easy now, because it's summer weather and there isn't a cloud in the sky and we're alone – but there'll be other people presently – we can't live our whole lives on this little island – other people are dangerous – they spoil true love, not consciously because they want to, but because they're themselves – out for all they can get – mischievous – you do see what I mean, don't you—?

VICKY: You mean they might make us want them one day instead of each other.

SIMON: Yes, but only a little – not like this – not all the way round—

VICKY: I can't imagine even that – I'm very single-tracked.

SIMON: Don't look sad – don't even have a flicker of unhappiness not for ages yet, anyway – but whenever you do – if I'm bad or foolish or unkind, or even unfaithful – just remember this, because this is what really matters – this lovely understanding of each other – it may be a jumping-off place for many future journeys – but however long the journey one's got to come back some time, and this is the white cliffs of Dover – hang on to the white cliffs of Dover—

VICKY: I'll try—

They hold hands for a moment across the table.

There is a burst of music which dies away on a discord. Then a dance tune starts and keeps up a steady rhythm during the ensuing scene. The light on SIMON and VICKY fades a little. They are sitting quite still gazing at each other. SIBYL HESTON and MICHAEL DOYLE dance on together out of the shadows. They are in a brilliant spotlight.

MICHAEL: We're a bit early, aren't we? They're still on their honeymoon.

SIBYL: Nonsense. The curtain will be lowered between scenes two and three to denote a lapse of four years—

The light on SIMON and VICKY goes out completely.

MICHAEL (*over his shoulder*): I'm so sorry.

SIBYL: It's impossible to dance here.

MICHAEL: They put so many tables on the floor.

SIBYL: There's no room at all.

MICHAEL: Let's go on to the Florida.

SIBYL: And the Coconut Grove.

MICHAEL: And the Four Hundred.

SIBYL: And the Blue Train.

SIMON *and* VICKY *dance on in another spotlight.*

SIMON: There's always the Florida.

VICKY: And the Coconut Grove.

SIMON: And the Four Hundred.

VICKY: And the Blue Train.

> *The rhythm gets slightly faster. The two couples circle round each other.*

SIBYL: The Florida.

SIMON: The Coconut Grove.

MICHAEL: The Four Hundred.

VICKY: The Blue Train.

SIBYL: The Florida.

VICKY: The Coconut Grove.

MICHAEL: The Four Hundred.

SIMON: The Blue Train.

> *The music gets faster still. They change partners.* SIMON *dances with* SIBYL *and* MICHAEL *with* VICKY – *then they change back to each other again* – *then once more* – *all saying together:* 'The Florida', 'The Coconut Grove', 'The Four Hundred', 'The Blue Train'. MICHAEL *and* VICKY *disappear and* SIBYL *and* SIMON *are left dancing round and round together, faster and faster. From the darkness can be heard voices shouting rhythmically:* 'The Florida', 'The Coconut Grove', 'The Four Hundred', 'The Blue Train', *coming to a crescendo and then a black-out.*
>
> LENA *appears on the right-hand side of the stage with a telephone.* MARTHA *appears on the opposite side, also with a telephone. Both in spotlights.*

MARTHA: Hallo – who is it?

LENA: It's Lena, madame.

MARTHA: Oh, Lena – yes – what is it?

LENA: Mr. Gayforth asked me to telephone to you, madame—

MARTHA: Is anything wrong?

LENA: It's Mrs. Gayforth, madame – those sleeping tablets – Mr. Gayforth wants to know if you can leave the party and come at once—

MARTHA: Good heavens! Is she ill?

LENA: Yes, madame – that is – she's not exactly ill but—

MARTHA: Have you sent for a doctor?

LENA: No, madame – Mr. Gayforth didn't want to send for a doctor until he'd seen you.

MARTHA: I'll come at once.

LENA: It was that extra Anytal tablet, madame – I knew she shouldn't have taken it—

MARTHA: I'll be there in a few minutes – in the meantime – give her some strong black coffee—

The lights fade.
In the darkness VICKY's *voice is heard.*

VICKY: Simon, Simon – where are you? – I'm lonely – I'm frightened – don't go away from me yet – in spite of what they say there is still time if only we're careful—

SIMON: There's something I want to say to you – I've been wanting to say it for quite a while—

VICKY: Don't say it – don't say it yet.

SIMON: I would like if possible to keep this conversation impersonal.

VICKY: I would so love to be clear at this moment. But nothing's clear at all—

SIMON: I didn't know you had taken anything—

VICKY: It was only to make me sleep – whenever I'm tired or unhappy, oh, Simon – Simon – come back – the White Cliffs of Dover – I'm trying so hard – I'm trying to hold on – don't leave me – don't leave me—

SIMON: Give her a little more, Lena.

LENA: Yes, sir.

SIMON: You don't think we ought to send for a doctor?

MARTHA: No, she'll be all right.

SIMON: It was awfully sweet of you to come back, Martha – I got in a panic – you were the only one I could think of—

VICKY: I shall be sick if I have any more of that damned coffee.

SIMON: That's a very good idea – be sick.

VICKY: No, no – I hate being sick – it's mortifying – I'm perfectly all right now – really I am.

The lights slowly go up on the bedroom.
    VICKY *is sitting on the edge of the bed.* SIMON *is sitting by her side with one arm round her, holding a cup of coffee in his other*

hand. MARTHA *is kneeling on the floor at her feet.* LENA *is standing anxiously at the foot of the bed holding a coffee pot.*

SIMON: There, darling – won't you lie down a bit?

VICKY: Don't fuss.

SIMON: You ought to be ashamed of yourself.

VICKY: What are you rolling about on the floor for, Martha? It looks very silly.

MARTHA (*rising*): You may well ask.

VICKY: I think I should like a cigarette.

SIMON: Then you will be sick.

VICKY: No, it's passed off.

LENA (*handing her a cigarette*): Here, madame.

VICKY: Thank you, Lena. Match, please.

SIMON: Here, Martha, take this cup, will you?

He gives MARTHA *the coffee and lights* VICKY's *cigarette.*

VICKY: That's lovely. (*She puffs.*)

SIMON: It's all right, Lena – you can go to bed again.

LENA: Are you sure, sir?

SIMON: Yes, thank you, Lena.

LENA: Good-night, sir.

SIMON: Good-night.

    LENA *goes out.*

VICKY: Now perhaps somebody will explain. What happened to me?

SIMON: You just went mad, that's all – raving.

VICKY (*interested*): Did I froth at the mouth?

SIMON: I don't know – I was too agitated to notice.

MARTHA: I think I'd better go back to Alice's.

VICKY: Alice's! Oh yes, of course. Oh, Simon – I remember now.

SIMON: Don't think of anything – just relax.

MARTHA (*kissing her*): Good-night, darling.

VICKY (*absently – her thoughts a long way away*): Good-night.

MARTHA: Good-night, Simon.

SIMON: Thanks awfully, Martha.

    MARTHA *goes out.*

VICKY: I'm so sorry, Simon – I'm feeling quite tranquil now – let's talk about the divorce in the morning.

SIMON: Divorce? What do you mean?

VICKY: You asked me to divorce you, didn't you?

SIMON: Certainly not.

VICKY: Are you trying to make me believe that that was part of the dream?

SIMON: I don't know what you're talking about.

VICKY: It's sweet of you to lie – but it won't wash.

SIMON sits on the bed again and puts his arms round her.

SIMON: Please forgive me.

VICKY (*sleepily*): We'll talk it all over calmly – to-morrow.

SIMON: All right.

VICKY (*resting her head on his shoulder*): If you really love her all that much I'll try not to be beastly about it—

SIMON: I don't love anybody that much.

VICKY: What did I do when I went mad? I'm so interested.

SIMON: You talked a lot – I thought it was nonsense at first and then I realised that it was true – then you began dancing about the room – then you really did go mad – and I got very frightened and told Lena to ring up Martha—

VICKY: It was certainly a very strange feeling—

She closes her eyes and the music starts again very softly.

SIMON: It will be all right now – it really will – I promise.

VICKY: The music's beginning again.

The music swells. SIMON lifts her gently on to the bed and covers her over with the counterpane. Then he kisses her, disentangles her cigarette from her fingers, tiptoes across the room and switches off the lights, all but a little lamp by the bed, and stretches himself on the sofa at her feet.

The music reaches a crescendo as—

THE CURTAIN FALLS

WAYS AND MEANS

A Light Comedy in Three Scenes

Ways and Means was produced in London at the Phoenix Theatre on 5 May 1936, with the following cast:

STELLA CARTWRIGHT	Miss Gertrude Lawrence
TOBY CARTWRIGHT	Mr Noël Coward
OLIVE LLOYD-RANSOME	Miss Joyce Carey
LORD CHAPWORTH (Chaps)	Mr Alan Webb
NANNY	Miss Everley Gregg
MURDOCH	Mr Anthony Pelissier
STEVENS	Mr Edward Underdown
PRINCESS ELÈNA KRASSILOFF	Miss Moya Nugent
GASTON	Mr Kenneth Carten

————

The action of the play takes place in a bedroom in the LLOYD-RANSOMES' *house, Villa Zephyre, on the Côte d'Azur.*

TIME: The present.

Scene I.   *11.30 a.m. on an April morning.*
Scene II.   *1.30 a.m. the following morning.*
Scene III. *Two hours later.*

Scene I

The scene is a bedroom in the Villa Zephyre on the Côte d'Azur. The Villa Zephyre belongs to MRS LLOYD-RANSOME, *who is excessively rich, comparatively pleasant and entirely idle, the bedroom therefore is luxurious and tastefully appointed. On the right there is a dressing-table with, above it, a door leading to the bathroom. On the left there is a french window leading on to a small verandah, above that, in the back wall, is a door leading to the passage and the rest of the house. There is a slight recess in the back wall containing a very wide and comfortable bed.*

This is occupied at the rise of the curtain by STELLA *and* TOBY CARTWRIGHT. *They are an attractive couple in the thirties. Between them there is a breakfast tray.* STELLA *is opening and reading letters.* TOBY *is scanning the* Continental Daily Mail. *A certain amount of pale sunshine is coming through the window, but this fails to banish from either of their faces an expression of gloomy dissatisfaction. After a considerable silence,* STELLA *speaks.*

STELLA: Here's a letter from Aunt Hester.

TOBY: Is she well and hearty?

STELLA: Apparently.

TOBY: To hell with her!

> *There is a further silence.*

STELLA (*pensively eating a brioche*): Why do other people's breakfasts always taste much nicer than one's own?

TOBY: Probably because they are.

> *There is another silence.*

STELLA: I knew marrying you was a mistake at least seven years ago, but I never realised the thoroughness of the mistake until now—

TOBY (*reading his paper*): You will be interested to hear that Mrs S.

J. Pendleton gave a small dinner party for Mr and Mrs Hubert Weir at the Hotel Normandie in Le Touquet last night—

STELLA: How thrilling.

TOBY: Among the guests were Lord and Lady Haven, Mrs George Durlap, the Countess Pantulucci, Mr Henry Bird, Mr and Mrs Harvey Lincoln, Miss Styles—

STELLA: Shut up!

TOBY: I beg your pardon?

STELLA: I said shut up.

TOBY (*continuing*): Mr and Mrs Sidney Alford have returned from Vichy and are staying at the Crillon—

STELLA: Toby—

TOBY: They are to be joined in a few days by Mrs Alford's sister, Lady Croker—

STELLA: Toby, please—

TOBY: Prince and Princess Jean Marie de Larichon have left the Hotel George Cinq en route for the Riviera—

     STELLA *snatches the paper from him.*

STELLA (*angrily*): Mr and Mrs Toby Cartwright have left the Villa Zephyre under a cloud—

TOBY (*complacently taking some coffee*): Not yet they haven't—

STELLA: Owing to the idiocy of Mr Toby Cartwright losing his shirt at the Casino—

TOBY: Oh, God, must we go back over that again!

STELLA: Yes, we must – don't you see – we've got to do something—

TOBY: Darling, what's the use—?

STELLA: Give me the pad and pencil – they're just by you—

TOBY (*taking a pencil and pad from the bedside table*): So what?

STELLA: Give it to me.

TOBY (*giving it to her*): Toby lost fifty pounds – Toby lost fifty pounds – Toby lost fifty pounds – write it down quickly, it would be awful if you happened to forget it—

STELLA (*near tears*): Oh, Toby!

TOBY (*relenting*): All right, darling – I am sorry – really I am.

     He leans towards her, nearly upsetting the breakfast-tray.

STELLA: Look out!

TOBY: Damn—

STELLA: It isn't that I want to rub in about the fifty pounds –
   really it isn't – but we are in the most awful jam, and we've
   got to concentrate.

TOBY: We concentrated up until four-thirty this morning and
   nothing came of it—

STELLA: Will you promise not to take offence at anything I say
   for ten minutes?

TOBY: That means you're going to be absolutely bloody.

STELLA: Promise.

TOBY: All right – I promise.

STELLA: We must face facts. Now then. Our combined incomes
   amount to seven hundred and fifty pounds a year—

TOBY: Until Aunt Hester dies.

STELLA: Aunt Hester will not die – she's outwitted life for
   seventy years and is now determined to outwit death.

TOBY: It's indecent.

STELLA: Never mind about that now – our combined overdrafts
   amount to roughly thirteen hundred pounds – in addition to
   which, you owe about three thousand—

TOBY: What about you?

STELLA (*writing*): Two thousand.

TOBY: I can't understand why you don't get a job of some sort –
   look at Liza Herrick – she at least made some effort – she
   opened a hat shop.

STELLA: And shut it again.

TOBY: No talent – that's what's wrong with you – no marketable
   talent whatsoever.

STELLA: You seem to forget that on a certain bleak day in 1928 I
   gave my life into your keeping.

TOBY: Marriage is a sacrament, a mystic rite, and you persist in
   regarding it as a sort of plumber's estimate.

STELLA: Be quiet. Where was I?

TOBY: Wandering along the paths of memory, dear, with a
   singularly nasty expression.

STELLA: You will admit, I suppose, that we live beyond our
   income?

TOBY: You have a genius for understatement.

STELLA: Having managed to rake up seventy-two pounds in

order to stay – God knows why – in this over-elaborate house—

TOBY: I don't agree. I think Olive, considering her innate vulgarity, has done this house with remarkable restraint.

STELLA: Olive is not vulgar – she's one of my oldest friends. She was at school with me, and—

TOBY: Well, let's just say that she was at school with you.

STELLA: Now look here, Toby—

TOBY: Go on – concentrate.

STELLA: You're maddening.

TOBY: Go on, write – write down the truth – face facts – put down our congenital idiocy in black and white – write down that we were brought up merely to be amiable and pleasant and socially attractive – that we have no ambition and no talent – except for playing games.

STELLA (*sharply*): And not enough of that.

TOBY: Toby lost fifty pounds – Toby lost fifty pounds—

STELLA: I wrote that down first – but what I didn't write down was that you were a silly, selfish, careless, bloody fool to do it—

TOBY (*furiously*): Look here, Stella—

He makes a violent movement.

STELLA: Look out!

TOBY: Damn!

STELLA: It's no use quarrelling. The fifty pounds has gone – we've already stayed over our time here – the Lorings are expecting us in Venice – we have, at the moment, one hundred and fourteen francs – and we are down two thousand four hundred francs in the Bridge Book.

TOBY: That's entirely your fault – you play Bridge too merrily, Stella.

STELLA: My merriment is entirely a social gesture. I loathe Bridge.

TOBY: That is no excuse for playing it as though it were lacrosse.

STELLA: I don't know what you mean.

TOBY: Your bids have a certain girlish devil-may-care abandon – you whoop through every rubber like a games mistress.

STELLA: What do you mean, whoop?

TOBY: What I say – whoop – W-H-O-O-P.

STELLA: Oh, do be quiet! What was I saying?

TOBY: You were saying that we were down two thousand four hundred francs in the Bridge Book. What you should have said was, that owing to your—

STELLA: Never mind about that now – within the next week we shall be asked definitely to leave – Olive was dropping hints all over the dinner-table last night.

TOBY: We can't leave.

STELLA: We'll have to.

TOBY: Chaps owes you some money, doesn't he?

STELLA: Yes. Backgammon – seven thousand francs.

TOBY: Thank God for that!

STELLA: If we travel to Venice second-class and send Nanny home—

TOBY: I can't think why you had to bring her in the first place; I don't have to have a valet, why should you have a maid?

STELLA: Nanny's not a maid – Nanny's saved our lives a million times.

TOBY: Wrongly.

STELLA: Anyhow—

> *There is a knock on the door and* GASTON *enters. He is a neatly dressed French valet.*

GASTON: Bon jour, monsieur.

TOBY: Bon jour, Gaston.

GASTON: Bon jour, madame.

STELLA: Bon jour.

GASTON: Lord Chapworth wish to speak to you.

TOBY: Is he there?

STELLA: Tell him to come in. (*She calls.*) Come in, Chaps!

> GASTON *stands aside to let* LORD CHAPWORTH *enter.* LORD CHAPWORTH *is an amiable-looking young man.*
>> GASTON *goes out.*

CHAPS: Good morning – how d'you feel?

TOBY: Frightful.

CHAPS: So do I.

TOBY: Good!

STELLA: You look very sweet, Chaps, darling, and very dapper – why are you up so early?

CHAPS: It's after eleven. I came to say goodbye—

STELLA: Of course, you're leaving today – I'd forgotten. Are you going to May Bainbridge?

CHAPS: Yes – Guy's picking me up.

STELLA: You must find out all about the chauffeur scandal and wire us immediately.

CHAPS: What chauffeur scandal?

STELLA: Don't be silly, darling, the whole coast is buzzing with it.

CHAPS: Oh, that! – I always thought it was a valet.

TOBY: Chauffeur-valet – a combined occupation rife, apparently, with the most delirious opportunities—

CHAPS: Do you think it's true? – I mean, do you think May really did—?

STELLA: Certainly – you only have to look at her.

TOBY: Don't be catty, Stella.

STELLA: As May Bainbridge has been consistently odious to me for years I really don't see why I shouldn't be as catty as I like.

TOBY: After all, Chaps is going to stay with them.

STELLA: Serve him right.

CHAPS: Oh, old May's not bad – she just has an unfortunate manner.

STELLA: To be not bad with an unfortunate manner is not enough—

CHAPS: You seem a bit scratchy this morning.

TOBY: Compared with what took place in the night, this is purring.

CHAPS: Well, it's a nice sunny day, anyhow.

STELLA: It had better be.

CHAPS: I had an awful evening – I got stuck with Pearl Brandt – she insisted on playing at the big table and I lost a packet.

TOBY: You what?

CHAPS: Just dropped about four hundred pounds – cleaned myself out.

STELLA: Oh, Chaps!

CHAPS: She kept on asking me to go in with her, she never ran a hand more than two coups except once, then she passed it after the fourth and it ran eleven times.

TOBY: Did it occur to you to strike her in the face?

CHAPS: So I wondered if you'd mind waiting for that seven thousand francs I owe you, Stella, until I get my allowance?

TOBY: When do you get your allowance?

CHAPS: First of May.

STELLA (*hurriedly*): Of course I don't, Chaps – it doesn't matter a bit.

TOBY: God is love, there is no pain.

CHAPS: It's awfully sweet of you.

STELLA: Don't be silly.

> OLIVE LLOYD-RANSOME's *voice is heard, outside.*

OLIVE (*outside*): Can we come in?

STELLA (*calling*): Of course!

TOBY: Send for a Bridge table and the Corinthian Bagatelle – don't let's waste a moment.

> OLIVE LLOYD-RANSOME *and* PRINCESS ELÈNA KRASSILOFF *enter.*
> OLIVE *is smartly dressed and dark.*
> ELÈNA *is fair and rather vague.*

OLIVE: Good morning, everybody – I'm suicidal.

STELLA: Why – what's the matter?

OLIVE: Everything's the matter. I went down twenty mille last night, Precious Bane's got distemper and I had to send him off to the vet at seven o'clock this morning, and on top of that I've had a telegram from Nicky and Vera to say they're arriving tomorrow.

TOBY: Tomorrow!

OLIVE: It's the most awful bore – it means that I shall have to turn you out, which I absolutely loathe – it also means that I shall have to put off Dolly, because she and Vera aren't speaking and—

STELLA: Why don't you put off Nicky and Vera?

OLIVE: Bob would never forgive me – he worships Nicky. They talk about international finance – also I've already put them off once – I feel absolutely dreadful about the whole business.

TOBY: Don't worry about us – we've got to go to the Lorings anyhow.

OLIVE: But I do – I adore you being here – you're the nicest guests I've ever had in my life.

ELÈNA (*scrutinising the breakfast-tray*): Do you mind if I take one of your lumps of sugar?

TOBY: Not at all – take the whole bowl.

ELÈNA: Angel!

> *She sits down quietly with the bowl of sugar and devours several lumps.*

OLIVE: And tonight we've got the Brandt dinner party – nobody wants to go – I tried to hint that we'd all rather stay in, but they're absolutely set on it – it's something to do with being Americans, I think, that passion for entertaining in restaurants.

TOBY: That means the Casino again.

STELLA: Yes, dear, that's what that means.

CHAPS: Have you got any messages for May, Olive?

OLIVE (*laughing*): None that I could possibly send her.

ELÈNA: He was lovely that chauffeur – he wore his cap bravely as though he wasn't afraid.

OLIVE: Wasn't afraid of what, darling?

TOBY: George Bainbridge.

ELÈNA: Anything – anything in the world. I remember he drove me to the station once, and I knew the back of his neck reminded me of someone, and who do you think it was?

STELLA (*wearily*): Who?

ELÈNA (*triumphantly*): Dimitri.

OLIVE: Everybody reminds you of Dimitri, darling.

ELÈNA: I loved him dreadfully. (*At the dressing-table.*) Do you mind if I take a little of your scent?

STELLA (*with false enthusiasm*): Do, dear!

> ELÈNA *sprays herself lavishly.*

OLIVE: We're going up to Vence to lunch – do you want to come?

STELLA: We shan't be ready in time.

OLIVE: I'll leave the small car for you – Irving and Pearl want to buy some of that awful pottery.

> MURDOCH *enters through the open door. He is a very correct English butler.*

MURDOCH: Excuse me, madame.

OLIVE: What is it, Murdoch?

MURDOCH: Mr Guy Forster has arrived, madame, for Lord Chapworth.

CHAPS: I must go.

OLIVE: Has his lordship's luggage gone down?

MURDOCH: Yes, madame.

ELÈNA: I love Guy, he's an angel. Where is he, Murdoch?

MURDOCH: In the bar, madame.

ELÈNA: I'll come down.

　　　MURDOCH *exits*.

CHAPS: Goodbye, Stella – Goodbye, Toby.

STELLA: Goodbye.

TOBY: Goodbye.

CHAPS: It's awfully sweet of you to hold that over. Goodbye, Olive.

OLIVE: I'll see you off – don't forget to write in the book – give Guy a drink.

CHAPS: He's probably had three already – come on, Elèna.

　　　ELÈNA *and* CHAPS *go out*.

OLIVE: I do feel so horrid about turning you out.

STELLA: Don't be silly, darling – we've overstayed frightfully, but we were having such a lovely time.

OLIVE: If it were anyone else but Vera and Nicky I'd tell them to go to hell, but Bob really has to discuss business with Nicky and – oh, well, I know you understand perfectly.

TOBY: Of course we do – when are they arriving?

OLIVE: Tomorrow afternoon – I must pop down and see Chaps off. The car will be waiting for you at twelve-thirty; we'd better meet in the main square.

STELLA: All right.

OLIVE: You *do* understand, don't you?

　　　She kisses her hand to them and goes out.
　　　There is silence for a moment.

STELLA: Dear Olive!

TOBY: She's done everything but throw us into the drive!

STELLA: We must think – we must think.

TOBY: What's the use of thinking – we haven't even enough to tip the servants.

STELLA: Oh, don't!

TOBY: If we asked Olive to lend us five thousand francs, do you think she would?

STELLA: Of course she would, and she'd dine out on it for a week – I'd rather die than ask her. Anyway, five thousand francs wouldn't be enough – not nearly enough. We've got to pay our train fares – Nanny's fare home – our Bridge debts – the servants – Oh, God!

There is a knock on the door.

Yes, who is it?

MURDOCH: Murdoch, madame.

TOBY: Come in!

MURDOCH *enters.*

MURDOCH: Mrs Lloyd-Ransome asked me to come and see you, madame, about your reservations.

STELLA: Reservations?

MURDOCH: On the afternoon train tomorrow. I took the liberty of telephoning in to the hall porter of the Majestic about them.

TOBY: How thoughtful of you, Murdoch.

STELLA: Why the hall porter at the Majestic?

MURDOCH: He happens to be a personal friend of mine, madame – he does a lot of odd jobs.

TOBY: This one may be odder than he bargained for.

MURDOCH: I beg your pardon, sir?

STELLA (*hurriedly*): When did you order these reservations, Murdoch?

MURDOCH: Last night, madame, directly Mrs Lloyd-Ransome told me.

STELLA (*with an attempt at light-hearted naturalness*): What have you got for us?

MURDOCH: Two single sleepers and one for your maid – that is what Mrs Lloyd-Ransome told me you required.

TOBY: It's a pity they don't have sitting-rooms on Continental trains.

STELLA: I'm afraid you'll have to change them, Murdoch. You see, we're not going back to London – we're going to Venice.

MURDOCH: That's all right, madame, Mrs Lloyd-Ransome told me that, too.

STELLA: She didn't happen to mention in passing that my sister was going to have a baby in July?

MURDOCH: I'll send the tickets up to you the moment they arrive; there's a small laundry bill as well – I've given that to your maid.

TOBY: You think of everything, Murdoch.

MURDOCH: Thank you, sir.

STELLA: Thank *you*, Murdoch.

MURDOCH bows and goes out.

TOBY: Dear Olive!

STELLA: Last night – she had it all arranged last night.

TOBY (*pensively*): I think I should like something quite dreadful to happen to Olive, you know – something really humiliating, like being sick at a Court Ball.

STELLA: How dare she!

TOBY: It's unsufferable.

STELLA: After all, she badgered us to come.

TOBY: Now she's badgering us to go.

STELLA: Isn't there anyone we could cable to?

TOBY: Don't be silly, dear – we've exhausted every possible telegraphic saviour years ago.

STELLA: Do you think I could do a little light prostitution in the Casino tonight?

TOBY: You'd have to work hard to raise ten thousand francs by tomorrow morning.

STELLA: There's no need to be rude.

TOBY: If you'd thought of that at the beginning of our stay things might have been much easier.

STELLA: You have the moral standards of a warthog.

TOBY: Think – think – there must be some way out.

STELLA: There isn't – it's no use – nothing's any use.

TOBY: Listen, darling, this is desperate – we've got to take a chance.

STELLA: What do you mean?

TOBY: Your bracelet.

STELLA: Don't be so absurd – it wouldn't fetch fifteen pounds.

TOBY (*ringing the bell*): We'll send Nanny into Cannes with it this afternoon.

STELLA: But I tell you—

TOBY: Shut up. Listen, at worst we can get a couple of thousand francs on it.

STELLA: I bet we couldn't.

TOBY: With my waistcoat buttons we could.

STELLA: Even then – what's the use?

TOBY: This is the use – listen – I'll gamble tonight.

STELLA: Oh, no, Toby – no!

TOBY: It's our only chance. I'll be careful, I promise. We'll have enough for three goes of the minimum at the big table—

STELLA: Oh, not the big table!

TOBY: The biggest—

> *He springs out of bed and goes over to the dressing-table.*
> NANNY *enters. She is a capable-looking, middle-aged woman.*

STELLA: Nanny, we're in the most awful trouble!

NANNY: I don't wonder – lying about in bed on a lovely morning like this.

TOBY (*springing at her with the bracelet and buttons*): Here, Nanny—

NANNY: What's this?

TOBY: Go into Cannes this afternoon and pop them.

NANNY: Oh, I couldn't – I really couldn't!

TOBY: You must.

NANNY: That lovely bracelet your Aunt Agnes left you.

STELLA: Listen, Nanny, we've got to leave tomorrow and we haven't got any money at all – we owe a lot as well – you must do this for us – go in by the twelve o'clock bus – please, Nanny.

NANNY: I could let you have a little, you know.

TOBY: We wouldn't hear of it, Nanny.

STELLA: Anyhow, a little's no good – we've got to have a lot.

NANNY: I shan't get much on these.

STELLA: Get what you can – promise you will, Nanny.

NANNY: That man in the pawnshop will split his sides when he sees me again.

TOBY: Never mind, Nanny – please!

NANNY: Won't you let me advance you a little? – I could go up to seven pounds.

TOBY: I tell you, Nanny, we couldn't possibly dream of such a thing.

NANNY: Oh, very well.

STELLA: How much do we owe you already?

NANNY: Three hundred and forty-two pounds all told.

STELLA: Oh, dear! (*She collapses on to the bed in helpless laughter.*)

TOBY: Go on, Nanny – go like the wind.

> *He pushes her out of the room.* GASTON *enters and crosses over to run the bath – he disappears into the bathroom.* TOBY *gets into bed again.*

STELLA: It's madness – stark, staring madness!

> TOBY *casually starts to read the paper again.*

You'll lose it, I know you will. Oh, God, I wish I could play the damned game—

> *There is a pause.*

TOBY (*reading*): Mr and Mrs Eugene B. Oglander arrived yesterday at the Hotel Maurice with their daughters Margaret and Helen—

STELLA: It's too humiliating – I wish I were dead!

TOBY: I wonder what the B stands for?

STELLA (*bitterly*): I *know*!

THE LIGHTS FADE

Scene II

The scene is the same.

> TOBY *is lying on the bed, smoking. He is in his dressing-gown and pyjamas.* STELLA, *in a negligee, is doing her face at the dressing-table.*
> *The time is about 1.30 a.m.*

TOBY: Is there no justice in the universe? No decency?

169

STELLA: Absolutely none, dear. I remember remarking that to Nanny only the other day when the stopper came out of my nail varnish and made the inside of my handbag look like Bortsch.

TOBY: There was no reason in what happened – it had nothing to do with the law of logic or the law of compensation or the law of anything – it was just low, senseless bad luck.

STELLA: Never mind, darling.

TOBY: Mind! I shall mind to the end of my days. The whole beastly scene is etched on to my brain in blood. (*Reconstructing his despair.*) I went up to the table – seven, my lucky number, was miraculously vacant – I sat down and waited for the shoe to come round – just as it was two away from me that New Jersey hag tapped me on the shoulder. 'It's terrible,' she said. 'I can't find a place anywheres – will you be a dear and let me have yours just for a little while? I'm feeling so lucky tonight.'

STELLA: She was right.

TOBY: Right! She ran the bank seventeen times – collected one hundred and seventy thousand francs with all the delicacy of a starving jaguar let loose in a butcher's shop – and graciously gave me back my place.

STELLA: Whereupon you proceeded to lose our two thousand francs in the brief space of four minutes, borrow five hundred francs from Bertie Gifford, who will never let us forget it, lose that too, and join me in the bar wearing what might be moderately described as a 'set look'.

TOBY: Correct. Have you anything more to say?

STELLA: Not for the moment.

TOBY: Good! Then we might talk of something else.

STELLA: I can't see any necessity to talk at all.

TOBY: That is only because you are temporarily exhausted by your own verbosity. Your natural flow will return in a minute.

STELLA: I was fond of Aunt Agnes and she was fond of me.

TOBY: That rather cloying relationship belongs mercifully to the days before I met you.

STELLA: She left me that bracelet in her will.

TOBY: It seems odd that she should symbolise her almost

incestuous love for you by such an undistinguished little trinket.

STELLA: You have a disgusting mind, Toby.

TOBY: I said almost.

STELLA: Aunt Agnes was the most generous woman in the world.

TOBY: I suspect that your memory of her has been softened by time. To the impartial observer she appears to have been a mean old bitch.

STELLA: Toby!

TOBY: If it's all the same to you, I would prefer to leave Aunt Agnes where she rightly belongs, warbling through eternity with the Feathered Choir.

STELLA: It seems a pity that you can't turn your devastating wit to a more commercial advantage – you should write a gossip column.

TOBY: I haven't got a title.

STELLA: Oh, shut up!

TOBY: That was merely rude.

STELLA: There's no sense in going on like this – snapping at each other – we've got to face facts—

TOBY (*rolling over*): Oh, God!

STELLA (*turning round*): Toby, don't you see—

TOBY: Your passion for facing facts is rapidly becoming pathological. You'll go mad, that's what you'll do, and spend your declining years being led about some awful institute by a keeper – facing the fact that you're the Empress Eugènie.

STELLA: Don't be so idiotic.

TOBY: I'm sick of facing facts; in future I shall cut every fact I meet stone dead – I intend to relax, to live in a lovely dream world of my own where everything is hilariously untrue. After all, at least three-quarters of the civilised world do it, why shouldn't I?

STELLA: Why shouldn't you what?

TOBY: Delude myself! I'm going to start deluding myself this very minute. I'm going to begin with the Old Testament and believe every word of it – I'm going to believe in Jehovah and Buddha and Krishna and Mahomet and Luther and Mary

Baker Eddy and Aimèe Semple Macpherson – I'm even going to believe in Aunt Agnes!

STELLA: Will you shut up about Aunt Agnes!

TOBY: It is possible, in my present state of splendid detachment, that I might go off into a Yogi trance and stay upside down for several days – in that case all our troubles would be over – even Olive's social conscience would jib at one of her guests being carried out of the house in a sort of sailor's knot.

STELLA: Darling, darling Toby!

She rushes to him and flings her arms round his neck.

TOBY: Look out – you're strangling me.

STELLA: I've been wanting to strangle you for hours and now I'm doing it – it's heaven!

TOBY: This might lead to almost anything.

STELLA (*in his arms*): Fiddling while Rome's burning – that's what we're doing.

TOBY: In the present circumstances fiddling sounds singularly offensive.

STELLA: I didn't mean that sort of fiddling.

TOBY: Really, Stella—

STELLA: Oh, darling, what are we to do?

TOBY: Let's go quietly but firmly along the passage and murder Pearl Brandt.

STELLA: We should be hanged.

TOBY: It would be worth it.

STELLA: She sleeps alone, you know – Irving is separated from her by the bathroom – it would be deliciously easy.

TOBY (*wistfully*): I hate her so. There's a certain austere scientific beauty about my hatred for that shrill harpy – like higher mathematics.

STELLA: I'd like to fasten that wad of thousand-franc notes to her nose with a safety-pin.

TOBY: I had other plans for them.

STELLA: Hush, darling.

TOBY (*jumping up and striding about the room*): I can't bear it – I really can't!

STELLA: Well, now let's talk about something else. I consider this particular topic exhausted and I don't want to get angry again.

TOBY: Angry! – Again! I shall never stop being angry until the
    end of my days.

STELLA: Being angry is very bad for you – I believe that when
    you are angry all the red corpuscles in your blood fight with
    the white ones.

TOBY: If that's so, my circulation at the moment would make the
    battle of Mons look like a Morris dance.

STELLA: It's dreadfully late, we'd better go to sleep.

TOBY: I shall never sleep again.

STELLA: Nonsense! – go and brush your teeth.

TOBY: We must think of something.

STELLA: No, we mustn't – we're worn out – go on.

TOBY: But, darling—

STELLA: Go on – leave the door open – the noise of your
    gargling will give me a sense of security, as though everything
    was all right.

> TOBY *goes into the bathroom, leaving the door open.* STELLA *gives a
> few final pats to her face and tries to spray herself with scent, but
> there isn't any left.*

Toby!

TOBY: What?

STELLA: Were Russians always predatory – even before the
    Revolution, I mean?

TOBY: I expect so. Why?

STELLA: Elèna's splashed herself from head to foot with the last
    precious drops of my scent this morning.

TOBY: Personally, I'm very glad – I never cared for it.

STELLA: That's beside the point.

TOBY: It smells like bad salad dressing.

STELLA: Smelt, dear – you can use the past tense now.

TOBY: Good – from now onwards I intend to live in the past
    anyhow – the present is too unbearable. I intend to go back to
    the happy scenes of my boyhood.

STELLA: I'm sorry I'm not a rocking-horse.

TOBY: You underrate yourself, darling.

STELLA (*getting into bed*): Witty to the last.

TOBY (*after a pause, during which the sound of gargling is heard*): Stella!

STELLA: What?

TOBY: What are we going to do?

STELLA: I told you just now – I refuse to discuss it – I'm too tired.

TOBY: If you broke your leg we should have to stay, shouldn't we?

STELLA: I have no intention of breaking my leg.

TOBY: Modern women have no courage – in olden times women did brave things for their menfolk every day of the week.

STELLA: I don't look upon you as my menfolk.

TOBY: Think of the girl who put her arm through the latches of the door to save Bonnie Prince Charlie.

STELLA: In my opinion a misguided ass.

TOBY: I won't hear a word against Flora Macdonald.

STELLA: It wasn't Flora Macdonald.

TOBY: Don't be so ignorant, of course it was. Flora Macdonald never stopped doing things like that.

STELLA: It was not.

TOBY: Who was it, then?

STELLA: I don't know who it was, but it was *not* Flora Macdonald.

TOBY (*appearing with a toothbrush*): I suppose you'll tell me it was Grace Darling in a minute.

STELLA: I see no reason for you to suppose any such thing.

TOBY: It was Flora Macdonald.

STELLA: It's a matter of supreme indifference to me whether it was Nell Gwynn or Marie Antoinette.

TOBY: Well, we're getting on – by a process of tedious elimination – we might ultimately arrive at who you think it was.

STELLA: I tell you I don't know who it was, I only know who it wasn't, and it wasn't Flora Macdonald.

TOBY: Oh, God!

> *He slams into the bathroom in a rage. There is a moment's pause then a crash. Then* TOBY *gives a wail of pain.*

STELLA: What's happened?

TOBY: I'm hurt.

STELLA: What sort of hurt?

TOBY: Badly hurt.

STELLA: Oh, darling!

She jumps out of bed and rushes into the bathroom. The following dialogue takes place off stage.

TOBY (*groaning*): It was the door of that blasted little cupboard—

STELLA: My poor sweet!

TOBY: Do something – it's bleeding.

STELLA: Where's the iodine?

TOBY: How do I know?

STELLA: Wait a minute – no, that's eye-drops – here—

TOBY: It's agony.

STELLA: Stand still.

TOBY: I don't want to stand still – I want to jump out of the window. This is the end—

STELLA: Don't be so silly!

TOBY: Cotton-wool.

STELLA: There isn't any.

TOBY: There ought to be.

STELLA: Wait a minute – I've got some.

She comes running in and goes to the dressing-table. She rummages in the drawers for a moment and produces some cotton-wool. TOBY *comes in carrying a bottle of iodine. There is an enormous bruise on his forehead which is bleeding slightly.*

Here we are.

TOBY: God, what a crack!

STELLA: Stand still.

TOBY: Do stop telling me to stand still.

STELLA: Don't be so irritable.

TOBY (*as she dabs him with iodine*): Ow! – hell! – ow!—

STELLA: Stand still.

TOBY: Shut up!

STELLA: I'm doing my best – don't be so childish. There!

TOBY (*looking in the glass*): For this to happen – on top of everything else – it's too much!

STELLA: Never mind, darling.

TOBY: It's not even bad enough to keep us here.

STELLA: You might pretend it had given you concussion and behave very peculiarly tomorrow morning.

TOBY: I couldn't carry it through – I'm too depressed.

STELLA: Get into bed, darling.

TOBY: The light's on in the bathroom.

STELLA: I'll turn it out.

> *She goes into the bathroom and does so, while he takes off his dressing-gown and gets into bed.* STELLA *returns.*

TOBY: You don't think we ought to bandage it?

STELLA: No – let the air get to it.

TOBY: Open the window.

STELLA: All right – I was just going to.

TOBY: If you're beastly to me I swear to God I'll yell the place down.

> STELLA *opens the window, switches out all lights except one by the bed, and gets into bed.*

STELLA: Does it hurt?

TOBY: Was that question merely rhetorical or do you really care?

STELLA: Of course I care – it's horrid for you.

TOBY: It does hurt, Stella – it hurts dreadfully.

STELLA: Try to forget about it.

TOBY: That remark was just plain silly.

STELLA: Do you want to read?

TOBY: Read! I doubt if I shall ever be able to read again.

STELLA: I'll turn out the light then.

TOBY: It would make no appreciable difference to me if the light of the world went out. My mind is a trackless waste of impenetrable darkness.

STELLA: That's right, dear.

> *There is a pause.* STELLA *switches out the bed light.*

TOBY: Stella – what *are* we to do?

STELLA: We'll deliver ourselves over to Olive bound and gagged in the morning. We'll meet her delighted, patronising contempt with fortitude – we'll humiliate ourselves without flinching – we'll add up how much we need and borrow it from her gaily, as though we enjoyed it – no matter how broken we are we'll never let her see—

TOBY (*drowsily*): Like Flora Macdonald.

STELLA: It was *not* Flora Macdonald!

THE LIGHTS FADE

Scene III

The scene is the same about two hours later. Moonlight is streaming into the room.

TOBY and STELLA are fast asleep. There is a slight noise on the verandah, a shadow falls across the moonlight. A man steps softly into the room. His face is muffled. He tiptoes across and trips over the stool in front of the dressing-table.

TOBY (*switching on the light*): Who's there?

STELLA (*waking*): Oh, dear!

STEVENS (*covering them with a revolver*): Keep quiet.

TOBY: Scream, dear, he wouldn't dare to shoot.

STELLA: Scream yourself.

STEVENS: Oh yes, I would.

TOBY: What do you want?

STEVENS: I want you to keep quiet.

TOBY: Naturally you do – I meant apart from that.

STEVENS: Where's your jewellery?

TOBY: Number 18, Rue Mirabeau, Cannes.

STELLA: We haven't a thing here – you've chosen probably the worst room to burgle in the whole world.

STEVENS: Come on – tell me where it is.

STELLA makes a sudden movement; he switches his gun towards her. TOBY throws a pillow and knocks it out of his hand – he leaps out of bed, there is a scuffle and TOBY gets the revolver – he covers the man with it.

TOBY: Now then!

STEVENS: Look out – it's loaded!

TOBY: I should damn well hope it was.

STELLA: Why aren't you French? We're in France – you ought to be French.

TOBY: Take off his muffler, Stella. (*To* STEVENS.) Keep your hands up.

STELLA (*approaching*): Excuse me.

TOBY: Keep them up.

STELLA undoes the scarf from round his mouth.

STELLA: There now!

TOBY: Turn on the other lights, Stella.

STELLA (*doing so*): It's a very expensive scarf. (*She looks at the man.*) My God, it's Stevens!

STEVENS: Oh, madame!

STELLA: Stevens, how *could* you!

TOBY: You ought to be ashamed of yourself.

STEVENS: I had no idea, sir – madame – I didn't realise you was staying here.

STELLA: Did you really mean to burgle this house?

STEVENS: Yes, madame.

STELLA: But why? You can't suddenly become a burglar all in a minute – you were a respectable chauffeur last week.

STEVENS: That was before the crash came, madame.

TOBY: You mean it was before George Bainbridge threw you out.

STEVENS: Yes, sir.

STELLA (*reproachfully*): Oh, Stevens!

STEVENS: He sacked me straight away – without even a reference.

STELLA: You should have applied to Mrs Bainbridge.

TOBY: Stella!

STEVENS: I'm desperate, madame – I haven't got a bob.

STELLA: That's no excuse for becoming a criminal.

STEVENS: It's the usual excuse – begging your pardon, madame.

STELLA: Do you mean to tell me Mrs Bainbridge didn't give you so much as a—

TOBY: Stella, be quiet – your behaviour is in the worst possible taste.

STELLA: I think it's a dirty shame – you have my sympathy, Stevens.

STEVENS: Thank you, madame.

TOBY: You'd better get out, Stevens – I'll keep the gun, if you don't mind.

STEVENS: It belongs to Meadows, sir – Mr Bainbridge's butler – I pinched it. If you wouldn't mind returning it to him I should be much obliged.

TOBY: We ought to hand you over to the police.

STEVENS: Oh, please don't do that, sir. I've had an awful time. I've got a wife and child in Walthamstow, I've got to get back somehow.

STELLA: We can't help you – we would if we could, but—

TOBY: Be quiet, Stella.

STEVENS: Thank you, madame – you're very kind.

TOBY: Go on – get out as quickly as you can.

STEVENS: Yes, sir. Thank you, sir.

TOBY: Go on.

      STEVENS *goes to the window.*

STELLA: Stop!

TOBY: Stella!

STELLA: Come back a minute.

TOBY: Don't be an idiot, Stella.

STELLA: Leave this to me – I know what I'm doing.

TOBY: What are you talking about?

STELLA: Sit down, Stevens.

TOBY: Have you gone mad?

STELLA: Shut up – sit down, Stevens.

STEVENS (*bewildered*): Yes, madame. (*He sits down.*)

STELLA: Now then—

TOBY: Look here—

STELLA: Put that gun down, Toby, and don't keep on waving it about like pampas grass – Stevens may be a potential thief, but he isn't a murderer and even if he were, he wouldn't murder us, he likes us, don't you, Stevens?

STEVENS: Very much, madame.

STELLA: You seem to forget, Toby, that when we were staying with the Bainbridges in Scotland last September, Stevens lent you seven pounds.

TOBY: I paid it back.

STEVENS: You certainly did, sir; within the month.

STELLA: Do you trust us, Stevens?

STEVENS: Trust you, madame?

STELLA: Yes – I mean will you trust us if we trust you?

STEVENS: I don't understand, madame.

STELLA: I'll explain. We're broke – cleaned out.

STEVENS: Yes, madame.

STELLA: You're broke too – in addition to which you've involved yourself in one of the juiciest scandals the Riviera has known for years.

STEVENS: It wasn't my fault, madame – I—

STELLA: I never imagined for one moment that it was.

TOBY: Look here, Stella – what is the use—?

STELLA: Toby, don't be such a fool – don't you see!

TOBY: See what?

STELLA: God sent Stevens to us tonight, Toby – or it may have been Buddha, or Mahomet or Mary Baker Eddy, but whoever it was he's here hale and hearty and ready to help us – you are ready to help us, aren't you, Stevens!

STEVENS: Help you, madame?

STELLA: If you can help yourself at the same time.

STEVENS: Anything you say, madame – you can rely on me.

TOBY (*at last realising what she means*): Stella – we can't!

STELLA: We can – and we will.

TOBY: You're raving.

STELLA: I'd rather face prison than Olive's patronising sneer tomorrow morning.

STEVENS (*noticing* TOBY's *wound*): Oh, sir, what have you done to your head?

TOBY: Never mind about that now.

STELLA: Mind about it – it's the most important thing in the world. You did it, Stevens – you knocked him out—

STEVENS: Oh, madame, I'd never do such a thing.

STELLA: Yes, you would – if you were an intelligent professional burglar you would – you'd knock him out; then you'd bind and gag us both – then you'd burgle the house and get away with the swag.

STEVENS: Swag, madame?

STELLA: That's what it's called.

STEVENS: What what's called, madame?

STELLA: The money that you're going to take from this house tonight.

STEVENS (*rising*): Oh, madame!

STELLA: Sit down and listen.

    STEVENS *sinks back again.*

A few yards away from this room there is wrapped in plebeian slumber a lady from New Jersey called Mrs Irving Brandt—

TOBY: Go on, darling – I'm with you.

STELLA: In the top right hand drawer of her dressing-table, just to the left of the door, there is a bundle of one hundred and seventy thousand francs—

STEVENS: Oh, dear!

STELLA: Halves, Stevens, halves!

STEVENS: Oh, madame – I don't think I dare.

TOBY: Be a man, Stevens.

STELLA: Go now – it's the last door on the right at the end of the passage.

TOBY: The carpet is ostentatiously soft, so you won't be heard.

STELLA: If by any chance she wakes up and screams, double back here and out of the window – I'll scream, too, and bathe my husband's head. If, on the other hand, you get away with it – come back here, give us half, tie us both up and get out.

STEVENS: All right, madame – I'll do it.

TOBY: Think of Walthamstow.

STELLA: Go on – last door on the right – dressing-table on left of the door – top right hand drawer.

TOBY (*holding out his hand*): Good luck.

STEVENS *shakes it.*

STELLA (*also shaking his hand*): Good luck, Stevens.

TOBY: Turn out the lights.

STELLA (*doing so*): There.

STEVENS *slips out of the room. They listen anxiously for a moment.*

STELLA (*in a whisper*): Quick – get the bedclothes off the bed – and your dressing-gown cord—

TOBY (*also in a whisper*): My feet are cold.

STELLA (*wrestling with the bedclothes*): Put on your slippers.

TOBY (*doing so*): Handkerchiefs for gags.

He rummages in the dressing-table drawers.

STELLA: Don't make such a row.

TOBY: My God!

STELLA: What is it?

TOBY: Stevens might bind and gag us and then take all the money.

STELLA: Don't be so absurd – he's utterly honest – you only have to look at him. His moral values may wobble a bit on the sex side, but otherwise I'm certain his integrity is beyond question. Why, he was a valet before he was a chauffeur – he's been trained as a gentleman's gentleman – they're always much more reliable than gentlemen.

TOBY: Hush! – did you hear anything?

STELLA: He's coming back.

> *They stand in silence for a moment.* STEVENS *creeps back into the room. He closes the door softly after him.*

Got it?

STEVENS: Yes.

STELLA: Switch on the bed-light, Toby.

TOBY (*doing so*): Was she asleep?

STEVENS: Snoring, sir.

STELLA: I'm *glad!*

STEVENS: Here you are, madame.

> *He flings the wad of notes on to the bed.*

TOBY: Come on – help divide them.

STEVENS: I'd rather not, sir, if you don't mind – I'd rather you had the money. I happened to find these on the dressing-table – they'll do me nicely.

> *He produces several diamond bracelets, some rings and a jewelled cigarette-case.*

STELLA: Stevens, for shame! – take them back at once!

TOBY: They can be traced.

STEVENS: I'll manage all right, sir.

STELLA: You must take half the money.

STEVENS: I'd really rather not.

TOBY: It's extraordinarily generous of you, Stevens.

STEVENS: You and Madame have always been very nice to me, sir – it feels somehow as if we was old friends.

STELLA: Thank you, Stevens.

TOBY (*giving him some bills*): Here, you must take these, for travelling expenses.

STEVENS: Very well, sir – if you insist.

TOBY: Where shall I put the rest?

STELLA: Put eleven thousand in the drawer and the rest in the inside pocket of your dinner jacket.

STEVENS: Allow me, sir.

TOBY: Thank you, Stevens.

> STEVENS *puts some notes in the dressing-table drawer and stuffs the rest into* TOBY's *dinner-coat; he then proceeds to fold it neatly and lay it on the chair.*

STELLA: Never mind about that now, Stevens – bind and gag us.

> *The following dialogue takes place while they are being bound and gagged.*

TOBY: Do you intend to go direct to England?

STEVENS: Yes, sir. I thought of going by boat from Marseilles. I've never seen Gibraltar.

TOBY: It's very impressive.

STELLA: The P & O boats always stop at Marseilles, don't they? I remember Blanche came home on one.

STEVENS: I think I shall try another line this time, madame. I once went P & O as far as Egypt with Mr Bainbridge – and I didn't fancy it.

TOBY: Why not, Stevens?

STEVENS: All them bugles got me down, sir – it was like being in the army all over again.

STELLA: You must look us up when you come to London – we might be able to help you to find a job.

STEVENS: Thank you, madame.

TOBY: We're in the book.

STEVENS: As a matter of fact, I've been thinking for a long time of giving up domestic service – I'd rather get a job that was more steady – more respectable, if you know what I mean.

STELLA: I couldn't know better.

STEVENS: I think my brother will be able to help me.

TOBY: Oh – what does he do?

STEVENS: He's got a very nice position in Barclays Bank, sir.

TOBY: Oh, I see.

> *By this time they are both successfully tied to two chairs.*

STEVENS: Now for the gags.

STELLA: They're on the dressing-table.

>STEVENS *politely gags them.*

STEVENS: Let me know if they're too tight.

TOBY: They ought to be pretty tight.

STEVENS: I think we might allow ourselves a little poetic licence, don't you, sir?

TOBY: Thank you, Stevens.

STEVENS (*regarding them*): Quite comfy?

>*They both nod.*

Light on or off? – One nod for on – two nods for off.

>*They both nod once.*

Well, I'll be getting along now – thank you very much, sir and madame – it's been a great pleasure meeting you again. Goodnight.

>*He bows politely and goes out of the window.*
>
>*They are left tied to the chairs. Behind their gags it is apparent that they are convulsed with laughter.* STELLA *loosens her gag enough to speak.*

STELLA: If I'd been May Bainbridge, I'd have married him!

CURTAIN

STILL LIFE

A Play in Five Scenes

Still Life was produced in London at the Phoenix Theatre on 18 May 1936, with the following cast:

LAURA JESSON	Miss Gertrude Lawrence
MYRTLE BAGOT	Miss Joyce Carey
BERYL WATERS	Miss Moya Nugent
STANLEY	Mr Kenneth Carten
ALBERT GODBY	Mr Alan Webb
ALEC HARVEY	Mr Noël Coward
YOUNG MAN	Mr Charles Peters
BILL	Mr Edward Underdown
JOHNNIE	Mr Anthony Pelissier
MILDRED	Miss Betty Hare
DOLLY MESSITERS	Miss Everley Gregg

The action of the play takes place in the refreshment room of Milford Junction Station.

TIME: The present.

Scene I

The scene is the refreshment room of Milford Junction Station. On the left of the stage is a curved counter piled with glass cases containing sandwiches, rock cakes, etc. There are rows of tea-cups and glasses symmetrically arranged, an expression of the fanciful side of MYRTLE'S *imagination. Schweppes' bottles of soda and Tonic water have been placed in circles and squares. Even the rock cakes mount each other on the glass stands in a disciplined pattern. There is a metal machine which gushes hot tea, a sort of cylindrical samovar.*

For drinking hours there are the usual appurtenances for the drawing of draught beer, and the wall behind the counter, except for a door upstage, is lined with looking-glass shelves supporting bottles, packets of chocolate, packets of cigarettes, etc.

There are two windows in the back wall. Their lower panes are frosted and their upper ones tastefully plastered with stained glass paper. There is another similar window on the right-hand wall which is at a slight angle. In this there is also a door leading on to the platform. There are three tables against the back wall, a stove in the corner, and two more tables against the right-hand wall, then the door and another table set below it. There are several advertisements and calendars in frames, and artificial flowers.

MYRTLE BAGOT *herself is a buxom and imposing widow. Her hair is piled high, and her expression reasonably jaunty except on those occasions when her strong sense of refinement gets the better of her.*

BERYL WATERS, *her assistant, is pretty but dimmed, not only by* MYRTLE'S *personal effulgence, but by her firm authority.*

When the curtain rises it is about 5.25 p.m. on an evening in April. The evening sunlight streams through the right-hand window illuminating gaily the paraphernalia on the counter.

A YOUNG MAN *in a mackintosh is finishing his tea at one of the upstage tables and reading an evening paper.*

> LAURA JESSON *is sitting at the downstage table having tea. She is an attractive woman in the thirties. Her clothes are not particularly smart but obviously chosen with taste. She looks exactly what she is, a pleasant, ordinary married woman, rather pale, for she is not very strong, and with the definite charm of personality which comes from natural kindliness, humour and reasonable conscience. She is reading a Boots library book at which she occasionally smiles. On the chair beside her there are several parcels as she has been shopping.*
>
> STANLEY *enters from the platform. He wears a seedy green uniform and carries a tray strapped to his shoulders. He goes to the counter. He addresses* MYRTLE *with becoming respect,* BERYL, *however, he winks at lewdly whenever the opportunity.*

STANLEY: I'm out of 'Marie's, Mrs Bagot, and I could do with some more Nestlé's plain.

MYRTLE (*scrutinising the tray*): Let me see.

STANLEY: An old girl on the 4.10 asked if I'd got an ice-cream wafer. I didn't 'arf laugh.

MYRTLE: I don't see that there was anything to laugh at – a very natural request on a faine day.

STANLEY: What did she think I was, a 'Stop me and buy one'?

> BERYL *sniggers.*

MYRTLE: Be quiet, Beryl – and as for you, Stanley, don't you be saucy – you were saucy when you started to work here, and you've been getting saucier and saucier ever since. Here you are — (*She gives him some packets of biscuits and Nestlé's chocolate.*) Go on now.

STANLEY (*cheerfully*): Righto.

> *He winks at* BERYL *and goes out.*

MYRTLE: And see here, Beryl Waters, I'll trouble you to remember you're on duty —

BERYL: I didn't do anything.

MYRTLE: Exactly – you just stand there giggling like a fool – did you make out that list?

BERYL: Yes, Mrs Bagot.

MYRTLE: Where is it?

BERYL: I put it on your desk.

MYRTLE: Where's your cloth?

BERYL: Here, Mrs Bagot.

MYRTLE: Well, go and clean off Number 3. I can see the crumbs on it from here.

BERYL: It's them rock cakes.

MYRTLE: Never you mind about the rock cakes, just you do as you're told and don't argue.

> BERYL *goes over to clean No. 3 table.*
>
> ALBERT GODBY *enters. He is a ticket inspector, somewhere between thirty and forty. His accent is north country.*

ALBERT: Hullo!

MYRTLE: Quite a stranger, aren't you?

ALBERT: I couldn't get in yesterday.

MYRTLE (*bridling*): I wondered what had happened to you.

ALBERT: I 'ad a bit of a dust-up.

MYRTLE (*preparing his tea*): What about?

ALBERT: Saw a chap getting out of a first-class compartment, and when he come to give up 'is ticket it was third-class, and I told 'im he'd 'ave to pay excess, and then he turned a bit nasty and I 'ad to send for Mr Saunders.

MYRTLE: Fat lot of good he'd be.

ALBERT: He ticked him off proper.

MYRTLE: Seeing's believing —

ALBERT: He's not a bad lot, Mr Saunders, after all you can't expect much spirit from a man who's only got one lung and a wife with diabetes.

MYRTLE: I thought something must be wrong when you didn't come.

MYRTLE: I'd have popped in to explain but I had a date and 'ad to run for it the moment I went off.

MYRTLE (*frigidly*): Oh, indeed!

ALBERT: A chap I know's getting married.

MYRTLE: Very interesting, I'm sure.

ALBERT: What's up with you, anyway?

MYRTLE: I'm sure I don't know to what you're referring.

ALBERT: You're a bit unfriendly all of a sudden.

MYRTLE (*ignoring him*): Beryl, hurry up – put some coal in the stove while you're at it.

BERYL: Yes, Mrs Bagot.

MYRTLE: I'm afraid I really can't stand here wasting my time in idle gossip, Mr Godby.

ALBERT: Aren't you going to offer me another cup?

MYRTLE: You can 'ave another cup and welcome when you've finished that one. Beryl'll give it to you – I've got my accounts to do.

ALBERT: I'd rather you gave it to me.

MYRTLE: Time and Taide wait for no man, Mr Godby.

ALBERT: I don't know what you're huffy about, but whatever it is I'm very sorry.

MYRTLE: You misunderstand me – I'm not —

> ALEC HARVEY *enters. He is about thirty-five. He wears a moustache, a mackintosh and a squash hat, and he carries a small bag. His manner is decisive and unflurried.*

ALEC: A cup of tea, please.

MYRTLE: Certainly. (*She pours it out in silence.*) Cake or pastry?

ALEC: No, thank you.

MYRTLE: Threepence.

ALEC (*paying*): Thank you.

> *He takes his cup of tea and goes over to a table. He takes off his hat and sits down.* LAURA *glances at the clock, collects her parcels in a leisurely manner and goes out on to the platform.* BERYL *returns to her place behind the counter.*

BERYL: Minnie hasn't touched her milk.

MYRTLE: Did you put it down for her?

BERYL: Yes, but she never came in for it.

MYRTLE: Go out the back and see if she's in the yard.

ALBERT (*conversationally*): Fond of animals?

MYRTLE: In their place.

ALBERT: My landlady's got a positive mania for animals – she's got two cats, one Manx and one ordinary, three rabbits in a hutch in the kitchen, they belong to her little boy by rights, and one of them foolish-looking dogs with hair over its eyes.

MYRTLE: I don't know to what breed you refer.

ALBERT: I don't think it knows itself —

> *There is a rumbling noise in the distance, and the sound of a bell.*

MYRTLE: There's the boat train.

There is a terrific clatter as the express roars through the station.

ALBERT: What about my other cup? I shall have to be moving –
the five-forty-three will be in in a minute.

MYRTLE: Who's on the gate? (*She pours him out another cup.*)

ALBERT: Young William.

MYRTLE: You're neglecting your duty, you know – that's what
you're doing.

ALBERT: A bit of relaxation never did anyone any harm —

LAURA *enters hurriedly holding a handkerchief to her eye.*

LAURA: Please could you give me a glass of water – I've got
something in my eye and I want to bathe it.

MYRTLE: Would you like me to have a look?

LAURA: Please don't trouble. I think the water will do it.

MYRTLE (*handing her a glass of water*): Here.

MYRTLE *and* ALBERT *watch her in silence as she bathes her eye.*

ALBERT: Bit of coal dust, I expect.

MYRTLE: A man I knew lost the sight of one eye through getting
a bit of grit in it.

ALBERT: Painful thing – very painful.

MYRTLE (*as* LAURA *lifts her head*): Better?

LAURA (*obviously in pain*): I'm afraid not – oh!

ALEC *rises from his table and comes over.*

ALEC: Can I help you?

LAURA: Oh, no, please – it's only something in my eye.

MYRTLE: Try pulling down your eyelid as far as it'll go.

ALBERT: And then blowing your nose.

ALEC: Please let me look. I happen to be a doctor.

LAURA: It's very kind of you.

ALEC: Turn round to the light, please – now – look up – now
look down – I can see it. Keep still — (*He twists up the corner of
his handkerchief and rapidly operates with it.*) There —

LAURA (*blinking*): Oh, dear – what a relief – it was agonising.

ALEC: It looks like a bit of grit.

LAURA: It was when the express went through – thank you very
much indeed —

ALEC: Not at all.

There is the sound of a bell on the platform.

ALBERT (*gulping down his tea*): There we go – I must run.

LAURA: How lucky for me that you happened to be here.

ALEC: Anybody could have done it.

LAURA: Never mind, you did and I'm most grateful. There's my
    train. Good-bye.

> *She puts out her hand and he shakes it politely. She goes out followed
> at a run by* ALBERT GODBY.
>
> ALEC *looks after her for a moment and then goes back to his table.
> There is the noise of the train rumbling into the station as the lights
> fade.*

Scene II

The scene is the same and the time is about the same.

*Nearly three months have passed since the preceding scene, and
it is now July.*

MYRTLE *is resplendent in a light overall.* BERYL'S *appearance
is unaltered. The tables are all unoccupied.*

MYRTLE (*slightly relaxed in manner*): It's all very faine, I said,
    expecting me to do this that and the other, but what do *I* get
    out of it? You can't expect me to be a cook-housekeeper and
    char rolled into one during the day, and a loving wife in the
    evening just because you feel like it. Oh, dear no. There are
    just as good fish in the sea, I said, as ever came out of it, and I
    packed my boxes then and there and left him.

BERYL: Didn't you ever go back?

MYRTLE: Never. I went to my sister's place at Folkestone for a
    bit, and then I went in with a friend of mine and we opened a
    tea-shop in Hythe.

BERYL: And what happened to him?

MYRTLE: Dead as a door-nail inside three years!

BERYL: Well, I never!

MYRTLE: So you see, every single thing she told me came true –
    first them clubs coming together, an unexpected journey, then

the Queen of diamonds and the ten – that was my friend and the tea-shop business. Then the Ace of spades three times running —

STANLEY *enters*.

STANLEY: Two rock and an apple.

MYRTLE: What for?

STANLEY: Party on the up platform.

MYRTLE: Why can't they come in here for them?

STANLEY: Ask me another. (*He winks at* BERYL.)

MYRTLE: Got something in your eye?

STANLEY: Nothing beyond a bit of a twinkle every now and again.

BERYL (*giggling*): Oh, you are awful!

MYRTLE: You learn to behave yourself, my lad. Here are your rock cakes. Beryl, stop sniggering and give me an apple off the stand.

BERYL *complies*.

Not off the front, silly, haven't you got any sense. Here — (*She takes one from the back of the stand so as to leave the symmetry undisturbed.*)

STANLEY: This one's got a hole in it.

MYRTLE: Tell 'em to come and choose for themselves if they're particular – go on now.

STANLEY: All right – give us a chance.

MYRTLE: What people want to eat on the platform for I really don't know. Tell Mr Godby not to forget his tea.

STANLEY: Righto!

He goes out as ALEC *and* LAURA *come in.* LAURA *is wearing a summer dress,* ALEC, *a grey flannel suit.*

ALEC: Tea or lemonade?

LAURA: Tea, I think – it's more refreshing, really. (*She sits down at the table by the door.*)

ALEC *goes to the counter.*

ALEC: Two teas, please.

MYRTLE: Cakes or pastry?

ALEC (*to* LAURA): Cakes or pastry?

LAURA: No, thank you.

193

ALEC: Are those bath buns fresh?

MYRTLE: Certainly they are – made this morning.

ALEC: Two, please.

> MYRTLE *puts two bath buns on a plate, meanwhile* BERYL *has drawn two cups of tea.*

MYRTLE: That'll be eightpence.

ALEC: All right. (*He pays her.*)

MYRTLE: Take the tea to the table, Beryl.

ALEC: I'll carry the buns.

> BERYL *brings the tea to the table.* ALEC *follows with the buns.*

ALEC: You must eat one of these – fresh this morning.

LAURA: Very fattening.

ALEC: I don't hold with such foolishness.

> BERYL *returns to the counter.*

MYRTLE: I'm going over my accounts. Let me know when Albert comes in.

BERYL: Yes, Mrs Bagot.

> BERYL *settles down behind the counter with* Peg's Paper.

LAURA: They do look good, I must say.

ALEC: One of my earliest passions – I've never outgrown it.

LAURA: Do you like milk in your tea?

ALEC: Yes, don't you?

LAURA: Yes – fortunately.

ALEC: Station refreshments are generally a wee bit arbitrary, you know.

LAURA: I wasn't grumbling.

ALEC (*smiling*): Do you ever grumble – are you ever sullen and cross and bad-tempered?

LAURA: Of course I am – at least not sullen exactly – but I sometimes get into rages.

ALEC: I can't visualise you in a rage.

LAURA: I really don't see why you should.

ALEC: Oh, I don't know – there are signs you know – one can usually tell —

LAURA: Long upper lips and jaw lines and eyes close together?

ALEC: You haven't any of those things.

LAURA: Do you feel guilty at all? I do.

ALEC (*smiling*): Guilty?

LAURA: You ought to more than me, really – you neglected your work this afternoon.

ALEC: I worked this morning – a little relaxation never did anyone any harm. Why should either of us feel guilty?

LAURA: I don't know – a sort of instinct – as though we were letting something happen that oughtn't to happen.

ALEC: How awfully nice you are!

LAURA: When I was a child in Cornwall – we lived in Cornwall, you know – May, that's my sister, and I used to climb out of our bedroom window on summer nights and go down to the cove and bathe. It was dreadfully cold but we felt very adventurous. I'd never have dared do it by myself, but sharing the danger made it all right – that's how I feel now, really.

ALEC: Have a bun – it's awfully bad for you.

LAURA: You're laughing at me!

ALEC: Yes, a little, but I'm laughing at myself, too.

LAURA: Why?

ALEC: For feeling a small pang when you said about being guilty.

LAURA: There you are, you see!

ALEC: We haven't done anything wrong.

LAURA: Of course we haven't.

ALEC: An accidental meeting – then another accidental meeting – then a little lunch – then the movies – what could be more ordinary? More natural?

LAURA: We're adults, after all.

ALEC: I never see myself as an adult, do you?

LAURA (*firmly*): Yes, I do. I'm a respectable married woman with a husband and a home and three children.

ALEC: But there must be a part of you, deep down inside, that doesn't feel like that at all – some little spirit that still wants to climb out of the window – that still longs to splash about a bit in the dangerous sea.

LAURA: Perhaps we none of us ever grow up entirely.

ALEC: How awfully nice you are!

LAURA: You said that before.

ALEC: I thought perhaps you hadn't heard.

LAURA: I heard all right.

195

ALEC (*gently*): I'm respectable too, you know. I have a home and a wife and children and responsibilities – I also have a lot of work to do and a lot of ideals all mixed up with it.

LAURA: What's she like?

ALEC: Madeleine?

LAURA: Yes.

ALEC: Small, dark, rather delicate —

LAURA: How funny! I should have thought she'd be fair.

ALEC: And your husband? What's he like?

LAURA: Medium height, brown hair, kindly, unemotional and not delicate at all.

ALEC: You said that proudly.

LAURA: Did I? (*She looks down.*)

ALEC: What's the matter?

LAURA: The matter? What could be the matter?

ALEC: You suddenly went away.

LAURA (*brightly*): I thought perhaps we were being rather silly.

ALEC: Why?

LAURA: Oh, I don't know – we are such complete strangers, really.

ALEC: It's one thing to close a window, but quite another to slam it down on my fingers.

LAURA: I'm sorry.

ALEC: Please come back again.

LAURA: Is tea bad for one? Worse than coffee, I mean?

ALEC: If this is a professional interview, my fee is a guinea.

LAURA (*laughing*): It's nearly time for your train.

ALEC: I hate to think of it, chugging along, interrupting our tea party.

LAURA: I really am sorry now.

ALEC: What for?

LAURA: For being disagreeable.

ALEC: I don't think you could be disagreeable.

LAURA: You said something just now about your work and ideals being mixed up with it – what ideals?

ALEC: That's a long story.

LAURA: I suppose all doctors ought to have ideals, really – otherwise I should think the work would be unbearable.

ALEC: Surely you're not encouraging me to talk shop?

LAURA: Do you come here every Thursday?

ALEC: Yes. I come in from Churley, and spend a day in the hospital. Stephen Lynn graduated with me – he's the chief physician here. I take over from him once a week, it gives him a chance to go up to London and me a chance to observe and study the hospital patients.

LAURA: Is that a great advantage?

ALEC: Of course. You see I have a special pigeon.

LAURA: What is it?

ALEC: Preventive medicine.

LAURA: Oh, I see.

ALEC (*laughing*): I'm afraid you don't.

LAURA: I was trying to be intelligent.

ALEC: Most good doctors, especially when they're young, have private dreams – that's the best part of them, sometimes though, those get over-professionalised and strangulated and – am I boring you?

LAURA: No – I don't quite understand – but you're not boring me.

ALEC: What I mean is this – all good doctors must be primarily enthusiasts. They must have, like writers and painters, and priests, a sense of vocation – a deep-rooted, unsentimental desire to do good.

LAURA: Yes – I see that.

ALEC: Well, obviously one way of preventing disease is worth fifty ways of curing it – that's where my ideal comes in – preventive medicine isn't anything to do with medicine at all, really – it's concerned with conditions, living conditions and common-sense and hygiene. For instance, my speciality is pneumoconiosis.

LAURA: Oh, dear!

ALEC: Don't be alarmed, it's simpler than it sounds – it's nothing but a slow process of fibrosis of the lung due to the inhalation of particles of dust. In the hospital here there are splendid opportunities for observing cures and making notes, because of the coal mines.

LAURA: You suddenly look much younger.

ALEC (*brought up short*): Do I?

LAURA: Almost like a little boy.

ALEC: What made you say that?

LAURA (*staring at him*): I don't know – yes, I do.

ALEC (*gently*): Tell me.

LAURA (*with panic in her voice*): Oh, no – I couldn't, really. You were saying about the coal mines —

ALEC (*looking into her eyes*): Yes – the inhalation of coal dust – that's one specific form of the disease – it's called Anthracosis.

LAURA (*hypnotised*): What are the others?

ALEC: Chalicosis – that comes from metal dust – steel works, you know —

LAURA: Yes, of course. Steel works.

ALEC: And Silicosis – stone dust – that's gold mines.

LAURA (*almost in a whisper*): I see.

> *There is the sound of a bell.*

There's your train.

ALEC (*looking down*): Yes.

LAURA: You mustn't miss it.

ALEC: No.

LAURA (*again the panic in her voice*): What's the matter?

ALEC (*with an effort*): Nothing – nothing at all.

LAURA (*socially*): It's been so very nice – I've enjoyed my afternoon enormously.

ALEC: I'm so glad – so have I. I apologise for boring you with those long medical words —

LAURA: I feel dull and stupid, not to be able to understand more.

ALEC: Shall I see you again?

> *There is the sound of a train approaching.*

LAURA: It's the other platform, isn't it? You'll have to run. Don't worry about me – mine's due in a few minutes.

ALEC: Shall I see you again?

LAURA: Of course – perhaps you could come over to Ketchworth one Sunday. It's rather far, I know, but we should be delighted to see you.

ALEC (*intensely*): Please – please —

> *The train is heard drawing to a standstill.*

LAURA: What is it?

ALEC: Next Thursday – the same time —

LAURA: No – I can't possibly – I —

ALEC: Please – I ask you most humbly —

LAURA: You'll miss your train!

ALEC: All right. (*He gets up.*)

LAURA: Run —

ALEC (*taking her hand*): Good-bye.

LAURA (*breathlessly*): I'll be there.

ALEC: Thank you, my dear.

> *He goes out at a run, colliding with* ALBERT GODBY, *who is on his way in.*

ALBERT: 'Ere – 'ere – take it easy now – take it easy — (*He goes over to the counter.*)

> LAURA *sits quite still staring in front of her as the lights fade.*

Scene III

It is now October. Three months have passed since the preceding scene.

The refreshment room is empty except for MYRTLE, *who is bending down putting coal into the stove.*

ALBERT GODBY *enters. Upon perceiving her slightly vulnerable position, he slaps her lightly on the behind – she springs to her feet.*

MYRTLE: Albert Godby, how dare you!

ALBERT: I couldn't resist it.

MYRTLE: I'll trouble you to keep your hands to yourself.

ALBERT: You're blushing – you look wonderful when you're angry, like an avenging angel.

MYRTLE: I'll give you avenging angel – coming in here taking liberties —

ALBERT: I didn't think after what you said last Monday you'd object to a friendly little slap.

MYRTLE: Never you mind about last Monday – I'm on duty now.

A nice thing if Mr Saunders had happened to be looking through the window.

ALBERT: If Mr Saunders is in the 'abit of looking through windows, it's time he saw something worth looking at.

MYRTLE: You ought to be ashamed of yourself!

ALBERT: It's just high spirits – don't be mad at me.

MYRTLE (*retiring behind the counter*): High spirits indeed!

ALBERT (*singing*):

'I'm twenty-one to-day – I'm twenty-one to-day,
I've got the key of the parlour door –
I've never been twenty-one before —'

MYRTLE (*retiring behind the counter*): Don't make such a noise – they'll hear you on the platform.

ALBERT (*singing*):

'Picture you upon my knee and tea for two and two for tea'.

MYRTLE: Now look here, Albert Godby, once and for all, will you behave yourself!

ALBERT (*singing*):

'Sometimes I'm 'appy – sometimes I'm blue-oo —'

(*He breaks off.*) This is one of my 'appy moments —

MYRTLE: Here, take your tea and be quiet.

ALBERT: It's all your fault, anyway.

MYRTLE: I don't know to what you're referring, I'm sure.

ALBERT: I was thinking of tonight —

MYRTLE: If you don't learn to behave yourself there won't be a tonight – or any other night, either —

ALBERT (*singing*):

'I'm in love again, and the spring is coming.
I'm in love again, hear my heart-strings humming —'

MYRTLE: Will you hold your noise?

ALBERT: Give us a kiss.

MYRTLE: I'll do no such thing.

ALBERT: Just a quick one – across the counter. (*He grabs her arm across the counter.*)

MYRTLE: Albert, stop it!

ALBERT: Come on – there's a love.

MYRTLE: Let go of me this minute.

ALBERT: Come on, just one.

> They scuffle for a moment, upsetting a neat pile of cakes on to the floor.

MYRTLE: Now look at me Banburys – all over the floor.

> ALBERT bends down to pick them up. STANLEY enters.

STANLEY: Just in time – or born in the vestry.

MYRTLE: You shut your mouth and help Mr Godby pick up them cakes.

STANLEY: Anything to oblige. (*He helps* ALBERT.)

> ALEC and LAURA come in. LAURA goes to their usual table. ALEC goes to the counter.

ALEC: Good afternoon.

MYRTLE (*grandly*): Good afternoon.

ALEC: Two teas, please.

MYRTLE: Cake or pastry?

ALEC: No, thank you – just the tea.

ALBERT (*conversationally*): Nice weather.

ALEC: Very nice.

ALBERT: Bit of a nip in the air, though.

> MYRTLE, having given ALEC two cups of tea, and taken the money for it, turns to STANLEY.

MYRTLE: What are you standing there gaping at?

STANLEY: Where's Beryl?

MYRTLE: Never you mind about Beryl, you ought to be on Number 4, and well you know it.

ALBERT (*reflectively*): Love's young dream!

> ALEC, meanwhile, has carried the two cups of tea over to the table and sat down.

STANLEY: There's been a run on the Cardbury's nut milk this afternoon; I shall need some more.

MYRTLE (*looking at his tray*): How many have you got left?

STANLEY: Only three.

MYRTLE: Take six more then, and don't forget to mark 'em down.

STANLEY: Righto.

> STANLEY *goes behind the counter and collects six packets of chocolate, then he goes out whistling.*

ALEC: I didn't mean to be unkind.

LAURA: It doesn't matter.

> *A* YOUNG MAN *comes in and goes to the counter.*

YOUNG MAN: Cup of coffee, please, and a beef sandwich.

MYRTLE: We're out of beef – will ham do?

YOUNG MAN: Yes – ham'll do.

> ALBERT *winks at* MYRTLE *over his tea-cup.* MYRTLE *draws a cup of coffee for the* YOUNG MAN *and takes a sandwich out of one of the glass stands.*

ALEC: We can't part like this.

LAURA: I think it would be better if we did.

ALEC: You don't really mean that?

LAURA: I'm trying to mean it – I'm trying with all my strength.

ALEC: Oh, my dearest dear —

LAURA: Don't – please don't —

MYRTLE (*to* YOUNG MAN): Fourpence, please.

YOUNG MAN: Thank you. (*He pays, and carries his coffee and sandwich over to the table near the stove.*)

ALBERT: It is all right about tonight, isn't it?

MYRTLE: I'll think about it.

ALBERT: It's Claudette Colbert, you know.

MYRTLE: Fat chance I shall get of enjoying Claudette Colbert with you hissing in me ear all the time.

ALBERT: I'll be as good as gold.

> BERYL *enters in a coat and hat – she goes behind the counter.*

ALEC: It's no use running away from the truth, darling – we're lovers, aren't we? If it happens or if it doesn't, we're lovers in our hearts.

LAURA: Can't you see how wrong it is? How dreadfully wrong!

ALEC: I can see what's true – whether it's wrong or right.

BERYL (*taking off her hat and coat*): Mr Saunders wants you, Mr Godby.

ALBERT: What for?

BERYL: I don't know.

MYRTLE: You'd better go, Albert, you know what he is.

ALBERT: I know 'e's a bloody fool, if that's what you mean.

MYRTLE: Be quiet, Albert – in front of Beryl.

BERYL: Don't mind me.

MYRTLE: Go on – finish up your tea.

ALBERT: No peace for the wicked —

MYRTLE: Go on —

ALBERT: I'll be back —

MYRTLE: That'll be nice, I'm sure —

> ALBERT *goes.*
>
> MYRTLE *retires to the upper end of the counter.* BERYL *goes off and comes on again laden with various packages of comestibles. She and* MYRTLE *proceed to stack them on the upstage end of the counter.*

ALEC (*urgently*): There's no chance of Stephen getting back until late – nobody need ever know.

LAURA: It's so furtive to love like that – so cheap – much better not to love at all.

ALEC: It's too late not to love at all – be brave – we're both in the same boat – let's be generous to each other.

LAURA: What is there brave in it – sneaking away to someone else's house, loving in secret with the horror of being found out hanging over us all the time. It would be far braver to say good-bye and never see each other again.

ALEC: Could you be as brave as that? I know I couldn't.

LAURA (*breathlessly*): Couldn't you?

ALEC: Listen, my dear. This is something that's never happened to either of us before. We've loved before and been happy before, and miserable and contented and reckless, but this is different – something lovely and strange and desperately difficult. We can't measure it along with the values of our ordinary lives.

LAURA: Why should it be so important – why should we let it be so important?

ALEC: We can't help ourselves.

LAURA: We can – we can if only we're strong enough.

ALEC: Why is it so strong to deny something that's urgent and real – something that all our instincts are straining after – mightn't it be weak and not strong at all to run away from such tremendous longing?

LAURA: Is it so real to you? So tremendous?

ALEC: Can't you see that it is.

LAURA: It's so difficult, so strained. I'm lost.

ALEC: Don't say that, darling.

LAURA: Loving you is hard for me – it makes me a stranger in my own house. Familiar things, ordinary things that I've known for years like the dining-room curtains, and the wooden tub with a silver top that holds biscuits and a water-colour of San Remo that my mother painted, look odd to me, as though they belonged to someone else – when I've just left you, when I go home, I'm more lonely than I've ever been before. I passed the house the other day without noticing and had to turn back, and when I went in it seemed to draw away from me – my whole life seems to be drawing away from me, and – and I don't know what to do.

ALEC: Oh, darling —

LAURA: I love them just the same, Fred I mean and the children, but it's as though it wasn't me at all – as though I were looking on at someone else. Do you know what I mean? Is it the same with you? Or is it easier for men —

ALEC: I don't know.

LAURA: Please, dear, don't look unhappy. I'm not grumbling, really I'm not —

ALEC: I don't suppose being in love has ever been easy for anybody.

LAURA (*reaching for his hand*): We've only got a few more minutes – I didn't mean to be depressing.

ALEC: It isn't any easier for me, darling, honestly it isn't.

LAURA: I know, I know – I only wanted reassuring.

ALEC: I hold you in my arms all the way back in the train – I'm angry with every moment that I'm not alone – to love you uninterrupted – whenever my surgery door opens and a patient comes in, my heart jumps in case it might be you. One of them I'm grateful to – he's got neuritis, and I give him sun-

ray treatment – he lies quite quietly baking, and I can be with
  you in the shadows behind the lamp.
LAURA: How silly we are – how unbearably silly!
ALEC: Friday – Saturday – Sunday – Monday – Tuesday –
  Wednesday —
LAURA: Thursday —
ALEC: It's all right, isn't it?
LAURA: Oh, yes – of course it is.
ALEC: Don't pass the house again – don't let it snub you. Go
  boldly in and stare that damned water-colour out of counte-
  nance.
LAURA: All right – don't bake your poor neuritis man too long –
  you might blister him.

> *The continuation of their scene is drowned by the noisy entrance of
> two soldiers,* BILL *and* JOHNNIE. *They go to the counter.*

BILL: Afternoon, lady.
MYRTLE (*grandly*): Good afternoon.
BILL: A couple of splashes, please.
MYRTLE: Very sorry, it's out of hours.
JOHNNIE: Come on, lady – you've got a kind face.
MYRTLE: That's neither here nor there.
BILL: Just sneak us a couple under cover of them poor old
  sandwiches.
MYRTLE: Them sandwiches were fresh this morning, and I shall
  do no such thing.
BILL: Come on, be a sport.
JOHNNIE: Nobody'd know.
MYRTLE: I'm very sorry, I'm sure, but it's against the rules.
BILL: You could pop it into a couple of tea-cups.
MYRTLE: You're asking me to break the law, young man.
JOHNNIE: I think I've got a cold coming on – we've been
  mucking about at the Butts all day – you can't afford to let the
  army catch cold, you know.
MYRTLE: You can have as much as you want after six o'clock.
BILL: An 'eart of stone – that's what you've got, lady – an 'eart of
  stone.
MYRTLE: Don't you be cheeky.

JOHNNIE: My throat's like a parrot's cage – listen! (*He makes a crackling noise with his throat.*)

MYRTLE: Take some lemonade then – or ginger-beer.

BILL: Couldn't touch it – against doctor's orders – my inside's been most peculiar ever since I 'ad trench feet – you wouldn't give a child carbolic acid, would you? That's what ginger-beer does to me.

MYRTLE: Get on with you!

JOHNNIE: It's true – it's poison to him, makes 'im make the most 'orrible noises – you wouldn't like anything nasty to 'appen in your posh buffay —

MYRTLE: May licence does not permit me to serve alcohol out of hours – that's final!

JOHNNIE: We're soldiers we are – willing to lay down our lives for you – and you grudge us one splash —

MYRTLE: You wouldn't want to get me into trouble, would you?

BILL: Give us a chance, lady, that's all – just give us a chance.

    They both roar with laughter.

MYRTLE: Beryl, ask Mr Godby to come 'ere for a moment, will you?

BERYL: Yes, Mrs Bagot.

    She comes out from behind the counter and goes on to the platform.

BILL: Who's 'e when 'e's at home?

MYRTLE: You'll soon see – coming in here cheeking me.

JOHNNIE: Now then, now then, naughty naughty —

MYRTLE: Kaindly be quiet!

BILL: Shut up, Johnnie —

JOHNNIE: What about them drinks, lady?

MYRTLE: I've already told you I can't serve alcoholic refreshment out of hours —

JOHNNIE: Come off it, mother, be a pal!

MYRTLE (*losing her temper*): I'll give you mother, you saucy upstart —

BILL: Who are you calling an upstart!

MYRTLE: You – and I'll trouble you to get out of here double quick – disturbing the customers and making a nuisance of yourselves.

JOHNNIE: 'Ere, where's the fire – where's the fire!

ALBERT GODBY *enters, followed by* BERYL.

ALBERT: What's going on in 'ere!

MYRTLE (*with dignity*): Mr Godby, these gentlemen are annoying me.

BILL: We 'aven't done anything.

JOHNNIE: All we did was ask for a couple of drinks —

MYRTLE: They insulted me, Mr Godby.

JOHNNIE: We never did nothing of the sort – just 'aving a little joke, that's all.

ALBERT (*laconically*): 'Op it – both of you.

BILL: We've got a right to stay 'ere as long as we like.

ALBERT: You 'eard what I said – 'Op it!

JOHNNIE: What is this, a free country or a bloody Sunday school?

ALBERT (*firmly*): I checked your passes at the gate – your train's due in a minute – Number 2 platform — 'Op it.

JOHNNIE: Look 'ere now —

BILL: Come on, Johnnie – don't argue with the poor little basket.

ALBERT (*dangerously*): 'Op it!

BILL *and* JOHNNIE *go to the door.* JOHNNIE *turns.*

JOHNNIE: Toodle-oo, mother, and if them sandwiches were made this morning, you're Shirley Temple —

They go out.

MYRTLE: Thank you, Albert.

BERYL: What a nerve talking to you like that!

MYRTLE: Be quiet, Beryl – pour me out a nip of Three Star – I'm feeling quite upset.

ALBERT: I've got to get back to the gate.

MYRTLE (*graciously*): I'll be seeing you later, Albert.

ALBERT (*with a wink*): Okay!

He goes out.

A train bell rings. BERYL *brings* MYRTLE *a glass of brandy.*

MYRTLE (*sipping it*): I'll say one thing for Albert Godby – he may be on the small side, but 'e's a gentleman.

She and BERYL *retire once more to the upper end of the counter and continue their arrangement of bottles, biscuits, etc. There is the sound of a train drawing into the station.*

LAURA: There's your train.

ALEC: I'm going to miss it.

LAURA: Please go.

ALEC: No.

LAURA (*clasping and unclasping her hands*): I wish I could think clearly. I wish I could know – really know what to do.

ALEC: Do you trust me?

LAURA: Yes – I trust you.

ALEC: I don't mean conventionally – I mean really.

LAURA: Yes.

ALEC: Everything's against us – all the circumstances of our lives – those have got to go on unaltered. We're nice people, you and I, and we've got to go on being nice. Let's enclose this love of ours with real strength, and let that strength be that no one is hurt by it except ourselves.

LAURA: Must we be hurt by it?

ALEC: Yes – when the time comes.

LAURA: Very well.

ALEC: All the futiveness and the secrecy and the hole-in-corner cheapness can be justified if only we're strong enough – strong enough to keep it to ourselves, clean and untouched by anybody else's knowledge or even suspicions – something of our own for ever – to be remembered —

LAURA: Very well.

ALEC: We won't speak of it any more – I'm going now – back to Stephen's flat. I'll wait for you – if you don't come I shall know only that you weren't quite ready – that you needed a little longer to find your own dear heart. This is the address.

He scribbles on a bit of paper as the express thunders through the station. He gets up and goes swiftly without looking at her again. She sits staring at the paper, then she fumbles in her bag and finds a cigarette. She lights it – the platform bell goes.

MYRTLE: There's the 5.43.

BERYL: We ought to have another Huntley and Palmer's to put in the middle, really.

MYRTLE: There are some more on the shelf.

BERYL fetches another packet of biscuits and takes it to MYRTLE. There is the noise of the 5.43 – LAURA's train – steaming into the

station. LAURA *sits puffing her cigarette. Suddenly she gets up –*
gathers up her bag quickly, and moves towards the door. She pauses
and comes back to the table as the whistle blows. The train starts, she
puts the paper in her bag and goes quietly out as the lights fade.

Scene IV

The time is about 9.45 on an evening in December.
    There are only two lights on in the refreshment room as it is
nearly closing time.
    When the scene starts the stage is empty. There is the noise of a
fast train rattling through the station.
    BERYL *comes in from the upstage door behind the counter armed*
with several muslin cloths which she proceeds to drape over the
things on the counter. She hums breathily to herself as she does so.
STANLEY *enters, he has discarded his uniform and is wearing his*
ordinary clothes.

STANLEY: Hallo!
BERYL: You made me jump.
STANLEY: Are you walking home?
BERYL: Maybe.
STANLEY: Do you want me to wait?
BERYL: I've got to go straight back.
STANLEY: Why?
BERYL: Mother'll be waiting up.
STANLEY: Can't you say you've been kept late?
BERYL: I said that last time.
STANLEY: Say it again – say there's been a rush on.
BERYL: Don't be so silly – Mother's not that much of a fool.
STANLEY: Be a sport, Beryl – shut down five minutes early and
    say you was kept ten minutes late – that gives us a quarter of
    an hour.
BERYL: What happens if Mrs Bagot comes back?
STANLEY: She won't – she's out having a bit of a slap and tickle
    with our Albert.

BERYL: Stan, you are awful!

STANLEY: I'll wait for you in the yard.

BERYL: Oh, all right.

> STANLEY *goes out.*
>> BERYL *resumes her song and the draping of the cake stands.*
> LAURA *enters – she looks pale and unhappy.*

LAURA: I'd like a glass of brandy, please.

BERYL: We're just closing.

LAURA: I see you are, but you're not quite closed yet, are you?

BERYL (*sullenly*): Three Star?

LAURA: Yes, that'll do.

BERYL (*getting it*): Tenpence, please.

LAURA (*taking money from her bag*): Here – and – have you a piece of paper and an envelope?

BERYL: I'm afraid you'll have to get that at the bookstall.

LAURA: The bookstall's shut – please – it's very important – I should be so much obliged —

BERYL: Oh, all right – wait a minute.

> *She goes off.*
>> LAURA *sips the brandy at the counter, she is obviously trying to control her nerves.* BERYL *returns with some notepaper and an envelope.*

LAURA: Thank you so much.

BERYL: We close in a few minutes, you know.

LAURA: Yes, I know.

> *She takes the notepaper and her brandy over to the table by the door and sits down. She stares at the paper for a moment, takes another sip of brandy and then begins to write.* BERYL *looks at her with exasperation and goes off through the upstage door.* LAURA *falters in her writing, then breaks down and buries her face in her hands.* ALEC *comes in – he looks hopelessly round for a moment, and then sees her.*

ALEC: Thank God – oh, darling!

LAURA: Please go away – please don't say anything.

ALEC: I can't let you go like this.

LAURA: You must. It'll be better – really it will.

ALEC (*sitting down beside her*): You're being dreadfully cruel.

LAURA: I feel so utterly degraded.

ALEC: It was just a beastly accident that he came back early – he doesn't know who you are – he never even saw you.

LAURA: I listened to your voices in the sitting-room – I crept out and down the stairs – feeling like a prostitute.

ALEC: Don't, dearest – don't talk like that, please —

LAURA (*bitterly*): I suppose he laughed, didn't he – after he got over being annoyed? I suppose you spoke of me together as men of the world.

ALEC: We didn't speak of you – we spoke of a nameless creature who had no reality at all.

LAURA (*wildly*): Why didn't you tell him the truth? Why didn't you say who I was and that we were lovers – shameful secret lovers – using his flat like a bad house because we had nowhere else to go, and were afraid of being found out! Why didn't you tell him we were cheap and low and without courage – why didn't you —

ALEC: Stop it, Laura – pull yourself together!

LAURA: It's true – don't you see, it's true!

ALEC: It's nothing of the sort. I know you feel horrible, and I'm deeply, desperately sorry. I feel horrible, too, but it doesn't matter really – this – this unfortunate, damnable incident – it was just bad luck. It couldn't affect us really, you and me – we know the truth – we know we really love each other – that's all that matters.

LAURA: It isn't all that matters – other things matter, too, self-respect matters, and decency – I can't go on any longer.

ALEC: Could you really – say good-bye – not see me any more?

LAURA: Yes – if you'd help me.

> There is silence for a moment. ALEC gets up and walks about – he stops and stands staring at a coloured calendar on the wall.

ALEC (*quietly, with his back to her*): I love you, Laura – I shall love you always until the end of my life – all the shame that the world might force on us couldn't touch the real truth of it. I can't look at you now because I know something – I know that this is the beginning of the end – not the end of my loving you – but the end of our being together. But not quite yet, darling – please not quite yet.

LAURA: Very well – not quite yet.

ALEC: I know what you feel – about this evening, I mean – about the beastliness of it. I know about the strain of our different lives, our lives apart from each other. The feeling of guilt – of doing wrong is a little too strong, isn't it? Too persistent – perhaps too great a price to pay for the few hours of happiness we get out of it. I know all this because it's the same for me, too.

LAURA: You can look at me now – I'm all right.

ALEC (*turning*): Let's be careful – let's prepare ourselves – a sudden break now, however brave and admirable, would be too cruel – we can't do such violence to our hearts and minds.

LAURA: Very well.

ALEC: I'm going away.

LAURA: I see.

ALEC: But not quite yet.

LAURA: Please not quite yet.

> BERYL *enters in hat and coat.*

BERYL: I'm afraid it's closing time.

ALEC: Oh, is it?

BERYL: I shall have to lock up.

ALEC: This lady is catching the 10.10 – she's not feeling very well, and it's very cold on the platform.

BERYL: The waiting-room's open.

ALEC (*going to counter*): Look here – I'd be very much obliged if you'd let us stay here for another few minutes.

BERYL: I'm sorry – it's against the rules.

ALEC (*giving her a ten-shilling note*): Please – come back to lock up when the train comes in.

BERYL: I'll have to switch off the lights – someone might see 'em on and think we were open.

ALEC: Just for a few minutes – please!

BERYL: You won't touch anything, will you?

ALEC: Not a thing.

BERYL: Oh, all right.

> *She switches off the lights. The lamp from the platform shines in through the window so it isn't quite dark.*

ALEC: Thank you very much.

BERYL *goes out by the platform door, closing it behind her.*

LAURA: Just a few minutes.

ALEC: Let's have a cigarette, shall we?

LAURA: I have some. (*She takes her bag up from the table.*)

ALEC (*producing his case*): No, here. (*He lights their cigarettes carefully.*) Now then – I want you to promise me something.

LAURA: What is it?

ALEC: Promise me that however unhappy you are, and however much you think things over that you'll meet me next Thursday as usual.

LAURA: Not at the flat.

ALEC: No – be at the Picture House café at the same time. I'll hire a car – we'll drive out into the country.

LAURA: All right – I promise.

ALEC: We've got to talk – I've got to explain.

LAURA: About going away?

ALEC: Yes.

LAURA: Where are you going? Where can you go? You can't give up your practice!

ALEC: I've had a job offered me – I wasn't going to tell you – I wasn't going to take it – but I must – I know now, it's the only way out.

LAURA: Where?

ALEC: A long way away – Johannesburg.

LAURA (*hopelessly*): Oh God!

ALEC (*hurriedly*): My brother's out there – they're opening a new hospital – they want me in it. It's a fine opportunity, really. I'll take Madeleine and the boys, it's been torturing me for three weeks, the necessity of making a decision one way or the other – I haven't told anybody, not even Madeleine. I couldn't bear the idea of leaving you, but now I see – it's got to happen soon, anyway – it's almost happening already.

LAURA (*tonelessly*): When will you go?

ALEC: In about two months' time.

LAURA: It's quite near, isn't it?

ALEC: Do you want me to stay? Do you want me to turn down the offer?

LAURA: Don't be foolish, Alec.

ALEC: I'll do whatever you say.

LAURA: That's unkind of you, my darling. (*She suddenly buries her head in her arms and bursts into tears.*)

ALEC (*putting his arms round her*): Oh, Laura, don't, please don't!

LAURA: I'll be all right – leave me alone a minute.

ALEC: I love you – I love you.

LAURA: I know.

ALEC: We knew we'd get hurt.

LAURA (*sitting up*): I'm being very stupid.

ALEC (*giving her his handkerchief*): Here.

LAURA (*blowing her nose*): Thank you.

> *The platform bells goes.*

There's my train.

ALEC: You're not angry with me, are you?

LAURA: No, I'm not angry – I don't think I'm anything, really – I feel just tired.

ALEC: Forgive me.

LAURA: Forgive you for what?

ALEC: For everything – for having met you in the first place – for taking the piece of grit out of your eye – for loving you – for bringing you so much misery.

LAURA (*trying to smile*): I'll forgive you – if you'll forgive me —

> *There is the noise of a train pulling into the station.* BERYL *enters.* LAURA *and* ALEC *get up.*

ALEC: I'll see you into the train.

LAURA: No – please stay here.

ALEC: All right.

LAURA (*softly*): Good-night, darling.

ALEC: Good-night, darling.

> *She goes hurriedly out on to the platform without looking back.*

ALEC: The last train for Churley hasn't gone yet, has it?

BERYL: I couldn't say, I'm sure.

ALEC: I'll wait in the waiting-room – thank you very much.

BERYL: I must lock up now.

ALEC: All right. Good-night.

BERYL: Good-night.

The train starts as he goes out on to the platform. BERYL *locks the door carefully after him, and then goes off upstage as the lights fade.*

Scene V

The time is between 5 and 5.30 on an afternoon in March. MYRTLE *is behind the counter.* BERYL *is crouching over the stove putting coals in it.* ALBERT *enters.*

ALBERT (*gaily*): One tea, please – two lumps of sugar, and a bath bun, and make it snappy.

MYRTLE: What's the matter with you?

ALBERT: Beryl, 'op it.

MYRTLE: Don't you go ordering Beryl about – you haven't any right to.

ALBERT: You heard me, Beryl – 'Op it.

BERYL (*giggling*): Well, I never!

MYRTLE: Go into the back room a minute, Beryl.

BERYL: Yes, Mrs Bagot.

    She goes.

MYRTLE: Now then, Albert – you behave – we don't want the whole station laughing at us.

ALBERT: What is there to laugh at?

MYRTLE: Here's your tea.

ALBERT: How d'you feel?

MYRTLE: Don't talk so soft – how should I feel?

ALBERT: I only wondered — (*He leans towards her.*)

MYRTLE: Look out – somebody's coming in.

ALBERT: It's only Romeo and Juliet.

    LAURA *and* ALEC *come in.* LAURA *goes to the table,* ALEC *to the counter.*

ALEC: Good afternoon.

MYRTLE: Good afternoon – same as usual?

ALEC: Yes, please.

MYRTLE (*drawing tea*): Quite Springy out, isn' it?

ALEC: Yes – quite.

> *He pays her, collects the tea and carries it over to the table – something in his manner causes* ALBERT *to make a grimace over his tea-cup at* MYRTLE. ALEC *sits down at the table, and he and* LAURA *sip their tea in silence.*

ALBERT: I spoke to Mr Saunders.

MYRTLE: What did he say?

ALBERT: 'E was very decent as a matter-of-fact – said it'd be all right —

> MILDRED *comes in hurriedly. She is a fair girl wearing a station overall.*

MILDRED: Is Beryl here?

MYRTLE: Why, Mildred, whatever's the matter?

MILDRED: It's her mother – she's bad again – they telephoned through to the Booking Office.

MYRTLE: She's inside – you'd better go in. Don't go yelling in at her now – tell her gently.

MILDRED: They said she'd better come at once.

MYRTLE: I thought this was going to happen – stay here, Mildred. I'll tell her. Wait a minute, Albert.

> MYRTLE *vanishes into the inside room.*

ALBERT: Better get back to the bookstall, hadn't you?

MILDRED: Do you think she's going to die?

ALBERT: How do I know?

MILDRED: Mr Saunders thinks she is – judging by what the doctor said on the telephone.

ALBERT: 'Ow do you know it was the doctor?

MILDRED: Mr Saunders said it was.

ALBERT: She's always being took bad, that old woman.

MILDRED: Do you think Beryl would like me to go along with her?

ALBERT: You can't, and leave nobody on the papers.

MILDRED: Mr Saunders said I might if it was necessary.

ALBERT: Well, go and get your 'at then, and don't make such a fuss.

> MYRTLE *comes back.*

MYRTLE: She's going at once, poor little thing!

ALBERT: Mildred's going with her.

MYRTLE: All right, Mildred – go on.

MILDRED (*half-way to the door*): What about me 'at?

MYRTLE: Never mind about your 'at – go this way.

>   MILDRED *rushes off upstage.*

MYRTLE: Poor child – this has been hanging over her for weeks. (*She puts her head round the door.*) Mildred, tell Beryl she needn't come back tonight, I'll stay on.

ALBERT: 'Ere, you can't do that, we was going to the Broadway Melody of 1936.

MYRTLE: For shame, Albert – thinking of the Broadway Melody of 1936 in a moment of life and death!

ALBERT: But look 'ere, Myrtle —

MYRTLE: I dreamt of a hearse last night, and whenever I dream of a hearse something happens – you mark my words —

ALBERT: I've got reserved tickets —

MYRTLE: Send Stanley to change them on his way home. Come in 'ere when you go off and I'll make you a little supper inside.

ALBERT (*grumpily*): Everybody getting into a state and fussing about —

MYRTLE: You shock me, Albert, you do really – go on, finish up your tea and get back to the gate. (*She turns and goes to the upper end of the counter.*)

>   ALBERT *gulps his tea.*

ALBERT (*slamming the cup down on the counter*): Women!

>   *He stamps out on to the platform.*

ALEC: Are you all right, darling?

LAURA: Yes, I'm all right.

ALEC: I wish I could think of something to say.

LAURA: It doesn't matter – not saying anything, I mean.

ALEC: I'll miss my train and wait to see you into yours.

LAURA: No – no – please don't. I'll come over to your platform with you – I'd rather.

ALEC: Very well.

LAURA: Do you think we shall ever see each other again?

ALEC: I don't know. (*His voice breaks.*) Not for years, anyway.

LAURA: The children will all be grown up – I wonder if they'll ever meet and know each other.

ALEC: Couldn't I write to you – just once in a while?

LAURA: No – please not – we promised we wouldn't.

ALEC: Please know this – please know that you'll be with me for ages and ages yet – far away into the future. Time will wear down the agony of not seeing you, bit by bit the pain will go – but the loving you and the memory of you won't ever go – please know that.

LAURA: I know it.

ALEC: It's easier for me than for you. I do realise that, really I do. I at least will have different shapes to look at, and new work to do – you have to go on among familiar things – my heart aches for you so.

LAURA: I'll be all right.

ALEC: I love you with all my heart and soul.

LAURA (*quietly*): I want to die – if only I could die.

ALEC: If you died you'd forget me – I want to be remembered.

LAURA: Yes, I know – I do, too.

ALEC: Good-bye, my dearest love.

LAURA: Good-bye, my dearest love.

ALEC: We've still got a few minutes.

LAURA: Thank God —!

> DOLLY MESSITER *bustles into the refreshment room. She is a nicely dressed woman, with rather a fussy manner. She is laden with parcels. She sees* LAURA.

DOLLY: Laura! What a lovely surprise!

LAURA (*dazed*): Oh, Dolly!

DOLLY: My dear, I've been shopping till I'm dropping – that sounds like a song, doesn't it? My feet are nearly falling off, and my throat's parched. I thought of having tea in Spindle's, but I was terrified of losing the train. I'm always missing trains, and being late for meals, and Bob gets disagreeable for days at a time. Oh, dear — (*She flops down at their table.*)

LAURA: This is Doctor Harvey.

ALEC (*rising*): How do you do!

DOLLY (*shaking hands*): How do you do! Would you be a perfect dear and get me a cup of tea! I don't think I could drag my poor old bones as far as the counter. I must get some chocolates for Tony, too, but I can do that afterwards – here's sixpence —

ALEC (*waving it away*): No, please —

> *He goes drearily over to the counter, gets another cup of tea from* MYRTLE, *pays for it and comes back to the table, meanwhile* DOLLY *continues to talk.*

DOLLY: My dear – what a nice-looking man. Who on earth is he? Really, you're quite a dark horse. I shall telephone Fred in the morning and make mischief – that is a bit of luck. I haven't seen you for ages, and I've been meaning to pop in, but Tony's had measles, you know, and I had all that awful fuss about Phyllis – but of course you don't know – she left me! Suddenly upped and went, my dear, without even an hour's warning, let alone a month's notice.

LAURA (*with an effort*): Oh, how dreadful!

DOLLY: Mind you, I never cared for her much, but still Tony did. Tony adored her, and – but, never mind, I'll tell you all about that in the train.

> ALEC *arrives back at the table with her tea – he sits down again.*

Thank you so very much. They've certainly put enough milk in it – but still it's wet and that's all one can really ask for in a refreshment room — (*She sips it.*) Oh, dear – no sugar.

ALEC: It's in the spoon.

DOLLY: Oh, of course – what a fool I am – Laura, you look frightfully well. I do wish I'd known you were coming in to-day, we could have come together and lunched and had a good gossip. I loathe shopping by myself, anyway.

> *There is the sound of a bell on the platform.*

LAURA: There's your train.

ALEC: Yes, I know.

DOLLY: Aren't you coming with us?

ALEC: No, I go in the opposite direction. My practice is in Churley.

DOLLY: How interesting! What sort of a doctor are you? I mean, are you a specialist at anything or just a sort of general family doctor?

ALEC: I'm a general practitioner at the moment.

LAURA (*dully*): Dr Harvey is going out to Africa next week.

DOLLY: But, my dear, how thrilling! Are you going to operate on the Zulus or something? I always associate Africa with Zulus, but I may be quite wrong.

> *There is the sound of* ALEC'S *train approaching.*

ALEC: I must go.

LAURA: Yes, you must.

ALEC: Good-bye.

DOLLY: Good-bye.

> *He shakes hands with* DOLLY, *looks at* LAURA *swiftly once, then presses her hand under cover of the table and leaves hurriedly as the train is heard rumbling into the station.* LAURA *sits quite still.*

DOLLY: He'll have to run – he's got to get right over to the other platform. How did you meet him?

LAURA: I got something in my eye one day, and he took it out.

DOLLY: My dear – how very romantic! I'm always getting things in my eye and nobody the least bit attractive has ever paid the faintest attention – which reminds me – you know about Harry and Lucy Jenner, don't you?

LAURA (*listening for the train to start*): No – what about them?

DOLLY: My dear – they're going to get a divorce – at least I believe they're getting a conjugal separation, or whatever it is to begin with, and the divorce later on.

> *The train starts, and the sound of it dies gradually away in the distance.*

It seems that there's an awful Mrs Something or other in London that he's been carrying on with for ages – you know how he was always having to go up on business. Well, apparently Lucy's sister saw them, Harry and this woman, in the Tate Gallery of all places, and she wrote to Lucy, and then gradually the whole thing came out.

> *There is the sound of a bell on the platform.*

Is that our train? (*She addresses* MYRTLE.) Can you tell me, is that the Ketchworth train?

MYRTLE: No, that's the express.

LAURA: The boat train.

DOLLY: Oh, yes – that doesn't stop, does it? Express trains are Tony's passion in life – he knows them all by name – where they start from and where they go to, and how long they take to get there. Oh, dear, I mustn't forget his chocolate. (*She jumps up and goes to the counter.*)

>   LAURA *remains quite still.*

(*At counter.*) I want some chocolate, please.

MYRTLE: Milk or plain?

DOLLY: Plain, I think – or no, perhaps milk would be nicer. Have you any with nuts in it?

>   *The express is heard in the distance.*

MYRTLE: Nestlé's nut milk – shilling or sixpence?

DOLLY: Give me one plain and one nut milk.

>   *The noise of the express sounds louder –* LAURA *suddenly gets up and goes swiftly out on to the platform. The express roars through the station as* DOLLY *finishes buying and paying for her chocolate. She turns.*

DOLLY: Oh! where is she?

MYRTLE (*looking over the counter*): I never noticed her go.

>   DOLLY *comes over to the table,* LAURA *comes in again, looking very white and shaky.*

DOLLY: My dear, I couldn't think where you'd disappeared to.

LAURA: I just wanted to see the express go through.

DOLLY: What on earth's the matter – do you feel ill?

LAURA: I feel a little sick.

DOLLY: Have you any brandy?

MYRTLE: I'm afraid it's out of hours.

DOLLY: Surely – if someone's feeling ill —

LAURA: I'm all right, really.

>   *The platform bell goes.*

That's our train.

DOLLY: Just a sip of brandy will buck you up. (*To* MYRTLE.) Please —

MYRTLE: Very well. (*She pours out some brandy.*)

DOLLY: How much?

MYRTLE: Tenpence, please.

DOLLY (*paying her*): There!

She takes the brandy over to LAURA, *who has sat down again at the table.*

Here you are, dear.

LAURA (*taking it*): Thank you.

As she sips it the train is heard coming into the station. DOLLY *proceeds to gather up her parcels as the Curtain falls.*

FAMILY ALBUM

A Victorian Comedy with Music

Family Album was produced in London at the Phoenix Theatre on 9 January 1936, with the following cast:

JASPER FEATHERWAYS	Mr. Noël Coward
JANE, *his wife*	Miss Gertrude Lawrence
LAVINIA FEATHERWAYS	Miss Alison Leggatt
RICHARD FEATHERWAYS	Mr. Edward Underdown
HARRIET WINTER	Miss Everley Gregg
CHARLES WINTER	Mr. Anthony Pelissier
EMILY VALANCE	Miss Moya Nugent
EDWARD VALANCE	Mr. Kenneth Carten
BURROWS	Mr. Alan Webb

———

The action of the play passes in the drawing-room of the Featherways' house in Kent on an Autumn evening in the year 1860.

The scene is the drawing-room of the FEATHERWAYS' *house in Kent not very far from London.*

It is an Autumn evening in the year 1860.

When the curtain rises the entire family is assembled. They are all in deep mourning. The music plays softly; an undercurrent to grief. The family group would be static were it not for an occasional slight movement from one or other of them. Apart from the music there is silence for quite a while. EMILY, *who is by the window, breaks it.*

EMILY: It has stopped raining.

RICHARD (*moving to the window*): Not quite, Emily, but it is certainly clearing.

LAVINIA: It was fitting that it rained to-day. It has been a sad day and rain became it.

JASPER: True, very true.

JANE: A little sunshine would have been much pleasanter nevertheless.

JASPER: Lavinia has a tidy mind. She likes life to be as neat as her handkerchief drawer.

HARRIET: I hope Mr. Lubbock reached London safely.

JANE: Dear Mr. Lubbock.

LAVINIA: Really Jane!

JANE: I think he's a sweet man. He read the will with such sympathy.

HARRIET: He coughed a great deal, I thought. I wanted to give him one of my pastilles.

CHARLES: I'm glad you didn't, my dear, they have an alarming flavour and he was already considerably nervous.

HARRIET: They're very efficacious.

EMILY (*pensively – at the window*): I wonder if he knew.

EDWARD: What was that, my love?

EMILY: Papa – I wonder if he knew it was raining?

LAVINIA: Perhaps he was watching – from somewhere above the trees.

HARRIET: Oh! Do you suppose he was!

LAVINIA: I like to think it.

JANE: Do you, Lavinia?

LAVINIA: Of course.

JANE: When I die I hope I shall go swiftly and not linger above familiar trees. It must be painful to watch those you have left, in black and weeping.

EMILY: Oh, don't, Jane, don't! (*She weeps.*)

EDWARD (*comforting her*): There, there, my dear.

HARRIET: Poor Papa.

EMILY: Poor dear Papa.

> *The door opens quietly and* BURROWS, *a very aged butler, enters staggering under the weight of a heavy tray on which is a decanter containing Madeira, and the requisite number of glasses.*
> RICHARD *goes quickly and relieves him of it.*

RICHARD: Oh, Burrows, you should have let Martin carry the tray, it's too heavy for you.

BURROWS (*cupping his hear with his hand*): Pardon, Master Richard?

JASPER (*bending down to him and speaking clearly*): You should have let Martin carry the tray, Burrows, it's too heavy for you.

BURROWS: Martin is young, Mr. Jasper. He would have been out of tune with the evening's melancholy. His very bearing would have been an intrusion.

LAVINIA: Thank you, Burrows, that was very considerate of you.

BURROWS: I beg your pardon, Miss Lavvy?

LAVINIA (*loudly*): I said thank you, Burrows, that was very considerate of you.

BURROWS: Your servant to the grave, Miss Lavvy.

JANE: Oh, Burrows!

BURROWS: I beg your pardon, ma'am?

JANE (*loudly*): I only said 'Oh, Burrows', Burrows.

BURROWS: Very good, ma'am.

> BURROWS *goes out.*

HARRIET: Poor Burrows looks very depressed.

JASPER: Burrows has looked depressed for at least thirty years.

JANE: One could scarcely expect him to be hilarious now.

LAVINIA: Hilarious! Really, Jane.

HARRIET: I think sorrow has increased his deafness.

JASPER: He was just as deaf last Christmas really, and that was a gay occasion.

JANE (*with meaning*): Gay!

JASPER (*reprovingly*): Hush, Jane.

HARRIET: A bereavement in the house must affect the servants profoundly, although I must admit I heard Sarah singing in the pantry this morning.

EMILY (*horrified*): This morning!

HARRIET: It was quite early.

LAVINIA: Disgraceful.

HARRIET: She was singing very softly, and it *was* a hymn.

LAVINIA: Nevertheless, I hope you scolded her.

HARRIET: I hadn't the heart, she has such a pretty voice.

CHARLES: What hymn was it?

HARRIET: 'For Those In Peril On The Sea'.

LAVINIA: Most inappropriate.

JASPER: Sarah's young man is a sailor, you know, he's on the *Brilliant*.

CHARLES (*with interest*): That's a Three Decker.

EDWARD: She carries 114 thirty-two pounders, 2 sixty-eight pounders and 4 eighteen pounders.

EMILY: Oh, Edward, how clever of you to know.

RICHARD: A fine ship, I have seen her at anchor.

CHARLES: Surely not a hundred and twenty guns?

EDWARD: Yes, she is the same class as the *Britannic* and the *Prince Regent*.

RICHARD: Cast-iron muzzle loaders, I presume?

EDWARD (*enthusiastically*): Yes, their recoil is checked by stout rope breechings.

CHARLES: How are they elevated?

EDWARD: Quoins – and trained by handspikes.

RICHARD: Oh – handspikes.

JANE (*with slight mockery*): Handspikes, Lavinia – do you hear that? – they're trained by handspikes!

LAVINIA: I declare I'm more at sea than Sarah's young man.

JANE: Oh, Lavvy – a joke – how sweet!

EMILY (*hugging her*): Darling Lavvy!

LAVINIA: Behave, Emily – let me alone.

JASPER: It seems odd that the solemnity of this particular family reunion should be dissipated by gunnery.

LAVINIA: Such irrelevance, on such a day.

EDWARD: It was my fault, I apologise.

JANE: With so much to be done, so much to be decided.

LAVINIA (*raising her handkerchief to her eyes*): Oh, dear!

JASPER: Steel yourself, Lavinia – be brave.

LAVINIA: I'll try.

HARRIET: We must all try.

> CHARLES *and* RICHARD *go to the table on which* RICHARD *has placed the tray.*

CHARLES: Jane – a little wine?

JANE: Thank you, Charles.

CHARLES: Harriet?

HARRIET: Thank you, Charles.

RICHARD: A little Madeira, Emily?

EMILY: Just a drop, please.

RICHARD: Lavinia?

LAVINIA: No, thank you.

HARRIET: Oh, Lavvy, a little sip would warm you.

LAVINIA: I am not cold.

JASPER (*brusquely*): Come, Lavvy, don't be annoying.

LAVINIA: How can you, Jasper—

JASPER: I insist – here— (*He gives her a glass.*)

JANE: We should drink a toast.

LAVINIA: You should be ashamed.

JANE: Don't be alarmed, I meant quite a gentle toast.

RICHARD: An excellent idea.

CHARLES: Why not?

LAVINIA: As though this were a moment for celebrating.

CHARLES: Again – why not?

JASPER (*sternly*): Charles – behave yourself!

JANE: Charles is right. Why not indeed!

LAVINIA: I am at a loss to understand your behaviour this evening, Jane.

JANE: A billiard room – I heard Charles and Harriet discussing it – they're going to have a billiard room—

228

HARRIET: It's an extravagance – I told Charles it was an extravagance.

JANE: Never mind, you can afford it now.

CHARLES: That's what I say.

JANE: Isn't it splendid! – Isn't it absolutely splendid?

LAVINIA (*immeasurably shocked*): What!

JANE: About Charles and Harriet being able to afford a billiard room, about Emily and Edward being able to send John and Curly to Eton, about you, Lavinia, being able to buy a little house anywhere you like, about Jasper and me living here—

RICHARD: What about me?

JASPER: I think Crockford's should be congratulated – that's where all your money goes.

RICHARD: Touché, Jasper – a new black fleece, though, for the blackest of black-sheep.

EMILY: Where will you go, Lavvy?

LAVINIA: I feel this conversation to be abominably out of place.

JANE: Darling, don't be stuffy.

LAVINIA: It is my father who has passed away, remember.

JANE: Jasper's too, and Emily's and Richard's and Harriet's.

JASPER: Leave Lavinia her decorum, Jane, polite grief should be respected.

LAVINIA: Polite! Oh, Jasper!

JASPER: I am your brother, dear, I know your heart.

JANE: Smile, Lavinia – just once.

EMILY: Yes, Lavvy, just one smile.

LAVINIA: You are disgraceful, all of you – all of you – unfeeling and disgraceful – I am ashamed of you.

JASPER: Smile, then, and you can be ashamed of yourself as well.

HARRIET: Please, Lavvy.

RICHARD: Come along, Lavvy.

JASPER: Think, Lavvy – a little house in some gay country – France or Italy – you've always loved foreigners – a little villa in the sun – you can paint your pictures – blue seas and cypresses – you could take tabby with you, she's an insular cat but I doubt whether French or Italian mice taste so very different—

JANE: We'll all come and stay with you, Lavinia.

RICHARD: Hurrah, Lavinia – smile and say Hurrah!

LAVINIA (*struggling*): No – no—

EMILY (*flinging her arms round her*): Yes – yes—

LAVINIA: Be still, Emily – for shame!

HARRIET: Her mouth twitched – I saw it.

JASPER (*tickling the back of her neck*): Come along, Lavvy—

LAVINIA (*slapping his hand away*): How dare you, Jasper!

JANE: Think of Mrs. Hodgson's bonnet at the funeral – do you remember? – I nudged you—

LAVINIA (*breaking at last into laughter*): Oh, dear – how horrid you all are – I hate you – it was the most ridiculous bonnet I ever saw – like a little black pie – oh, dear—

JASPER: Are your glasses charged?

LAVINIA: No, Jasper, no – I don't approve—

JASPER (*raising his glass*): To Mrs. Hodgson's little black pie!

ALL (*raising their glasses*): Mrs. Hodgson's little black pie!

JASPER (*triumphantly, as* LAVINIA *drinks*): There!

> LAVINIA *chokes – everyone gathers round her and pats her on the back.*

Some more – quickly, Richard—

> RICHARD, CHARLES, EDWARD *and* JASPER *refill all the glasses.*

LAVINIA: This is so wrong – so dreadfully wrong—

JASPER: Another toast – be prepared—

LAVINIA: Please, stop, Jasper – the servants will hear.

JASPER (*raising his glass*): To ourselves – a closely united family and the dear strangers who have joined us – I allude to you, Jane, darling, and Charles and Edward—

CHARLES: Does that mean that we three may not drink?

JASPER: Certainly not – drink to yourselves – to each other – and the happiness of us all.

CHARLES: Good!

HARRIET: Do be quiet, Charles.

JASPER: Where was I?

JANE: The happiness of us all, my dear.

> JASPER *sings a short toast to each of them – everybody joins in. The tempo becomes more gay and there is much laughter as each individual is commented upon.*

The gaiety is interrupted by the clock on the mantelpiece striking ten.

The music drops to the minor. Everyone puts down his glass.

LAVINIA: Papa's eight-day clock – he would never allow anyone to wind it but himself – who will wind it now?

She bows her head. EMILY, JASPER, HARRIET *and* RICHARD *all sing sadly together.*

EMILY
JASPER
HARRIET
RICHARD

'Ah, who will wind it now – alack-a-day – who will wind it now!'

JANE: Jasper, of course – don't be so silly.

JASPER: Richard, be so kind as to ring for Burrows.

RICHARD: Now?

JASPER: Yes, now.

LAVINIA: The box?

JASPER: The box.

RICHARD: Very well.

He pulls the bell-rope by the fireplace.

EMILY: Oh, dear!

There is a gloomy silence for a moment. EDWARD *breaks it.*

EDWARD (*at the window*): Look – there's a squirrel!

CHARLES (*eagerly*): Where?

EDWARD: There – by the steps.

RICHARD (*joining them*): How can you tell – it's so dark.

EMILY: There's only a little moon but enough to see by, look – there he goes – back into the wood.

LAVINIA: Poor Papa – poor dear Papa – he'll never see a squirrel again.

HARRIET: Don't, Lavinia.

JANE: Do you think he would wish to? – I mean – not to see any more squirrels is surely one of the lesser disadvantages of dying.

LAVINIA (*coldly*): You take me too literally, Jane.

EMILY (*coming away from the window*): Oh, it's all so dreadful – death is so frightening.

LAVINIA: So lonely.

JASPER: Lonelier even than life.

JANE (*hurt*): Jasper!

JASPER: Forgive me, my love – it was a generalisation.

BURROWS *enters.*

BURROWS: You rang, Mr. Jasper?

JASPER: We are ready for the box now, Burrows.

BURROWS: Every one of them, Mr. Jasper – regulated to the minute – I did them myself.

JASPER: Not the clocks, Burrows, the box.

BURROWS: I had a mort of trouble with the one in the library – it struck fifteen three times – but I fixed it. (*He gives a slight cackle and then controls himself.*)

JASPER: The box, Burrows – we want the box – I told you to have it brought down from the attic this morning.

BURROWS: Oh, the trunk! Very well, Mr. Jasper.

He goes off.

LAVINIA: It seems callous somehow – so soon to pry upon Papa's secrets.

JASPER: Callous perhaps, but certainly necessary.

JANE: I observed one of his more open secrets at the back of the church this morning.

LAVINIA: What do you mean, Jane?

JANE: Mrs. Wynant.

HARRIET: That creature.

JASPER: Hush, Harriet – we cannot resent her grieving, too – in her own way.

HARRIET: Nevertheless, I do resent it.

LAVINIA: She should not have come.

EMILY: Poor Mrs. Wynant.

LAVINIA: Really, Emily – poor Mrs. Wynant indeed!

EMILY: I was thinking of the will.

RICHARD: It was perfectly just – she had no claim.

JASPER: No legal claim at any rate.

LAVINIA: Jasper!

JASPER: It would be unchristian to deny her a certain moral right.

CHARLES: Moral is hardly the word I should have chosen.

JASPER: Spoken like a soldier, Charles – and also, I'm afraid, like a gentleman.

BURROWS *enters.*

BURROWS: The box is outside, Mr. Jasper – if you and Mr. Richard – I would rather Martin did not enter—

JANE: Why, Burrows, it really wouldn't matter.

BURROWS: It isn't the clatter, ma'am, it's his face, it's so very hot and red – in this pale room – you understand?

JASPER: Very well, Burrows – come along, Richard.

RICHARD *and* JASPER *go out.*

BURROWS: Will there be any tea required, ma'am?

JANE: Yes, please, Burrows – a little later.

BURROWS (*cupping his ear with his hand*): I beg your pardon, ma'am?

JANE (*shouting*): A little later, Burrows.

BURROWS (*respectfully*): Oh, no, ma'am – certainly not – not for the world, ma'am.

BURROWS *goes out.*

JANE: What could he have thought I said?

CHARLES: I fear that we shall never know.

RICHARD *and* JASPER *return with a very dusty little trunk. They put it down.*

JASPER: Sarah has done her best with a duster, but I fear it needs scrubbing.

RICHARD: Never mind.

LAVINIA: The box.

HARRIET: Oh, dear – the box.

JASPER: Yes, there it sits – reproaching us – almost frowning at us.

JANE: That little strap makes it look even more disagreeable than it really is.

JASPER: You have the key, Lavinia. You took it from Father's chain.

LAVINIA: Yes, it's here. (*She hands it to* JASPER.) You're the eldest.

JASPER: Before opening it – before unearthing our dear Father's secrets – I must most earnestly enjoin – complete discretion.

CHARLES: Of course.

JASPER: You, Charles, and Edward, and my dear Jane—

JANE: Open it, Jasper, and don't be silly.

JASPER: You cut me short, Jane, in the most frivolous way.

JANE: Never mind.

CHARLES: We understand, Jasper – complete discretion.

JANE (*impatiently*): Open it!

JASPER (*on his knees*): Poor Papa! (*He wrestles with the lock.*) The key doesn't fit – (*He lifts the lid.*) It's already open – (*He puts his hand into the box and produces a gilt paper crown.*) It's the wrong box!

LAVINIA: Oh, how stupid of Burrows!

EMILY: A paper crown.

HARRIET: I remember it.

RICHARD: Where's the sceptre – there should be a sceptre, too – I made it myself from Uncle William's walking-stick— (*He searches in the box.*)

EMILY: He was very angry.

RICHARD (*finding it*): Here it is.

LAVINIA: There was a scarf with beads on it from India – I wore it when I was the Queen— (*She goes on her knees too, and searches in the box.*)

HARRIET: And there were four swords – flat ones – but one was broken—

> She joins LAVINIA *and searches in the box.*

EMILY (*rushing to the box*): Princes and Princesses – oh, how lovely!

JANE: What on earth are you talking about?

JASPER (*smiling*): Princes and Princesses – it was a dressing-up game – we played it when we were children—

HARRIET: On Sundays – only on Sundays—

> They sing a foolish little tune: 'Princes and Princesses'. They act a little too, fragments of the game they remember. LAVINIA *is crowned with the paper crown.* JASPER *and* RICHARD *fight a brisk duel with the swords. At the end* LAVINIA *tears off her crown and throws it on to the floor.*

LAVINIA: This is wicked – wicked – I shall never forgive myself to the end of my days—

> She sinks on to a sofa, in tears. The others look at her mutely.

RICHARD *rises from the floor where he has been lying since being killed in the duel and dusts himself down.*

JASPER: Don't cry, Lavvy – please don't.

LAVINIA (*tearfully*): —God must surely punish us for this heartlessness, dancing and singing and playing, with Father not yet cold in his grave.

JASPER: That is an emotional statement, my dear, understandable in the circumstances, but hardly accurate.

EMILY: The cemetery really is very exposed, Lavinia.

LAVINIA: Forgive us, Papa, forgive us—

RICHARD: A little more Madeira, Charles, our sister is becoming hysterical.

> CHARLES *pours out some Madeira and hands it to* RICHARD, *who takes it to* LAVINIA.

Here, my dear.

LAVINIA: No, no – I don't want it.

JASPER: Drink it, Lavinia, it will calm you.

JANE: I think I should like a little more, too.

CHARLES (*pouring it for her*): Very well – Harriet?

HARRIET: Yes, please.

JASPER (*to* LAVINIA): Come along, dear.

LAVINIA (*sipping the wine*): How shameful – oh, how shameful!

CHARLES: Emily, some more wine?

EMILY: May I, Edward?

EDWARD: Yes, my love, but only a little.

CHARLES: There is only a little left.

RICHARD: We had better ring for some more.

LAVINIA: No, Richard, no – I forbid it.

RICHARD: As you say, Lavvy, but my throat is cruelly dry.

CHARLES: Mine too – Jasper?

JASPER: Dry as dust.

LAVINIA (*bursting into tears again*): Dust! Oh, Jasper!

> *The door opens discreetly and* BURROWS *enters bearing another decanter of Madeira. Everyone looks at him in silence as he places it ceremoniously on the tray. He looks enquiringly at* CHARLES *who is holding the empty decanter.* CHARLES *gives it to him. He bows politely and goes to the door. He turns and regards them all lovingly for a moment then, from his cuff, he produces a large white*

handkerchief with which he wipes his eyes, but it is difficult to tell
whether he is laughing or weeping.
He goes out, closing the door behind him.

JASPER: With every advancing year Burrows grows wiser.

HARRIET: And kinder.

RICHARD: And more understanding.

JASPER: Surely, among ourselves, a little private toast to Burrows
would not be entirely without grace?

CHARLES: Hear, hear!

EMILY: I think Papa would have wished it.

EDWARD: Well spoken my love.

LAVINIA: Papa would not have approved at all – Jasper – I appeal
to you—

HARRIET: Oh, Lavvy, I know he would—

RICHARD: Tinge your grief with tolerance, Lavinia.

CHARLES: What harm is there, Lavinia?

JANE: Don't be silly, Lavinia.

JASPER: The 'Ayes' have it – charge your glasses.

Everybody refills their glasses.

(*Raising his glass.*) To Burrows – our first friend – don't you
remember, Lavinia? He made us toys in the woodshed. He read
us stories when we were ill; he gave us forbidden sweets from
the pantry. He loved us all – you particularly, Lavinia – have you
forgotten his tenderness when Mother died? Have you forgotten
his welcoming smile when we came home from school? Surely
this small gesture of affection to him can only be a pale sin in the
eyes of heaven. To Burrows, Lavinia.

LAVINIA (*rising to her feet*): To Burrows! (*She drinks.*)

ALL: To Burrows! (*They drink.*)

CHARLES: That was delicious.

RICHARD: I think it must have come from Papa's special cellar.

EMILY: I believe I should like a little more.

EDWARD: No, Emily.

EMILY (*gaily*): Spoilsport – I defy you!

She quickly pours herself out another glassful and drinks it before
anyone can stop her.

HARRIET: Emily!

LAVINIA: Behave, Emily.

JASPER: You shock me appallingly, Emily – I'm almost sure you do.

EMILY: Nonsense!

EDWARD: I apologise – I apologise to you all. Come to bed, Emily.

EMILY: Papa liked wine – he liked it to excess – I expect this is hereditary. (*She giggles.*)

EDWARD: Come to bed immediately.

EMILY: I shall do no such thing, my love, so there! I want to see what more there is in the box— (*She kneels on the floor beside it and begins to rummage about in it.*)

JANE: Poor Edward, I fear the grape has robbed you of your marital authority.

RICHARD: Vanquished, Edward – be a man and admit it.

LAVINIA: I feel a little faint – the heat, I think, and everyone behaving so strangely—

HARRIET (*going to her*): My dear—

JANE: Would you like me to take you upstairs?

LAVINIA: No, no, it will pass – it's nothing.

RICHARD: Some salts – some vinegar?

LAVINIA: No, no – I think perhaps a thimbleful more of that wine—

CHARLES (*pouring her out some*): Here, my dear—

LAVINIA: Thank you, Charles – how kind. (*She accepts it weakly.*)

JANE: I feel very curious myself.

JASPER: Beloved!

HARRIET: Open the window.

JANE: No – the air is damp – it would be dangerous—

RICHARD: Some wine?

JANE: Perhaps – perhaps that would revive me.

CHARLES (*pouring her out some*): Here, my dear.

JANE (*smiling gaily*): Thank you, Charles.

> They all casually take a little more wine.

EMILY (*at the box*): Oh, look – look—!

JASPER: What is it?

EMILY: The musical box – don't you remember?

RICHARD: I thought it had dropped to pieces years ago.

LAVINIA: Aunt Heathcote gave it to us – it was a Christmas present.

HARRIET: Papa forbade us to play it.

EMILY (*placing it on the table and winding it*): He can't forbid us now!

EDWARD (*reprovingly*): Emily!

EMILY: Shh! Be still – listen—

> *They all listen – no sound comes from the musical box.*

JASPER: It's old and tired, it's forgotten how to play.

RICHARD: No, no – there was a little catch – I'm sure there was—

EMILY: Make it play, Richard – please try—

> RICHARD *tinkers with it and it strikes one note. They all sing 'Let's play a tune on the music box'. They stop singing and the music box tinkles out a tinny little melody.*

RICHARD: There!

EMILY (*clasping her hands ecstatically*): Oh, how sweet – how sweet!

HARRIET: The red schoolroom curtains – I can suddenly see them – blowing out in the draught—

RICHARD: The hard pink sugar on the edge of the cake – I can suddenly taste it.

JASPER: Your hand in mine, Jane, when you were brought over to tea by your governess – I can suddenly feel it.

JANE (*taking his hand*): Oh, darling—

EMILY: Again, again – make it play again – I want to remember, too—

> RICHARD *tinkers with it again. It plays the same sticky little melody.*
> EMILY *begins to sing – they all join in – little snatches of melody come back to them out of their childhood.*

HARRIET: There was another tune as well – I remember distinctly – it played another tune—

RICHARD: We mustn't ask too much of it.

JASPER: Try the little catch again.

HARRIET: It was a waltz.

JANE (*looking at* JASPER): Of course it was – a waltz – don't you recall it, my dear love? We danced to it years later – at a ball – just before we were married – it was this – it was this—

She starts to sing – RICHARD *is still at work on the music box –*
suddenly it begins to play again – the tune that JANE *is singing.*

EMILY: It's remembered – oh, how clever of it!

RICHARD: Hush, Emily – that was their love song—

> JASPER *and* JANE *sing to each other the love song of their youth. The*
> *others join in, humming very softly, as they dance together. At the*
> *end of it* JANE *sinks to the floor in a deep curtsy,* JASPER *bows over*
> *her, taking her hand.*

JASPER: I love you, my heart.

JANE: 'Till death us do part—'

> *He raises her to her feet and takes her in his arms.* LAVINIA *sinks on*
> *to the sofa once more in tears.*

RICHARD: Oh, Lavvy!

LAVINIA: Don't mock me – these are true tears.

JASPER: Not sad ones though, I beg of you—

LAVINIA: Mama died when we were little, Papa died four days
    ago, but life isn't dead, is it – is it?

JASPER: Never, as long as it's gay, as long as it's happy.

EMILY: Poor Papa – poor dear Papa!

LAVINIA: To hell with Papa!

HARRIET: Lavinia!

RICHARD: Lavinia!

EMILY: Oh, Lavvy, how can you!

JASPER: Bravo, Lavvy!

LAVINIA: I mean it – give me some more Madeira, Charles.

CHARLES: Good heavens!

LAVINIA: I hated Papa, so did you, Jasper, and Harriet and
    Richard and Emily—

EMILY: Oh, Lavvy – don't – don't—

LAVINIA: He was cruel to Mama, he was unkind to us, he was
    profligate and pompous and worse still, he was mean—

CHARLES (*handing her some wine*): Here, my dear – drink this.

LAVINIA (*taking it*): Certainly I will— (*She raises her glass.*) Now I
    will propose a toast – To Papa – and to the truth, too – Papa
    and the truth together – for the first time.

JASPER: I do hope you will not regret this in the morning,
    Lavinia.

HARRIET: Don't you think you had better retire to bed?

EMILY: I feel frightened.

LAVINIA: This may be wicked. I expect it is – I expect I shall be punished for it – but I don't care. You escaped – all of you – you found husbands and wives and lives of your own – but I had to stay here – with him – For years he has scarcely spoken to me – I've counted the linen – I've added up the bills – I've managed the house – years ago I said good-bye to someone I loved because my miserable unkind conscience told me that it was my duty. I've sat here in this house week after week, month after month, year after year, while he insulted me and glowered at me and betrayed our name with common village loves. The will – the happy will which was read to us to-day was made ten years ago – you realise that, do you not?

JASPER: Lavinia – what in heaven's name—

LAVINIA: What you do not realise is that he made another – a week before he died—

HARRIET: What are you saying?

RICHARD: Lavinia – are you mad?

EMILY (*wailing*): Oh, Lavvy!

LAVINIA: None of us were even mentioned in it. Five thousand pounds was left to Mrs. Wynant. Six thousand pounds to Rose Dalton. Three thousand pounds to Mrs. Waterbury – I can only gather that she was less satisfactory than the others – and the rest to a fund for the erection of a new church containing a memorial of himself in black marble!

JASPER: Lavinia – are you sure of this?

LAVINIA: Quite sure. Burrows witnessed it.

JASPER: And would it be trespassing too far on your indiscretion to ask what became of it?

LAVINIA: Seven and a half minutes after Papa breathed his last, Burrows and I burnt it.

JASPER: Ring the bell, Richard.

RICHARD: Very well. (*He goes to the bell and pulls it.*)

EMILY: I think, Edward dear, another sip of wine would be pardonable in the circumstances.

HARRIET: I agree.

JANE: Black marble – how very nasty.

RICHARD: Black clay would have been more appropriate.

They all pour themselves out a little more Madeira.

EMILY: Poor Mrs. Waterbury.

JANE: Think of the humiliation she has been spared.

HARRIET: I wonder where Rose Dalton is now?

JASPER: In Scotland, I believe – she married a Baptist.

EDWARD: Do you suppose Mrs. Wynant suspects?

JASPER: Suspects what, Edward?

EDWARD: About the – er – about your father – about what Lavinia has just told us?

LAVINIA: I observed an expensive diamond brooch fastening her cloak in church to-day. That, I think, should be a sufficient reward for services rendered.

JASPER: How hard you are, Lavinia.

JANE: And how right.

BURROWS *enters.*

BURROWS: You rang, Mr. Jasper?

JASPER: Yes, Burrows.

RICHARD: We wish to ask you a question, Burrows.

BURROWS: Much better, thank you, Master Richard. A little herb tea soothes all disharmony.

JASPER: A question, Burrows.

BURROWS: Very well, Mr. Jasper.

JASPER: Miss Lavinia gives me to understand that you witnessed my late father's last Will and Testament.

BURROWS (*cupping his ear with his hand*): I beg your pardon, sir?

JASPER: Did you or did you not witness my late father's last Will and Testament?

BURROWS: My affliction is increasing bad, Mr. Jasper, I shall never be able to hear that particular question.

LAVINIA (*softly*): Thank you, Burrows.

BURROWS: Not at all, Miss Lavinia.

RICHARD: Some Madeira, Burrows?

He holds up the decanter.

BURROWS: I should be honoured, Master Richard.

RICHARD (*pouring him some*): Here, then.

BURROWS (*accepting it*): At your service always.

JASPER: Thank you, Burrows.

BURROWS (*catching sight of the musical box*): Have I your permission for a moment.

JASPER: Certainly – what is it?

BURROWS: There should be a little tune, a little tune from the years that are dead – allow me—

> *He starts the musical box. It plays the same gay little melody that it played before. He stands beside it, bending down to hear it more clearly, then he stands up with his head nodding to the tune and raises his glass.*

BURROWS: I drink to you all – (*Then to* JASPER *and* JANE.) And to you, sir, and ma'am – this house was happy when there were children in it—

> *He drinks.* EMILY *and* JANE *and* HARRIET *start to sing. All the others join in. The tune becomes gayer and swifter until they are all hand in hand and dancing round* BURROWS *as—*

THE CURTAIN FALLS

STAR CHAMBER

A Light Comedy in One Act

Star Chamber was produced in London at the Phoenix Theatre on 21 March 1936, with the following cast:

XENIA JAMES	Miss Gertrude Lawrence
JOHNNY BOLTON	Mr Noël Coward
HESTER MORE	Miss Moya Nugent
JULIAN BREED	Mr Alan Webb
DAME ROSE MAITLAND	Miss Everley Gregg
VIOLET VIBART	Miss Betty Hare
MAURICE SEARLE	Mr Edward Underdown
ELISE BRODIE	Miss Lumena Edwardes
J. M. FARMER	Mr Anthony Pelissier
JIMMIE HORLICK	Mr Kenneth Carten
PRESS PHOTOGRAPHER	Mr Charles Peters

———

The action of the play passes on the stage of a West End theatre.

TIME: The present.

The action of the play passes on the bare stage of a West End theatre in London.

The time is about twelve noon.

When the curtain rises JIMMIE HORLICK, *the stage-manager of the theatre, is arranging chairs round a long table. The stage is dim as there is only one working light on.*

J. M. FARMER *enters from the left. He is an amiable-looking man somewhere between thirty and forty. He wears a mackintosh, a bowler hat and glasses, and he carries a brief-case bulging with papers.*

MR. FARMER: Good morning.

JIMMIE: Good morning.

MR. FARMER: I'm Mr. Farmer.

JIMMIE (*shaking hands*): Pleased to meet you.

MR. FARMER: Mr. Bolton not here yet?

JIMMIE: No, nobody's here yet – it's only just twelve.

MR. FARMER: It's a bit dark, isn't it?

JIMMIE: I'll put a couple of battens on and you can have the floats up if you like.

MR. FARMER: Thanks.

JIMMIE *goes to the prompt corner and switches on more light.*

JIMMIE: That better?

MR. FARMER (*taking off his mackintosh*): That's fine. (*He surveys the table.*) Looks nice and businesslike.

JIMMIE: That's the table out of the party scene. Mr. Bolton does a buck and wing on it.

MR. FARMER: How's the show going?

JIMMIE: Wonderful. We dropped off a bit before Christmas, but we're back again now.

MR. FARMER: Are you Mr. Bolton's stage-manager?

JIMMIE: Yes.

MR. FARMER: How is he to work with?

JIMMIE: He's all right as long as you laugh at his gags.

MR. FARMER: I haven't seen him on the stage for years, not since he was at the Gaiety.

JIMMIE: He's still doing the same stuff.

HESTER MORE comes on to the stage. She is wearing tweeds, a turtle-neck jumper and a felt hat. A lot of fuzzy hair escapes from under the hat. Her manner is vague to the point of lunacy and she carries a small brown-paper parcel.

HESTER: These are my shoes.

MR. FARMER: Good morning.

HESTER: My feet got sopping wet so I had to buy a new pair, these are the wet ones – don't they look silly?

MR. FARMER: You're the first to arrive, except me.

HESTER: Who are you?

MR. FARMER: I'm Mr. Farmer, the Secretary of the Fund.

HESTER: Oh, I see.

There is a pause.

MR. FARMER: Nasty out, isn't it?

HESTER: I should have been here earlier still, only I went to the Lyceum, but there wasn't anybody there.

MR. FARMER: Oh.

There is another pause.

This is Mr. Horlick, Mr. Bolton's stage-manager.

HESTER (*shaking hands*): How lovely! Would you mind putting my hat somewhere? (*She takes it off and gives it to him.*)

JIMMIE: Certainly.

HESTER: I think hats are maddening, they get so wet and stupid.

MR. FARMER (*anxious to please*): Yes, I suppose they do really.

HESTER: I can never rehearse in a hat – I feel I want to shake and shake and shake my head until it flies through the air like a moon.

MR. FARMER: Yes, that puts you off, I expect.

HESTER: Nothing puts me off really once I start, because I shut off absolutely everything, but the getting to the shutting-off stage is sheer misery – you have to mean so much yourself before you can begin to make the play mean whatever it ought to mean – you see what I mean?

MR. FARMER (*lost*): Oh, yes – of course.

246

HESTER: Well, oughtn't we to do something?

MR. FARMER: I'm afraid we can't do much until the rest of the committee arrive.

HESTER: I love committee meetings – there's something sort of ponderous about them – they give me a feeling of complete inevitability, don't they you?

MR. FARMER: Yes, I suppose they do – in a way.

HESTER: Do you like being a Secretary?

MR. FARMER: Yes, very much.

HESTER: Does it give you a thrilling sense of power? I've often wondered what it would be like to be terrifically powerful. Who are you actually secretary to?

MR. FARMER: To the Fund.

HESTER: I always thought one had to be secretary to a person not a thing. Have you a portfolio?

MR. FARMER: A what?

HESTER: Portfolio – Of course, I see a portfolio as black and battered and made of watered silk – a sort of Victorian hold-all filled with Grandmother's sketches – You haven't got a safety-pin, have you?

MR. FARMER: I'm afraid I haven't.

HESTER: It doesn't matter in the least bit really, but this skirt actually belongs to my sister – I live with her when I'm rehearsing.

MR. FARMER: Are you starting a new play soon?

HESTER: Yes, but I'm deeply angry about it – it's a translation by Cedric Gibbons – they always make me do plays like that when all I ever want really is to be gay! Has anybody got a cigarette?

MR. FARMER (*offering her his case*): Here. I'm afraid they're only Gold Flake.

HESTER: I worship Gold Flake because they have lovely pictures of fish, and I worship fish, too – aren't I a fool?

MR. FARMER (*laughing deprecatingly*): Not at all – I quite agree – Fish can be very interesting – some fish, that is—

HESTER: I naturally didn't mean ordinary dull ones, like cod and those mad-looking flat things – I meant splendid, thrilling fish

247

like you see in aquariums – brilliantly coloured – silver and gold flake – Oh dear!

She goes off into gales of laughter.

JOHNNY BOLTON *comes briskly on to the stage. He is a star comedian of middle age, but perennial youthfulness. He is wearing plus-fours, a camel-hair coat, a check cap and a very bright scarf.*

JOHNNY: Hallo! hallo! hallo! – sorry to be late – good morning, old man! How are you, Miss More? – We seem to be the early birds—

HESTER (*weakly*): Birds and fish – Oh dear, oh dear—

JOHNNY (*puzzled*): Pardon?

MR. FARMER: It's nothing, Mr. Bolton – we were just talking about fish when you came in, that's all—

JOHNNY: We haven't met for ages, have we, Miss More? – I remember you as a little kiddie in *Peter Pan*. You've done great things since then!

HESTER: Everybody's been very kind – I can't think why.

JOHNNY: What's your new play?

HESTER: *Hurrah, We Die!*

JOHNNY: My God!

HESTER: It's more an investigation than a play really.

JOHNNY: What of?

HESTER: Oh, impulses and urges and foolish rowdiness.

JOHNNY: Oh, I see.

VIOLET VIBART *and* JULIAN BREED *come on to the stage.* VIOLET VIBART *is an elderly actress of considerable reputation.* JULIAN BREED *is known beyond a shadow of doubt to be the leading young actor of London. He has a beautiful speaking voice, and a manner that is only artistic in moments of stress. His clothes are casual and he moves with a certain modest authority.*

JULIAN: I'm terribly sorry to be late, but it was entirely Violet's fault really – hallo, Johnny – good morning, Hester darling—

HESTER: Julian – I'm going mad—

JULIAN: I've known that for a long time, dear—

VIOLET: It wasn't my fault at all – Julian promised to pick me up and then he said he hadn't and I had to telephone – Where's Xenia?

JOHNNY: Not here yet – what's the betting she'll be last? Any odds?

VIOLET: I do think dear Xenia, as President, ought to be here on time, don't you? – it's awfully naughty of her.

HESTER: I've been here for hours and hours and hours talking to Mr. Thing.

JULIAN: Who's missing?

MR. FARMER (*consulting a list*): Apart from our President, Miss James, there's Miss Brodie, Mr. Searle and Dame Rose Maitland—

VIOLET: Rosie will turn up all right, she's been on committees ever since I can remember—

JULIAN (*laughing*): Oh, Violet, you're superb!

VIOLET: Well, it's perfectly true, and after all she's not rehearsing now, is she?

MR. FARMER: I understand that Mr. Searle is doing a film at the moment.

JULIAN: Maurice is always doing a film – I'm furious with him.

VIOLET: You really can't blame him; after all, if he can't get quite the parts he wants in the theatre—

JULIAN: They wanted him to do a season at the Old Vic and he refused.

VIOLET: Oh, that *was* naughty of him—

JULIAN: And I myself offered him Petrovitch in *The Inspector from Tobolsk*.

VIOLET: I suppose you were playing Ivan?

JULIAN: Of course, but after all, Ivan dies in the second act.

VIOLET: Yes, and the play dies with him.

JOHNNY: This is all too highbrow for me, I shall have to go into me number in a minute—

HESTER: It must be heavenly to act with music all the time; I don't mean weird pipings, I mean jolly jiggerty-jig music—

JOHNNY: Come and work with me, Miss More – I'll teach you how to tap-dance – it would be a sensation – Miss Hester More – from Shakespeare to Schwartz—

HESTER: Who's Schwartz?

JOHNNY: The little chappie that wrote the show I'm doing here now – he's a wizard – all I have to do is to go to him and say:

'Bill, I want a couple of new gags for the second act' – most authors would say, 'Give me a few days, I got to go home and think.' Not so Bill Schwartz aren't I right, Jimmie? Out comes an envelope from his pocket – 'How's this, old boy?' he says – and there you are – a couple of sure-fire laughs; for instance, you know when I come on in the wheelbarrow just before the bathing number? well, it's old stuff, I know, they've seen it for years – but still I had to do something – I get out and do a pratt-fall – it's a laugh, of course, but you need something more there – I thought to myself, this is not so hot, so I go to Bill. 'Look here, old man,' I say – 'it's all very well relying on me to hold the show together, but after all, even I can't go on making bricks without straw till Kingdom Come; you've got to give me a laugh line that's going to knock 'em for a loop.' Well, I come down to the theatre that night, feeling a bit mad, you know, after all, it isn't as if I had another star to help me to carry the show; Maisie's all right, very pretty and all that, but it's a weak voice and she's got *no sense of comedy whatsoever*, she's got to have everything built up round her – Well, I come down to the theatre that night—

MAURICE SEARLE *comes hurriedly on to the stage. He is an exceedingly handsome, virile young man, but his looks are somewhat marred by the fact that, for the purposes of the film he is at present working on, he has had to grow his hair almost down to his shoulders.*

MAURICE (*loudly*): Don't look at me, anybody! I'm doing a film!

VIOLET: Oh, Maurice, is it *worth* it?

MAURICE (*taking off his coat*): I'm a sight – I'm ashamed to go out in the street—

HESTER: I think you look marvellous – I always said you had a period face—

JULIAN: There are periods and periods—

MAURICE: Don't be a cad, old boy – one's got to live—

VIOLET: It really is rather a shock, Maurice dear.

HESTER: You're mad, Violet – it's lovely – it suits his bone structure—

JULIAN: Why don't you go the whole hog, Maurice, and wear armour?

MAURICE: Shut up, you old fool, Julian, I didn't come here to be laughed at, I came to a committee meeting.

VIOLET (*with a look at* JOHNNY): Anyhow, you came in the *nick* of time!

HESTER: I long to do a film but nobody will let me.

MAURICE: Nonsense, Hester, they'd be damn glad to get you.

HESTER: No, they all say I'm *too* hideous.

JULIAN: I think that for us to do films is sheer money-grubbing anyhow, the theatre is our place and in the theatre we should stay.

VIOLET: If we can, Julian dear.

JOHNNY: I had a scenario sent me the other day – one of the funniest situations I've ever read – an absolute foolproof part for me—

JULIAN (*sotto-voce to* VIOLET): It would have to be.

JOHNNY: Pardon?

JULIAN: Nothing, I was only wondering whether we ought to get on with the meeting even without the President.

JOHNNY: —The situation's this, see – a Russian Grand Duke – exiled, you understand, during the Revolution – sold all his jewellery, hasn't got a bob and has to take a job as a salesman in a ladies' corset shop – there's a set-up for comedy if ever I saw one – and he meets this girl, see—

JULIAN: Which girl?

JOHNNY: A girl he met in Paris when he was on his uppers, and he doesn't know that she was one of the Imperial Ballet dancers who's also been exiled – that's to give Gracie Golden a chance to use her dancing – they've got her under contract, you see, and they've got to do something with her – so along they come to me – Ben Oelrichs came himself, as a matter of fact – 'Look here, old man,' he says, 'we're in a bit of a jam at Elstree – it's up to you to help us out – here's a part in a million for you and all you have to do is to write your own ticket.' 'All very fine,' I say, 'but I've got to have Bill Schwartz on that set every minute of the day to think out gags for me' – I've been in this profession long enough to know that it's no use trying to make people laugh if you haven't got the material there to do it with – so I call up Bill: 'Look here, old boy,' I say, 'you've got to stand by the old firm—'

At the beginning of this speech everyone has been reluctantly attentive, but by now they have drifted into individual conversations with each other, snatches of which are occasionally audible, such as:

MAURICE: I implored them to let me have a wig, but they said that it would always show in close-ups—

VIOLET: I don't see that it really matters as long as you are not seen about *too* much—

JULIAN: I've always thought him the unfunniest comedian in the world on the stage, but his dreariness off it amounts to genius—

HESTER: Shhh! he'll hear you—

JULIAN: That egomania is pathological—

HESTER: I think he's rather sweet, really, like a sort of rubber horse—

JOHNNY, by this time, is reduced to MR. FARMER, whom he pins down mercilessly.

JOHNNY: —'Okay!' he says. 'How about this for a start?' – and I give you my word he coughed up three of the funniest gags I've ever heard. For instance – two men are sitting in a cab shelter, see? As a matter of fact it needn't really be a cab shelter, it could be a bar or a café, or even a seat in the park – anyway, they're sitting there and a girl goes by – she stops a minute, looks at them and then walks on. 'See that bit of skirt?' says one—

At this moment DAME ROSE MAITLAND advances majestically on to the stage. She is imposingly dressed and slightly autocratic in manner. She is followed by ELISE BRODIE who is pretty but not particularly distinguished. She is obviously the type of star who plays leading parts adequately and whose home life is well known to be irreproachable.

DAME ROSE (*advancing*): Violet! I thought you were dead!

VIOLET (*as they kiss*): I really don't see why, dear—

DAME ROSE (*continuing her greetings*): —Hester – you look charming – Julian – darling boy – (*She kisses him.*) Mr. Bolton – it was generous and dear of you to lend us this stage for the meeting— (*She turns to MAURICE.*) —My God!

MAURICE: Don't look at me, Dame Rosie – I'm doing a film—

DAME ROSE: Cela va sans dire!

JULIAN: She met Rejane, you know.

HESTER: Hallo, Elise.

ELISE (*kissing her*): I had a dreadful time with John this morning, that's why I'm so late – he refused to go to school – and Patricia's had a rash for a whole week—

DAME ROSE: Mr. Farmer, I'm delighted to see you – I hope you have everything in order— (*She looks at* JIMMIE HORLICK.) Who is this?

JOHNNY (*bounding forward*): Jimmie Horlick, my stage-manager – son of the great Robert Horlick, you remember him, Dame Rose, I'm sure—

DAME ROSE (*taking both* JIMMIE'*s hands*): I should have known you anywhere! Your father was my friend, and when I say friend I mean friend. Well, well, well, let's get to business.

MR. FARMER: I am afraid our President, Miss James, is not here yet.

DAME ROSE: That doesn't matter in the least, we will proceed without her.

VIOLET: Don't you think that would be a little ultra vires, Rosie dear?

DAME ROSE: Ultra fiddlesticks! – we can't wait about all day. Kindly tell us where you want us to sit, Mr. Farmer.

ELISE (*to* JULIAN): —I was just telling Hester – if it was an ordinary rash I shouldn't worry, but it looks very angry to me and it's all over her poor little tummy—

DAME ROSE: Whose poor little tummy?

ELISE: Patricia's—

DAME ROSE: Who is Patricia?

ELISE: My child, Dame Rosie, my youngest child.

DAME ROSE: Poor little thing! Where do you want us to sit, Mr. Farmer?

HESTER: If I had children I should let them run wild in the woods all the year round.

VIOLET (*patronisingly*): Dear Hester—

HESTER (*with spirit*): Naked.

DAME ROSE: What did you say, my dear?

HESTER: Just naked.

DAME ROSE: Mr. Farmer, you had better take the foot of the table. Julian, darling boy, come and sit next to me – Mr. Bolton, will you be on my right—?

VIOLET: Surely our President should take the chair—?

DAME ROSE: My dear Violet, in the absence of the President it is my privilege, as Vice-President, to take the chair.

VIOLET: I am also a Vice-President.

DAME ROSE: That's beside the point – will everyone kindly be seated?

HESTER: I believe I'm a Vice-President, too, in a sort of way.

DAME ROSE (with polite firmness): I think if you consult the constitution of the Fund, my dear, you will find that you are merely a Trustee.

HESTER: All right, I'll be a Trustee then, I don't mind a bit.

JULIAN (to MAURICE): I'm going to do the whole production in different coloured tweed—

MAURICE: Are you using rostrums?

JULIAN: Yes – each scene will be played on different levels – the designs are marvellous—

JOHNNY: Don't use a revolve, that's all I can say; we had one in *Oh For To-night* and it held us up all the way through the show – I remember one matinee day I came on to do that cod soldier number with Dickie Black – you remember it came just at the opening of the last act – well, I come in to the theatre and start making up when Bob Fry comes flying into the room – he was my stage-manager then – 'Look here, old boy,' he says, 'we're up the spout, the bloody revolve's gone wonky—'

DAME ROSE (sternly): Mr. Bolton!

JOHNNY: Pardon?

DAME ROSE: I think we should really concentrate on the business that we are gathered together to discuss—

HESTER: Gathered together sounds awfully sweet, doesn't it? Almost religious—

DAME ROSE (in ringing tones): Mr. Farmer – I have much pleasure in declaring this meeting open.

> At this moment XENIA JAMES comes on to the stage. She is pretty, over-made-up, only slightly over-dressed and bursting with charm.

She is leading, or being led by a very large dog indeed, probably a Great Dane.

XENIA: My God! the traffic! – It took me over twenty-five minutes to get from Hertford Street to Antoine's and hours and hours to get from there to here and now I've kept you all waiting and you'll think I'm absolutely frightful – Oh, dear! – there are moments in life when I quite definitely wish I were dead – Darling Dame Rosie, please forgive me— (*She kisses her.*) —Violet – you are an angel to come— (*She kisses her.*) — Elise! I thought you were divine the other night; I couldn't come round to see you because I was with a party, but your second act wrecked me utterly, the mascara streamed down my face and Ronnie said I looked exactly like a zebra – Hester! you look perfectly lovely, have you just come up from the country? – how I wish I had hair like yours rushing away like that, mine has to be actually tortured to make it look like anything at all, I swear it does – Antoine hates me, he groans whenever I go into the shop, and whenever he groans Atherton growls and it's all too horrible – Julian darling, I've got a message for you from Marjorie but I'll give it to you afterwards – hold Atherton a minute – he's frightfully good – Maurice, darling, for God's sake don't sit where I can see you or I shall giggle and spoil everything – Hallo, Johnny, it was most awfully sweet of you to let us have this theatre for the meeting, I haven't seen your show yet because I've been away, but I'm coming next week I swear, we start rehearsing on Monday – I'm nearly frantic – Bobbie's in the country and can't be found and the last act's unplayable, positively unplayable, and you know what Bobbie is, he won't rewrite a word unless you hit him on the head – I promise you all here and now that I shall never do another play of his as long as I live – Mr. Farmer – where do I sit?

MR. FARMER: You take the chair, Miss James.

XENIA: It sounds awfully important, doesn't it? – I'm sure I ought to have a hammer – excuse me, Dame Rosie darling – Give me Atherton, Julian, he'll sit as quiet as a mouse – won't you, my angel? – he worships me, this dog, it's fantastic, it really is – Atherton Blake gave him to me just two weeks before he died, you know, and it was the most extraordinary thing, I felt that there was somehow a part of that Atherton in this Atherton, d'you know what I mean? – it was as though – Oh, I don't know, but anyhow from that moment onwards he's never left me—

DAME ROSE: Declare the meeting open, my dear, and let's get to business.

XENIA: Lie down, Atherton, who's a good dog? Come on – give Dame Rosie a paw – paw, Atherton – give paw— (*In sterner tones.*) Atherton, give Dame Rosie a paw at once and don't be a damn fool – all right, don't then, I'll talk to you about this later —(*To everybody.*) He's quite human, you know – we have the most awful rows – I sometimes think he's the only person in the whole wide world who really understands me – only the other night—

DAME ROSE: Xenia! we're wasting time – declare the meeting open.

XENIA: Darling Dame Rosie, I adore you – it's wide open as far as I'm concerned – Mr. Farmer – what do I say?

MR. FARMER: Just say 'I declare the meeting open.'

XENIA: I declare the meeting open – there now! (*She smiles radiantly.*) Lie down, Atherton, and don't be silly, it's no use pretending *you've* never been on a stage before – why, you're an old pro, aren't you, my darling? – he was with me in *Lady's Laughter*, you know—

JOHNNY: I don't trust animals on the stage, I learnt my lesson years ago in *Queen For A Day*; we had two horses in that and a flock of geese and what they didn't do was nobody's business—

VIOLET: I once played a whole scene with a parrot—

JULIAN: How lovely for you, darling—

Everybody laughs.

HESTER: I'd like to play a play with nothing but animals – think how heavenly it would be if only you could get them to moo and bark and neigh and do everything on cue—

JOHNNY: Try and stop 'em, that's all I say – just try and stop 'em—

DAME ROSE: Really, Mr. Bolton, you're disgraceful, you really are!— (*She breaks into laughter.*)

XENIA: Now we really must concentrate – I do see that – we really must – Mr. Farmer – will you begin, please?

MR. FARMER (*rising*): Certainly.

XENIA: First of all, before you start I should just like to say one thing and that is that I think we ought all to propose a vote of thanks to dear Mr. Farmer, not only for coming here today, but for all the wonderful work he has done for Garrick Haven.

Everybody mutters: 'Hear! hear!'

Thank you, Mr. Farmer. (*She smiles bewitchingly at him.*)

MR. FARMER (*deprecatingly*): I assure you I've done nothing, nothing at all—

JOHNNY: You can't get away with that, old boy, you've done wonders – the place wouldn't be standing if it hadn't been for you—

HESTER (*very loudly*): Hear! hear!

DAME ROSE: Hester! You made me jump.

MR. FARMER: Mr. President, ladies and gentlemen – as you all know, Garrick Haven was originally a private house and when the Garrick Haven Fund for a home for destitute actresses was established in the year nineteen hundred and two—

DAME ROSE: Yes, yes, yes, that was the year I went to His Majesty's.

MR. FARMER: —the executive committee of that time selected this fine old Georgian house on the outskirts of Ham Common—

XENIA: It's the sweetest house I've ever seen, you know, I went there last year—

MR. FARMER: —At that time the inmates numbered eleven, exclusive of the personnel which was comprised of Mrs. Ellsworth, matron—

VIOLET: Dear old Fanny – do you remember her, Rosie?

DAME ROSE: Drank like a fish.

MR. FARMER (*continuing*): —Dr. Harris, resident physician, and Mr. and Mrs. Grief, housekeeper and general handyman respectively. Mr. Horace Bevell was Honorary Secretary, the position that I have the privilege of holding at the present moment—

HESTER: Hear! hear!

JULIAN: Be quiet, darling—

HESTER (*in a loud whisper*): I love him – he's got a round, dear face—

JOHNNY: What happened to old Horace?

VIOLET: He died.

JOHNNY: Well, well, now I never knew that – he was a great pal of my dad's, you know, I remember being taken to see him when I was a kid at the old Rivoli, or rather Johnson's Music Hall as it was then – What a comedian! Whew! There wasn't any trick he didn't know – for instance, I remember one gag he cracked to this day – he came on dressed as a fireman and—

XENIA (*tapping the table, sweetly but firmly*): Johnny – order, please – Mr. Farmer wants to talk to us.

JOHNNY: Sorry! Exit Johnny Bolton, the man who made Kitchener laugh!

Everybody titters.

DAME ROSE: Continue, Mr. Farmer.

MR. FARMER (*clearing his throat*): In those days the total capital of the Fund amounted to just seventeen hundred pounds. In the year 1935 our assets were fifty-eight thousand pounds exclusive of certain slightly speculative investments with which I will not trouble you now—

HESTER: I think we ought to hear everything, *don't* you?

VIOLET: Isn't it wonderful—?

MR. FARMER: I need hardly tell you that, apart from a few outside subscriptions, this splendid financial security has been achieved entirely by the efforts of the Theatrical Profession at the annual Garrick Haven Fun Fayre.

XENIA: It's very gratifying, isn't it? I ran the roundabouts last year and I swear I've never enjoyed anything so much in my life.

VIOLET: Herrick's let met down dreadfully over my Tea Tent, Mr. Farmer – they sent me no sugar at all, and no spoons!

JULIAN: That made it all right then, didn't it, darling?

ELISE: I've been meaning to write to you for ages, Mr. Farmer, about my Lucky Dip—

DAME ROSE: Never mind about your Lucky Dip now, my dear—

ELISE: But I think Mr. Farmer ought to know. There were a lot of tin-tacks among the sawdust and some horrid sticky stuff as well—

JOHNNY: We did fine with our Hula-Hula Cabaret, but the tent was on the small side you know, old boy, on the small side—

XENIA: Darling Johnny, we must concentrate, we really must – Order – order! (*She raps on the table with her vanity-case.*) —oh, dear, I've broken the glass – seven years' bad luck—

JULIAN: Next year, Mr. Farmer, I should be very much obliged if you would put the Children's Opera at the *other* end of the grounds – Elizabeth and I could hardly hear ourselves speak – it's a little trying to have to do the Balcony scene with some beastly child banging a drum five yards away from you—

MAURICE: You didn't have to do the Balcony scene!

VIOLET: Any anyhow, dear Elizabeth's voice is louder than any drum!

JULIAN (*with a false laugh*): Oh, Violet, you're superb!

The conversation now becomes simultaneous.

MAURICE: My Roulette started off all right but the wheel kept sticking and I was down seventeen pounds by the end of the afternoon—

XENIA: Perhaps it doesn't count if it's only cracked—

ELISE: —it wasn't exactly jam and it wasn't exactly treacle, and we couldn't think what it was – but one old lady got it all over her gloves and made an awful scene—

VIOLET: They were waiting four deep in a long, long queue stretching right down as far as the Tombola, and there I was with only Jane and poor old Laura to help me and you know what a featherbrain she is, I sent her rushing off down the King's Road with an enormous basket—

JULIAN: —it wasn't my idea to do excerpts from Shakespeare, anyhow, but the public demand it – what I should really like to do next year is something jolly—

DAME ROSE: I should like to state here and now, Mr. Farmer, that the mismanagement over my Ice Creams was nothing short of disgraceful – It's all very well to buy them in blocks, but they don't stay in blocks unless you have an ice-box to put them in – I should have thought that would have been obvious to the meanest intelligence – it's a positive insult to the public to charge them two-and-six for a cardboard saucer of lukewarm custard with lumps in it—

ELISE: Robert – that's my husband, you know – brought both the children along – 'For God's sake don't let them put their hands in that,' I said, 'they might catch almost *anything*—'

MAURICE: Fourteen came up twenty-two times running and so consequently we were absolutely cleaned out before five o'clock—

XENIA: Order please, everybody – Oh, dear! – we *ought* to get on with the meeting—

JOHNNY (*loudly*): Order, there – Order!

XENIA: Thank you, Johnny dear—

JOHNNY (*jumping to his feet*): Excuse my butting in but as a subscriber of many years' standing I should just like to say that as far as I am concerned, and I sure as far as everyone here to-day is concerned, I should like to say that any work we any of us do for this particular charity is willing work and, what's more, glad work! These dear old souls – our own sisters in the profession – have, most of them, been faithful servants of the public for many long years – and for us to feel – all of us, that is, in the world of the theatre—

JULIAN (*sarcastically*): Tinsel world of the theatre—

JOHNNY: Pardon?

VIOLET: Hush, Julian.

DAME ROSE: You're perfectly right, Mr. Bolton, and we're all in complete agreement with you – please proceed, Mr. Farmer.

MR. FARMER: We now come to the purpose of this meeting. As you all know, no structural alterations, in fact no alterations of any kind, can be made in Garrick Haven without the approval and consent of the full Executive Committee. I have, therefore, acting on a letter received from our President, Miss James, on the twenty-fourth of November 1935, in reply to a letter of mine of the third of October of the same year – a proposal to put before you for the building of a new wing, and

I have with me the various builders' and plumbers' estimates which, with your consent, I will now read.

XENIA: Atherton! You smell awful – I've been wondering what it was for hours, and it's you! – What have you been doing, you naughty bad dog—?

DAME ROSE: Really, Xenia – it was a mistake to have brought him at all—

XENIA: Would somebody be really sweet and take him out or something? – I really can't bear it another minute— (*To Atherton.*) You're a filthy old pig, that's what you are, and Mother's livid with you—

JOHNNY: He'd be all right in the property-room, wouldn't he?

XENIA: I hope so.

JOHNNY: Jimmie – take Miss James's dog into the property-room.

JIMMIE: Does he bite?

XENIA: Bite! He wouldn't bite a child!

ELISE: I should just hope not.

XENIA: Go on, Atherton – go with the nice gentleman – here – take him by the lead—

JIMMIE *gingerly takes Atherton's lead.*

JIMMIE (*weakly*): Come on, old fellow.

XENIA (*as he is led away*): He breaks my heart every time I look at him, you know – those great mournful eyes – I swear he's the only real friend I have in the world – he's sensitive to every mood I have – when I'm sad he comes and puts his paw on my knee and when I'm gay he romps with me—

JULIAN: In those circumstances I should be permanently sad.

XENIA: It's all very fine to laugh, Julian, but that dog is definitely part of my life—

DAME ROSE: I still maintain that it was a mistake to bring him to a committee meeting.

XENIA: Dear Dame Rosie, he's my dog and I *am* the President!

DAME ROSE: Please proceed, Mr. Farmer.

MR. FARMER (*clearing his throat*): Before we deal with the estimates I feel that it is my duty to read you a round-robin letter signed by all the inmates of Garrick Haven with the exception of old Mrs. Baker—

ELISE: I wonder what her stage name was?

MR. FARMER: Joy Collins, I believe—

VIOLET: Good Heavens! I remember being taken to see her when I was a little tiny child—

DAME ROSE: Never mind that now, Violet – to our muttons, to our muttons.

MR. FARMER: She has, I believe, the reputation of being rather a rebellious spirit in the Home and refused to sign unless all her own personal complaints were included in the document; as these comprised several closely written sheets of foolscap, it was considered advisable—

XENIA: What ingratitude! It's really quite horrifying, isn't it? (*She laughs merrily.*)

MR. FARMER: At all events here is the letter – I read it without prejudice—

HESTER: That's absolutely sweet of you, and quite typical.

MR. FARMER: 'Dear Mr. Farmer, we the undersigned would be very glad if you would read the following letter to the Committee. We are very over-crowded in Garrick Haven and although we are very happy and contented here on the whole, we the undersigned feel that another bathroom and another indoor lavatory, as we only have one of each at the moment, would be not only more comfortable but really necessary, as the inside one is very inadequate and the outside one is rather a long way away and in the winter months very cold. We would be very glad if the Committee would look into this. We are – yours very sincerely – Mary Spink – Laura Richmond – Gloria Denton—', etc., etc.

XENIA: Poor angels – something must be done at once.

> JIMMIE HORLICK *returns, having deposited Atherton in the property-room.*

MR. FARMER: Their complaint, being perfectly reasonable—

VIOLET: Although a little high-handed in tone, don't you think?

MR. FARMER: I communicated with Miss James and have here the following estimates—

XENIA (*to* JIMMIE): Is he all right?

JIMMIE: Good as gold – he dropped off to sleep.

XENIA: We must all be very quiet.

MR. FARMER (*reading*): 'A report from Messrs. Belling, Sons and

Hapgood, embodying a summarised estimate for the proposed
new wing to be added to the west elevation of Garrick Haven,
Ham Common, on an approved design by Mr. Henry
Struthers, F.R.I.B.A., the building to be of red-faced brickwork
to harmonise with the Georgian exterior of the main
building—'

HESTER: Red-faced brick sounds so embarrassed somehow,
doesn't it?

DAME ROSE: Shh, Hester!

MR. FARMER: '—and to comprise a separate entrance, entrance
hall 10 feet 8 inches by 16 feet 2 inches, recreation-room 43 feet
by 28 feet 5 inches with raised platform-stage at far end.'

XENIA: How lovely for them, they'll be able to give little plays at
Christmas, won't they?

JOHNNY: It wouldn't be a bad idea if we all went down once a
month and gave a show for them – I mean – as far as I'm
concerned – I'm sure my little company would be only too
pleased—

MAURICE: Is the stage to have adequate lighting equipment?

JULIAN: I wonder we don't give them a revolve and they could
all ride round and round on it all day.

DAME ROSE: Don't be flippant, Julian. C'est une chose sérieuse!

MR. FARMER: '—Staircase 4 feet 6 inches wide to upper floor,
which will consist of landing, corridor 47 feet by 4 feet on to
which will give bedrooms (5 on each side) of approximately 10
feet square each, and leading to 2 bathrooms, 2 lavatories and
a washing and drying room, fittings for which are embodied
by Messrs. Joyce and Spence in their accompanying estimate
for all interior and exterior plumbing and sanitary work and
fitments—'

XENIA (in response to a whisper from JULIAN, goes off into gales of
laughter): —Julian – how can you! – you are dreadful—!

MR. FARMER (reading more quickly): '—The structural work to be
carried out in best quality English brick, rendered in Portland
cement and sand, 1 part to 4, reinforced against weather by the
addition of 'Pudlo'—'

MAURICE: Good God, what's Pudlo?

JULIAN: Shut up, Maurice.

MR. FARMER: '—the roof to be of red hung tiles, with gutters and damp-course of good quality lead – The specification includes cavity walls, metal window-frames and woodblock flooring to all rooms, hardwood interior woodwork, 3 coats white lead paint gloss finish and electric wiring, light and power points throughout. The plans may be inspected at Mr. Struthers's office, 6 Sedgwick Road, Richmond, between 10 a.m. and 4 p.m. on any day except Saturday. The estimated cost, including additional estimate from Messrs. Joyce and Spence, to be three thousand and eighty-two pounds, seventeen shillings and fourpence.'

XENIA: It all sounds absolutely perfect, Mr. Farmer – Do you think I ought to go and look at the plans?

DAME ROSE: You wouldn't understand them if you did, my dear.

XENIA: Darling Dame Rosie, as a matter of fact you're quite wrong – house-building happens to be one of my things, you know – my own house in Essex I did entirely by myself – every single brick—

MAURICE: I might drop off and cast an eye on them on my way back from the studio one night—

JULIAN (*rising to his feet*): Forgive me for interrupting, but there is just one thing I should like to suggest – I am perfectly sure the actual structural work would obviously be adequately carried out by any reputable firm, but what I want to make a plea for is the look of the thing from the *inside* – for instance, I have always found that the interiors of charity institutions are terribly austere and sort of cold – couldn't we appoint someone like Rex Whistler or Oliver Messel to do a sort of pageant of theatrical history all round the walls of the dormitory? – and if they could leave a few spaces in the painting I have a lot of old play bills that Mother left me in her will, which would look marvellous, and after all, it would be something for the poor old girls to look at—

JOHNNY (*springing to his feet*): —Better still, what about some of those old-time melodrama posters in colour? – you know – *The Fatal Wedding* and *The Girl from the Jam Factory* – I mean to say, it would make the dear old souls laugh their heads off – I mean—

DAME ROSE: Just a moment, Mr. Bolton – Have we all agreed to pass the estimate read to us by Mr. Farmer—?

XENIA (*in ringing tones*): Unconditionally – Passed unconditionally!

VIOLET: You don't think, perhaps, that three thousand and eighty-two pounds, seventeen shillings and fourpence is a shade expensive?

XENIA: Certainly not – if anything, I should say it was dirt cheap. Why, doing up that flat I had in Portland Place cost me more than that and all I had put in was two bathrooms and a telephone extension.

MR. FARMER: I take it that the estimate is passed?

XENIA (*gloriously*): Unanimously, Mr. Farmer.

JULIAN (*to* HESTER): You could start with the old barn-storming days and gradually work up to the Old Vic—

HESTER (*with spirit*): You're wrong, Julian – you're wrong – it would distract them – their lives are nearly over, they want peace, peace, peace. Gentle greys and broken white—

DAME ROSE: Well, when I'm on my last legs I certainly shan't want to look at pictures of the Old Vic!

XENIA: Mr. Farmer – Mr. Farmer – please let's get on – I have a lunch at one and a fitting at two – Silence, everybody, silence! Oh, dear!

MR. FARMER: Well, I have here the estimate from Messrs. Joyce and Spence—

ELISE: It's awfully sad, isn't it, when you analyse it? Those poor old darlings – I wish we could do more than we do—

HESTER: We ought to do much more – much much much more – Who knows but that some of us may be there one day – looking back at the past with mournful eyes—

JULIAN: Like Atherton.

XENIA: Oh, I wonder if he's all right? – Mr. Horlick, would you be an angel and just tiptoe in and have a look at him? – No, I think I'd better do it myself – go on with the estimate, Mr. Farmer, I shan't be a moment—

She creeps off in the direction of the property-room.

MR. FARMER (*reading, very hurriedly*): 'For work to be carried out at Garrick Haven, comprising removing of existing independent boiler in main building, supplying and fixing new no. 3 size

Hearts of Oak improved domestic boiler, connecting same with existing system in main building. To supplying new 60-gallon tank connecting up with 6 radiators in new wing and 4 in main building, to 220 feet lead piping, flow and return pipes, wiped soldered joints and branch joints for circulating, connecting from boiler to existing and new bathrooms and washroom with 213 feet $1\frac{1}{2}$-inch lead piping and testing—'

XENIA *comes tiptoeing back.*

XENIA: He's fast asleep and giving little jumps; I expect he's dreaming of some lovely wood filled with bunny rabbits – How's the estimate going?

MR. FARMER: '—To supplying and fitting 2 porcelain enamelled baths, chromium taps and fitments in new bathrooms—'

XENIA: Doesn't it sound luxurious? The old sweets will feel like the Queen of Sheba—

MR. FARMER: '—To supplying and erecting new cold water 60-gallon storage tank on the roof of north elevation new building, flanged edging and connecting to 2 new lavatories—'

XENIA: Darling Mr. Farmer, couldn't you cut it short now? – I'm sure it's all perfectly in order and I really have to fly—

JOHNNY (*rising*): Before this meeting breaks up, I should just like to say—

MR. FARMER: I fear that it would be out of order for you to pass the estimate unread—

JULIAN (*rising*): I'm afraid I must go, anyhow, Mr. Farmer – I have a very important appointment—

A PRESS PHOTOGRAPHER *comes on to the stage.*

PHOTOGRAPHER: Excuse me—?

XENIA: My goodness, just in time! – Go on reading, Mr. Farmer, and we'll all be listening—

MR. FARMER: But, Mr. President, ladies and gentlemen—

XENIA: Please, Mr. Farmer – I can't stay more than another minute—

JOHNNY: We ought to be signing a resolution, you know, give the picture a bit of action—

> MR. FARMER *reluctantly continues to read the estimate while* XENIA *and* JOHNNY *arrange a group for the* PHOTOGRAPHER; *the following dialogue takes place during the reading.*

MAURICE: Has anybody got a pen?

JULIAN: Here—

XENIA: We haven't got any paper – where's some paper?

DAME ROSE: Never again! Never again as long as I live will I come to a meeting like this – it's outrageous – nothing has been settled at all – talk talk talk – nobody does anything but talk – where do you want me to stand?

XENIA: Here, dear, by me—

VIOLET: I can't see what we're all being photographed for – surely it's rather waste of time—?

MAURICE: Let me get behind you, Julian – I can't be taken like this—

MR. FARMER (*reading dully*): '—To supplying and fixing in same good quality pedestal fitments, improved modern one-gallon flush cisterns connected soil pipes and main outdoor drainage. To complete in accordance with the plans approved by Mr. Henry Struthers, F.R.I.B.A., and the local council surveyors, which plans may be seen at Messrs. Joyce and Spence's office, West Acton Green, between 10 a.m. and 4 p.m. on any day except Saturday, will cost two thousand, one hundred and four pounds, thirteen shillings and eightpence.'

By this time the group has been satisfactorily posed and the PHOTOGRAPHER *takes the picture.*

XENIA (*charmingly, to the* PHOTOGRAPHER): Thank you *so* much.

VIOLET: Is that all, Mr. Farmer?

MR. FARMER: Well, there are one or two little matters—

JOHNNY: I should just like to say one thing—

JULIAN: Well, before you say it I really must go – Good-bye, Xenia dear – good-bye, Dame Rosie – Good-bye, everybody – Mr. Farmer, if you're interested in my idea for decorating the dormitory, just let me know—

MAURICE: Hold on a minute, can you give me a lift?

JULIAN: Yes – only I can't wait.

MAURICE: Good-bye – good-bye, everybody—

He and JULIAN *dash out, followed by the* PHOTOGRAPHER.

MR. FARMER: Am I to take it that you all pass the estimate?

XENIA: Dear Mr. Farmer, *of course* we do – there was never any question of it – Now I really must go – Do you want me to declare the meeting closed or anything?

MR. FARMER: There are just one or two little formalities—

JOHNNY: I just want to say one thing—

XENIA: Be quiet a minute, Johnny – I want to say just a few words – will you all sit down for a minute?

DAME ROSE: Look here, Xenia – I really do think—

XENIA (*firmly*): Please, Dame Rosie—

HESTER (*loudly*): Silence for the President! Oooh! Was that the right thing to say?

XENIA (*in ringing tones*): What I want to say to you all is this: first, how proud and honoured I am to have been elected the President of this wonderful charity. We have all known what it is to be poor and needy and a day may come when we may all know poverty again – therefore – I beg you all – together with me, put your shoulders to the wheel and give, give, give all you can – Garrick Haven must live – Garrick Haven must be flourishing long after we are dust and ashes, long after our names are but echoes from a forgotten tune – It is only a small thing really – but for us of the Theatre it is a part of our life's blood. You do see what I mean, don't you? I mean, here we are, all of us, on the top of the ladder of success, but who can tell when that ladder may not crash to the ground leaving us bruised and broken and oh! so terribly tired?

JOHNNY (*loudly*): Hear! hear!

XENIA: Thank you, Johnny – Now then – I am willing to lead off with a cheque for a hundred pounds and all I beg of you is to give just as much as you can afford, if not a little more! Mr. Farmer, how much do we need?

MR. FARMER: Nothing at all, Miss James; although, naturally, any contributions to the Fund would be gratefully accepted.

XENIA (*undaunted*): Well, whenever you're in trouble – whenever you are in need, remember we all are here, ready and eager to help. Thank you, Mr. Farmer, for everything you have done in the past and for everything you will do in the future— (*She glances at her wrist-watch.*) My God, it's nearly half-past – Good-bye – good-bye – darlings – good-bye—

She rushes off the stage.

JOHNNY (*rising*): May I take this opportunity of saying, Mr. Farmer, that I heartily endorse everything that our President has said – We have known each other for many years, Xenia and I, and you can take it from me that girl has a heart of pure gold – many a time in the past I have known her give all she had to help some poor soul who has fallen by the way—

> ELISE *and* HESTER, *after blowing a few kisses, leave at the beginning of this speech.* VIOLET *and* DAME ROSE *gather up their bags and furs.*

I know I can say with truth and conviction that all of us here to-day are working for one motive and one motive alone, that is the upholding of and the carrying on of this splendid work – I myself have no fish to fry – and I am sure that you, Dame Rosie, have no fish to fry—

DAME ROSE: I certainly have not.

JOHNNY: In fact, we are one and all animated by one desire – that is—

DAME ROSE: Good-bye, Mr. Bolton – I hope we shall meet again soon. Come Violet—

VIOLET: Good-bye, Mr. Bolton.

DAME ROSE: Good-bye, Mr. Farmer. You have been most kind.

MR. FARMER: Good-bye, Dame Rose.

VIOLET: Good-bye, Mr. Farmer – Good-bye, Mr. Bolton.

JOHNNY (*discouraged*): Oh – good-bye.

> DAME ROSE *and* VIOLET *sweep off the stage.*

MR. FARMER (*gathering up his papers*): Well, Mr. Bolton—

JOHNNY: Feel like a spot of lunch?

MR. FARMER: It's very kind of you.

JOHNNY: Come over to the club – I've got a few ideas I'd like to discuss with you—

MR. FARMER: Thanks very much—

JOHNNY: Lights, Jimmie.

JIMMIE: Yes, Mr. Bolton.

JOHNNY (*as he and* MR. FARMER *go off*): I was supposed to meet Bill Schwartz at one o'clock, he'll give me the raspberry all right for keeping him waiting – he doesn't give a damn for anybody – only the other night, I come into the theatre see, rather early for once – I wasn't feeling too good as a matter of fact – I open my dressing-room door—

By this time they have gone. JIMMIE *switches off the lights, leaving only one working light on, and goes off the stage, too.*

When the door has closed behind him, Atherton is heard howling dismally in the property-room as

THE CURTAIN FALLS

Methuen Drama Student Editions

Jean Anouilh *Antigone* • John Arden *Serjeant Musgrave's Dance*
Alan Ayckbourn *Confusions* • Aphra Behn *The Rover*
Edward Bond *Lear* • Bertolt Brecht *The Caucasian Chalk Circle*
Life of Galileo • *Mother Courage and her Children*
The Resistible Rise of Arturo Ui • *The Threepenny Opera*
Anton Chekhov *The Cherry Orchard* • *The Seagull* • *Three Sisters*
Uncle Vanya • Caryl Churchill *Serious Money* • *Top Girls*
Shelagh Delaney *A Taste of Honey* • Euripides *Elektra* • *Medea*
Dario Fo *Accidental Death of an Anarchist* • Michael Frayn *Copenhagen*
John Galsworthy *Strife* • Nikolai Gogol *The Government Inspector*
Robert Holman *Across Oka* • Henrik Ibsen *A Doll's House* • *Ghosts*
Hedda Gabler • Charlotte Keatley *My Mother Said I Never Should*
Bernard Kops *Dreams of Anne Frank* • Federico García Lorca
Blood Wedding • *Doña Rosita the Spinster* (bilingual edition) • *The House
of Bernarda Alba* • (bilingual edition) • *Yerma* (bilingual edition) • David
Mamet *Glengarry Glen Ross* • *Oleanna* • Patrick Marber *Closer* • John
Marston *The Malcontent* • Joe Orton *Loot* • Luigi Pirandello *Six
Characters in Search of an Author* • Mark Ravenhill *Shopping and
F***ing* • Willy Russell *Blood Brothers* • *Educating Rita* • Sophocles
Antigone • *Oedipus the King* • Wole Soyinka *Death and the King's
Horseman* • August Strindberg *Miss Julie* • J. M. Synge *The Playboy
of the Western World* • Theatre Workshop *Oh What a Lovely War* •
Timberlake Wertenbaker *Our Country's Good* • Arnold Wesker *The
Merchant* • Oscar Wilde *The Importance of Being Earnest* • Tennessee
Williams *A Streetcar Named Desire* • *The Glass Menagerie*

Methuen Drama Modern Plays

include work by

Edward Albee
Jean Anouilh
John Arden
Margaretta D'Arcy
Peter Barnes
Sebastian Barry
Brendan Behan
Dermot Bolger
Edward Bond
Bertolt Brecht
Howard Brenton
Anthony Burgess
Simon Burke
Jim Cartwright
Caryl Churchill
Complicite
Noël Coward
Lucinda Coxon
Sarah Daniels
Nick Darke
Nick Dear
Shelagh Delaney
David Edgar
David Eldridge
Dario Fo
Michael Frayn
John Godber
Paul Godfrey
David Greig
John Guare
Peter Handke
David Harrower
Jonathan Harvey
Iain Heggie
Declan Hughes
Terry Johnson
Sarah Kane
Charlotte Keatley
Barrie Keeffe

Howard Korder
Robert Lepage
Doug Lucie
Martin McDonagh
John McGrath
Terrence McNally
David Mamet
Patrick Marber
Arthur Miller
Mtwa, Ngema & Simon
Tom Murphy
Phyllis Nagy
Peter Nichols
Sean O'Brien
Joseph O'Connor
Joe Orton
Louise Page
Joe Penhall
Luigi Pirandello
Stephen Poliakoff
Franca Rame
Mark Ravenhill
Philip Ridley
Reginald Rose
Willy Russell
Jean-Paul Sartre
Sam Shepard
Wole Soyinka
Simon Stephens
Shelagh Stephenson
Peter Straughan
C. P. Taylor
Theatre Workshop
Sue Townsend
Judy Upton
Timberlake Wertenbaker
Roy Williams
Snoo Wilson
Victoria Wood

Methuen Drama Contemporary Dramatists

include

John Arden (two volumes)
Arden & D'Arcy
Peter Barnes (three volumes)
Sebastian Barry
Dermot Bolger
Edward Bond (eight volumes)
Howard Brenton
  (two volumes)
Richard Cameron
Jim Cartwright
Caryl Churchill (two volumes)
Sarah Daniels (two volumes)
Nick Darke
David Edgar (three volumes)
David Eldridge
Ben Elton
Dario Fo (two volumes)
Michael Frayn (three volumes)
John Godber (three volumes)
Paul Godfrey
David Greig
John Guare
Lee Hall (two volumes)
Peter Handke
Jonathan Harvey
  (two volumes)
Declan Hughes
Terry Johnson (three volumes)
Sarah Kane
Barrie Keefe
Bernard-Marie Koltès
  (two volumes)
Franz Xaver Kroetz
David Lan
Bryony Lavery
Deborah Levy
Doug Lucie

David Mamet (four volumes)
Martin McDonagh
Duncan McLean
Anthony Minghella
  (two volumes)
Tom Murphy (five volumes)
Phyllis Nagy
Anthony Neilson
Philip Osment
Gary Owen
Louise Page
Stewart Parker (two volumes)
Joe Penhall
Stephen Poliakoff
  (three volumes)
David Rabe
Mark Ravenhill
Christina Reid
Philip Ridley
Willy Russell
Eric-Emmanuel Schmitt
Ntozake Shange
Sam Shepard (two volumes)
Wole Soyinka (two volumes)
Simon Stephens
Shelagh Stephenson
David Storey (three volumes)
Sue Townsend
Judy Upton
Michel Vinaver
  (two volumes)
Arnold Wesker (two volumes)
Michael Wilcox
Roy Williams (two volumes)
Snoo Wilson (two volumes)
David Wood (two volumes)
Victoria Wood

Methuen Drama World Classics

include

Jean Anouilh (two volumes)
Brendan Behan
Aphra Behn
Bertolt Brecht (eight volumes)
Büchner
Bulgakov
Calderón
Čapek
Anton Chekhov
Noël Coward (eight volumes)
Feydeau
Eduardo De Filippo
Max Frisch
John Galsworthy
Gogol
Gorky (two volumes)
Harley Granville Barker
  (two volumes)
Victor Hugo
Henrik Ibsen (six volumes)
Jarry

Lorca (three volumes)
Marivaux
Mustapha Matura
David Mercer (two volumes)
Arthur Miller (five volumes)
Molière
Musset
Peter Nichols (two volumes)
Joe Orton
A. W. Pinero
Luigi Pirandello
Terence Rattigan
  (two volumes)
W. Somerset Maugham
  (two volumes)
August Strindberg
  (three volumes)
J. M. Synge
Ramón del Valle-Inclán
Frank Wedekind
Oscar Wilde

Methuen Drama Classical Greek Dramatists

Aeschylus Plays: One
(Persians, Seven Against Thebes, Suppliants,
Prometheus Bound)

Aeschylus Plays: Two
(Oresteia: Agamemnon, Libation-Bearers, Eumenides)

Aristophanes Plays: One
(Acharnians, Knights, Peace, Lysistrata)

Aristophanes Plays: Two
(Wasps, Clouds, Birds, Festival Time, Frogs)

Aristophanes & Menander: New Comedy
(Women in Power, Wealth, The Malcontent,
The Woman from Samos)

Euripides Plays: One
(Medea, The Phoenician Women, Bacchae)

Euripides Plays: Two
(Hecuba, The Women of Troy, Iphigeneia at Aulis,
Cyclops)

Euripides Plays: Three
(Alkestis, Helen, Ion)

Euripides Plays: Four
(Elektra, Orestes, Iphigeneia in Tauris)

Euripides Plays: Five
(Andromache, Herakles' Children, Herakles)

Euripides Plays: Six
(Hippolytos, Suppliants, Rhesos)

Sophocles Plays: One
(Oedipus the King, Oedipus at Colonus, Antigone)

Sophocles Plays: Two
(Ajax, Women of Trachis, Electra, Philoctetes)

For a complete catalogue of Methuen Drama titles
write to:

Methuen Drama
A & C Black Publishers Limited
36 Soho Square
London
W1D 3QY

or you can visit our website at:

www.acblack.com